Praise for *Radiant Mormonism*

Professor Muhammad Yunus

Nobel Peace Prize Laureate 2006, founder of the Grameen Bank of Bangladesh for rural women, member board of directors of the United Nations Foundation, Fulbright scholar, founder of dozens of Grameen businesses for the poor, recognized with a dozen major awards including the U.S. Presidential Medal of Freedom, the Congressional Gold Medal, the World Food Prize, India's Indira Gandhi Peace Prize, and more; he is a board member of Grameen America and has received dozens of honorary university degrees globally

Professor Woodworth became a great friend over the years. He invited me many times to speak to his students and conferences. It led to his many visits to Bangladesh to spend time with Grameen Bank. He and his band of Brigham Young University students have rolled out multiple NGOs around the globe, and this book explains how and why.

Joseph Grenny

Four-time author of *New York Times* best-selling books like *Crucial Conversations*, *Influencer*, and others; cofounder of global consulting firm Vital Smarts; Unitus

My life would be impoverished were it not for the good fortune of Warner Woodworth's previous books' landing on my desk 25 years ago. *Working Toward Zion* translated my abstract religious commitments into concrete moral duties that set me on a different life course—one that has infinitely enriched my life. And I am not alone. I know I speak for hundreds whose lives beat to another trajectory after encountering Woodworth's writings. *Radiant Mormonism* is destined to do the same for the next generation. The establishment of Zion is not just a prophecy, it is a commandment. And few men in our generation have attempted to obey it more completely than Warner Woodworth. This is not just an interesting account of intrepid do-gooders; it is a sure guide for filling the measure of our creation.

Richard Bushman

American historian and Gouverneur Morris Professor Emeritus of History at Columbia University, having also taught at Harvard, Boston University, and University of Delaware; winner of the Bancroft Prize; recipient of fellowships at the Smithsonian, Claremont, and Princeton; author of the best-selling *Joseph Smith: Rough Stone Rolling*

If Warner's book is taken seriously, readers will emerge with a greatly enlarged idea of what the Mormon movement can accomplish in the world. Mormonism is more potent than we have imagined.

Paul H. Thompson

Former president of Weber State University, Harvard Business School professor, vice president of BYU, dean at BYU's Marriott School of Management, LDS leader as a mission president and stake president, a leading management consultant, co-author of *Novations: Strategies for Career Management*, board member of MicroBusiness Mentors

I can think of no one who is better qualified to write a book about helping the poor. Warner has spent a great deal of time in the past 50 years working tirelessly in many parts of the world to help people at the bottom of the pyramid. This book describes a few of the NGOs with which he has worked to better the lives of many people and will inspire its readers to follow Warner's lead.

Sarah Carmichael Parsons

Canadian cofounder and manager of NGOs, Wave of Hope, Empowering Nations, board member of HELP International, founder of Dolls of Hope and the Undaunted Foundation

I have had the privilege of learning from Warner Woodworth as a graduate student at BYU and during a number of years as we worked together to respond to the devastation of the South-East Asian Tsunami through 'Wave of Hope,' as we worked to create the nonprofit Empowering Nations, and later as a board member of HELP International. Warner provided me with the means to do what has been in my heart for so long. I am grateful for his tutelage, mentoring, and support over the years and feel incredibly honored to have been able to work alongside him and to rub shoulders with him. His legacy has reached the tiniest of villages from the Philippines to Kenya, from Ghana to Peru, from Paraguay to Haiti. If anyone is qualified to write a book about how members of the LDS Church can more fully live out the gospel of Jesus Christ and build Zion, it is Warner.

Dave Ulrich

Rensis Likert Professor, Ross School of Business, University of Michigan; founder and partner of The RBL Group (consultants to the Fortune 500); ranked the #1 management educator and guru by *BusinessWeek*; co-author of books by such publishers as Harvard, McGraw-Hill, and others, including *How Leaders Build Value and Delivering Results: A New Mandate for Human Resource Professionals.*

Wow! Warner has spent a lifetime preaching the gospel to the poor, healing the brokenhearted, offering deliverance to the destitute, and setting at liberty the bruised. He (and his colleagues) are indeed 'latter-day' Saints whose words and deeds offer sustainable hope to the impoverished. This inspiring book chronicles this incredible mission and calls each of us to action to use our power to empower others and our strengths to strengthen others: *'Well done, thou . . .'*

Devin Thorpe

Well-known podcaster, motivational speaker, author of a number of books such as *Your Mark on the World*, *Crowdfunding for Social Good*, and *Adding Profit by Adding Purpose*

Radiant Mormonism describes aspirationally the Church I believe in, follow and preach. Author Warner Woodworth uses his articulate, respected voice to nudge us toward more Christlike lives, defined more by action and generosity than by hollow expressions of faith.

Matthew Bowman

Associate professor of history and religion, Howard W. Hunter Chair of Mormon Studies, Claremont Graduate University

Warner Woodworth's inspiring call for a religion that transforms not only ourselves, but the world around us into the image of God, is borne out by the work of his lifetime. This book will introduce you to the message and the messenger.

Louis M. Pope

Former CEO, Utah business leader, humanitarian globally but especially in Africa

Radiant Mormonism reawakens in us that knowledge that we should be doing more to help the poor. Dr. Warner Woodworth has given us insight into not only the 'why' but also the 'how' we can make a difference and make this world a better place for all.

Liz Wiseman

CEO of Wiseman Group, a leadership research and development firm headquartered in Silicon Valley; consultant to Fortune 500 firms globally; *New York Times* best-selling author of three books; recognized in 2019 as the top leadership thinker in the world

For years Dr. Woodworth has inspired his students to create organizations where people at all levels can contribute and flourish in meaningful ways. His teaching changed my vision. Now in *Radiant Mormonism*, he invites saints everywhere to set our sights higher and help build communities where poverty dies and humanity flourishes. This book is a powerful call to think bigger, to serve more expansively, and to stand for the highest ideals in the gospel of Jesus Christ. I hope *everyone* in the church reads this book.

Jaime Figueroa

Cusco, Peru, cofounder and Field Director in the Andes of what originally was the NGO called Chasqui Humanitarian named after the ancient Incas of Peru that later evolved into Eagle Condor Humanitarian

This will be a valuable book in educating thousands of volunteers and donors to establish future NGOs among the *pobrecitos* of my people. Hearts will increasingly turn to especially aid Lamanite communities in their struggles for emancipation. In our MPA courses, Dr. Woodworth helped us start innovative strategies to do rural development, set up schools, offer economic development through microenterprises, provide adult literacy, and in many other ways empower the ultra-poor of the Lamanite people. The programs continue their impacts today, 20 years later. Yes, change is possible. '*Sí, se puede!*'

Terryl L. Givens

Author of a dozen-plus books such as *Wrestling the Angel* and, with Fiona Givens, *All Things New*; professor emeritus of literature and religion at the University of Richmond

Joseph Smith referred to Zion as a global enterprise 'that has interested the people of God in every age.' Building Zion will require extraordinary efforts to transcend our historical proclivity toward self-concern, in order to alleviate suffering and build community across religions, cultures, and peoples. Warner Woodworth provides a marvelous template for the kind of innovations and creativity he and kindred souls have fostered to move us in that direction.

Margaret Young

Former president of the Association for Mormon Letters; author of works including the novels *House Without Walls*, *Salvador*, and *Heresies of Nature*; co-author of a trilogy of historical novels about Black Mormon pioneers titled *Standing on the Promises* and creator of the *Nobody Knows: The Untold Story of Black Mormons* shown on PBS and in film festivals; award-winning playwright of *I Am Jane*, about Black Mormon pioneer Jane Manning James; now living in the Democratic Republic of the Congo on a mission to work with Africans to relaunch the nation's film industry that was destroyed during the 1990s civil war there, as well as on literacy and educational projects

We have had no electricity or internet for a while, having to use a battery pack for internet now. Village violence claimed many lives, including children's lives, last week. A land dispute fomented the violence. One side was victimized, but then the victims 'became the executioners.' This is the cycle of violence and will be repeated until it is stopped not by a new policy or persuasive words, but by a change of heart. I have come to see the ideal of Zion as the real hope for the DR-Congo—and for all of us. Here in this part of Africa, the ideal seems like the only way out of the corruption and war, and indeed a matter of life and death. Violence in the USA has become more verbal than physical, but it is pervasive. I have long looked at Warner Woodworth as one who lives the ideal, who seeks to do good at all times, who has provided templates and patterns for unity and success throughout the world. This kind of 'Radiant Mormonism' shines like stars in an often dark world.

Robert A. Rees, Ph.D.

UCLA professor, assistant dean, poet, Fellow at the Center for Advanced Research, visiting professor at numerous schools, currently director of Mormon Studies at Graduate Theological Union, Berkeley; cofounder and vice president, Bountiful Children's Foundation

Apostle Jeffrey Holland stated, 'Jesus's first and foremost messianic duty [was] to bless the poor.... [He] has issued no more persistent call than for us to join Him in lifting this burden from the people.' I don't know of anyone in the modern church who has responded to Jesus's call more successfully and more consistently than Warner Woodworth. The title of his new book, *Radiant Mormonism*, is an apt summary of Warner's own life and ministry, not only as a supreme philanthropist, but as a teacher, inspirer, and leader of others to address the needs of the poor, the needy, the downtrodden, the forgotten—those Mother Theresa calls 'Jesus in disguise.' This book chronicles in a concrete way not only that such work must be done, but how it can be done—by anyone who chooses to follow Jesus. Get this book. Read it. Be inspired by it. Warner Woodworth is not only a Radiant Mormon, he is a radiant human being whose radiance has blessed and is blessing millions!

Martín Burt

Former mayor of Asunción, Paraguay; founder and CEO of Fundación Paraguaya, Poverty Stoplight, and Teach a Man to Fish (UK); recipient of the prestigious Skoll Award for Social Entrepreneurship at Oxford University, Ph.D.

This book adds a unique perspective to the conversation on poverty. With his persistent and unrelenting dedication to those experiencing poverty, Warner Woodworth is a beacon for all of us, and in this book he shares some of his most inspiring stories. I have been lucky enough to get to know some of Warner's work in person and am thrilled to see his expertise now available as a book for everyone to learn from. This book is bound to motivate and guide readers of all faiths to join the fight against poverty and to reduce human suffering.

Curt Bassett, JD

CEO of Impact Investment Leaders, founder of Purpose Investors Network and formerly a finance leader on Wall Street

Warner Woodworth, Ph.D., is the 'Johnny Appleseed' of social enterprise because no one can match him in starting up both nonprofit and for-profit social enterprises around the world—aided by his many admiring MBA students. He wanders through the world, planting tiny NGO seeds that grow into large, lasting oak trees. Today many economic analysts believe we're now in a 'Purpose Economy,' where the primary driver in successful business is social purpose. In his latest volume, *Radiant Mormonism*, Warner again shows he's one of the world's leading social entrepreneurs, and explains why LDS members are among the most socially minded people in the world and thereby prepared to excel in this new economy. The Church encourages the core pillars of 'Purpose' in the New Economy: volunteerism, service, and charitable giving to redistribute wealth to the poor.... But just as important, he explains how LDS teachings about the principles of responsibility and self-reliance must govern all wealth redistribution. When combining these principles with the Church's 'pioneer-culture,' 'can-do' attitude, and 'hard-work-ethic,' this has resulted not only in the Church and many of its members ranking high in affluence, but also in Utah's ranking #1 in social entrepreneurism around the world.

Sam Daley-Harris

Founder of RESULTS, Civic Courage, cofounder of the Microcredit Summit Campaign, author of Reclaiming Our Democracy

I first met Warner Woodworth more than 25 years ago at the University of Michigan where he'd driven a dozen BYU students to a microfinance conference and a chance to meet future Nobel Peace Prize laureate Muhammad Yunus. Since then, I have been inspired by his deep commitment to empowering students and Mormons from all walks of life to do 'More Good' and practice 'Radiant Mormonism' on behalf of the world's poor.

Afton Beutler

From Geneva, Switzerland, a longtime leader serving on the UN Committee on the Status of Women, Alliance for Health, and Freedom of Religion Committee

In 2004, the Nigerian women's leader Carol Ugochukwu of Worldwide Organization for Women (WOW) and I miraculously met Warner, and it changed my perspective toward global endeavors. My heart and life was never, ever the same. So, I am happy to support his new book on NGOs. He has always been my inspiration to continue such work in human rights by his great example of being an advocate and a voice for those whose voices at the grassroots are not always heard. Warner has been the voice guiding many of us at this time in history.

Jim McConkie

Attorney, a founder of the Refugee Justice League, a nonprofit organization of attorneys offering pro-bono legal help to refugees discriminated against because of religion, ethnicity, or national origin, which has a membership of over 800 lawyers and former Assistant US Attorneys; his law practice focuses on civil rights and personal injury; named Utah State Bar 'Lawyer of the Year'; coauthor of Whom Say Ye That I Am: Lessons from the Jesus of Nazareth and a Mormon history book, Looking at the Doctrine and Covenants Again for the First Time

Warner Woodworth's book *Radiant Mormonism* is an inspiring look at what individuals and groups can do to help alleviate the suffering and pain in this world. It makes you want to get up from your comfortable armchair and do something! It is a lesson on how to magnify good intentions and good works that are at the heart of Christianity and put into practice those same impulses that inspired our LDS forefathers to live the Law of Consecration and sacrifice for each other.

Gordon Shepherd

Co-author of *The Palgrave Handbook of Global Mormonism* and of *Growing Up in the City of the Saints*, professor at University of Central Arkansas

Through both word and action, Warner Woodworth challenges members of the Church of Jesus Christ of Latter-day Saints to live lives of compassion and service beyond their organizational roles in a demanding lay religion. *Radiant Mormonism* demonstrates the many ways that abstract concern for the welfare of underprivileged people worldwide has been effectively transformed into concrete modes of volunteer action for helping people in need to help themselves. The subtext of this inspiring book is the ethical demand required of church members—both individually and collectively—to actively embrace the unselfish standards signified by the designation of 'Latter-day Saints.'

Gary Shepherd

Co-author of *Binding Earth and Heaven* and *Talking with the Children of God*, professor of sociology and anthropology at Oakland University

Warner Woodworth has dedicated the entirety of his adult life not only to passionately advocating for the poor but, more significantly, to creating and implementing innovative ways that have improved and elevated the economic prospects for tens of thousands of impoverished people around the world. In this volume, he details case studies that show how he and others he has inspired have put into action core values of their LDS faith to bring about powerful economic and social improvement for people previously ensnared in the seemingly hopeless grip of structural-generational poverty. An apt subtitle for this book—aimed squarely at Warner's Mormon co-religionists—would be *Actualization of Faith, Hope, and Charity*.

Scott C. Hammond

Author of *Lessons of the Lost: Finding Hope and Resilience in Work, Life and the Wilderness*

Warner Woodworth shows how today's Mormon pioneers should keep walking, beyond 'This is the Place...,' beyond prosperity, beyond education, to a real Zion. Read, but don't expect to be comfortable! Expect to want to get busy.

João Bueno

Brazilian LDS Church leader, BYU master's of public administration graduate, executive director of Care for Life in Africa, an administrator of Native American Serving Non-Tribal Institutions with the US Department of Education adjacent to the Ute and Navajo reservations

I was in Warner's social entrepreneurship class where I learned about self-reliance and increased my lifelong desire to serve the poor. This book, like his many 'required articles,' helped me develop one of the most successful community development programs implemented in Africa: our NGO called Care for Life. Warner has become a friend, tutor, and mentor. I never could have imagined his influence on me and the villages of Mozambique.

Radiant
MORMONISM

By Common Consent Press is a non-profit publisher dedicated to producing affordable, high-quality books that help define and shape the Latter-day Saint experience. BCC Press publishes books that address all aspects of Mormon life. Our mission includes finding manuscripts that will contribute to the lives of thoughtful Latter-day Saints, mentoring authors and nurturing projects to completion, and distributing important books to the Mormon audience at the lowest possible cost.

WARNER WOODWORTH

Using Our Faith in Christ to Power
World-changing Service

Radiant Mormonism: Using Our Faith in Christ to Power World-changing Service
Copyright © 2022 by Warner Woodworth

All rights reserved. Printed in the United States of America. No part of this book may be used or reproduced in any manner whatsoever without written permission except in the case of brief quotations embodied in critical articles or reviews.

For information contact
By Common Consent Press
4900 Penrose Dr.
Newburgh, IN 47630

Cover design: D Christian Harrison
Book design: Andrew Heiss

www.bccpress.org
ISBN-13: 978-1-948218-51-1

10 9 8 7 6 5 4 3 2 1

To Kaye Colvin Woodworth

Contents

Acknowledgments   xi

Preface   xv

Glossary   xvii

1   The Need for Latter-day Saints to Change the World   1
(November 2020)

Drawing on the historian Richard Bushman's call for a more-"Radiant Mormonism," this chapter is an introduction to LDS theology that encourages—even insists on—living lives of consecration and stewardship by serving the poor, using our skills, and donating money and services to private initiatives for empowering those who suffer, principles taught by modern LDS prophets for over a century. Each of the cases in this book was initiated by the author, Warner Woodworth, in seeking to practice what we preach as Latter-day Saints. All the chapters describe inspiring efforts by church members and others to build a better quality of life, above and beyond formal programs of the institutional church that bless the global poor, thereby empowering them toward sustainable futures.

2   HELP International   21
(Honduras and Beyond, 1999–2022)

This chapter tells the courageous story of young Latter-day Saints responding to Central America's destruction by Hurricane Mitch in late 1998. Their work has since led to HELP International's growing efforts to serve victims of disaster for 22 years by applying microfinance, education, square-foot-gardening techniques, orphanage volunteerism, and other humanitarian tools to bless the poor. HELP has expanded to some 17 countries in the Americas, the Caribbean, Africa, the Middle East, and Asia.

3 Ouelessebougou Alliance — 55
(From Utah to Mali, West Africa, 1985–2022)

This chapter describes the amazing work of the Ouelessebougou Alliance, a nongovernmental organization (NGO) founded by a mixed group of LDS, Catholic, and Muslim Utahns who saw the Ethiopian crisis hit East Africa in 1985, leading to more than a million deaths from starvation and drought. This chapter describes how the Alliance has prompted Utahns to initiate sustainable programs for over three decades in Mali, saving many lives.

4 Sustain Haiti — 85
(Post-Haiti's Earthquake, 2010–2020)

This chapter heralds the dedicated efforts of LDS students in a Brigham Young University course following the horrendous 10.0-magnitude earthquake that flattened most buildings in the Caribbean island nation of Haiti, inspiring college-age adults to sacrifice time, effort, and money in seeking to rebuild schools, orphanages, and numerous other institutions. Known as Sustain Haiti, the effort has established a better future for new LDS converts and the Haitian people at large for the past decade.

5 Philippines Enterprise Development Foundation — 121
(Mentors International, 1990–2022)

The story of Mentors International began at the request of Filipino students whom the author was teaching in 1988 at BYU Hawaii, which led to forming a board with LDS executives who established an economic development strategy through training and microfinance. This chapter reports the story of their organization that has served more than five million people throughout the many islands of the Philippines for over three decades, having raised capital totaling some $168 million in microloans as a hand up, not a handout. It has gradually expanded to Central and South America, and beyond.

6 MicroBusiness Mentors — 151
(Utah Latino Immigrants and Refugees, 2003–2022)

This chapter tells of the author's efforts, with his graduate students in the MBA and MPA programs at the Marriott School of Business, BYU, who in 2003 set up a nonprofit and began serving poor families in Utah Valley, especially Latino immigrants and refugees, by designing a mentoring program for local residents. MicroBusiness Mentors has now applied microcredit and training approaches for nearly two decades to help such families settle in Utah, open bank accounts, receive microcredit capital, and launch their own tiny entrepreneurial businesses toward a better future.

7   Eagle Condor Humanitarian   173
     (Peru, 2002–2022)

This chapter tells the fascinating story of a Peruvian nonprofit, now known as Eagle Condor, which began in the author's NGO Management course some two decades ago. The objective was to mobilize LDS returned missionaries who had served indigenous villages in Andean countries, asking them to pool their money and helping them achieve career successes by returning to serve the descendants of Book of Mormon Lamanite ancestors. Assisting them with programs in agriculture, clean water, microcredit, and literacy training, the quest continues still today.

8   Unitus   207
     (1999–2022)

This chapter relates how the author and many of his LDS business associates designed and launched a big, new "microfinance accelerator"—the first of its kind in the world—which started in Mexico and spread to more than 20 nations and has raised $1.2 billion since the start of the new millennium. The chapter analyzes the rollout of large-scale efforts by Unitus to reduce extreme poverty, especially in the Third World, focusing on training, loans, jobs, and a more-sustainable future for some 21 million families.

9   How to Design Your Own NGO:
     Tools and Methods for Launching New NGOs   249
     (January 2022)

This chapter provides a range of ways to educate and inspire readers who want to start their own nonprofit organization to lift up those who struggle and to help poor families dig their way up from the lowest situations in society to achieving a better quality of life and economic justice. The chapter outlines steps for creating an organizational vision, mission, values, structure, marketing, managing, planning, financing, and evaluating—all critical processes for success. Ultimately, the goal is not to make poor people wealthy, but rather to aid them in becoming a little better off, helping them secure three meals per day, be able to send their children to school, have access to village healthcare and drinking clean water, and much more.

10 Conclusion—Practicing Personal Consecration Globally Through Private, Personal, and Social Innovations   275
(December 2021)

> This final chapter integrates the book's core themes and offers a few concluding thoughts as well as a call to action for readers who feel inspired to make a difference in the world. Learning about the various ecosystems and methods of doing international development and humanitarianism will help readers to find deeper meaning in their own lives while empowering others to lift themselves up. The goal is to help people achieve dignity, not subsist in dependency. Perhaps this book will help others reduce a bit of global suffering, by reaching out beyond their comfortable existence to show gratitude for their blessings and even to offer love and options for a better life for the world's have-nots.

Appendix I: Private NGOs with and without a Latter-day Saint Connection   289

Appendix II: Global Change Agents, Inc.   331

Appendix III: Sample NGO Work Expectations   337

Appendix IV: Sample NGO Legal Liabilities   343

Appendix V: Sample NGO Handout   349

Acknowledgments

How does one fully acknowledge the many supporters of my efforts to change the world? Starting with the God of Heaven Himself, I'd have to mention the Savior who has always inspired me, as well as the many prophets of the standard works of Latter-day Saint scripture I began reading as a youngster and continued studying throughout my life as a missionary in Brazil; a fulltime seminary and institute teacher for 15 years; a student at Brigham Young University, the University of Utah, the University of Michigan; and my decades of serving as an academic professor at various universities. Any and all credit for my life's scholarship belongs to my Heavenly Father.

With respect to the life-changing stories, research, and cases in this volume, I want to share my deep appreciation and love for many individuals.

It starts with acknowledging the millions of suffering people I've worked with, listened to, and learned from. They will always be my mentors and my personal heroes. They showed me what pain, suffering, and courage really are; how hunger and poverty affect human life; and the ways that I could be privileged to help empower them so that their children could live another day. Women I've labored with in hundreds of rural communities could develop tiny microenterprises and begin to be community leaders with more-sustainable lives. Men were able to become humbler, learning to listen to their spouses, support their families, and be true to great human values of ethics, kindness, trust, and giving. Thousands of impoverished and oppressed children in the many villages in which I've volunteered began to eat two or three meals per day, not just one, and were also able to go to school and have other experiences so they could enjoy real growth and new dreams instead of hopelessness and a life of squalor with no viable future. One hundred percent of the royalties from this book will be donated to several of our NGOs that have struggled during the global pandemic so they may become stronger, healthier, and have even greater impacts for good in the coming years.

My sweet wife, Kaye Woodworth, has greatly blessed my life through the years. As my amazing companion, she has taught me so much about love, honesty, ethical values, and gospel principles, all the while supporting our lifestyle of family service to the poor, disabled, and homeless, in our own community and state and far beyond. Whether I was building a successful career as a tenured full professor in the Marriott School of Business at Brigham Young University, doing a great deal of teaching and publishing, attending or presenting at conferences around the globe, or mentoring graduates as well as undergraduates, she was home managing the Woodworth "farm." Always supportive, helping us to have a meaningful marriage and partnership, Kaye has been amazing. She read and critiqued many of the books and articles I wrote. Over the decades, we were co-donors of hundreds of thousands of dollars to charities based in our home state and 96 nations. Equally important, Kaye traveled the world with me to serve the poor and develop a global perspective together. I'll never forget her dancing in Mali, West Africa, after the women came out of their mud huts and wrapped a baby in a shawl on her back as men beat their drums and many clapped to the music's beat. Or her singing performances for indigenous villagers high in the Andes where descendants of the ancient Inca civilization still exist today. Or when she ran our wood shop in Thailand after the 2004 Asian tsunami where she worked all the equipment and trained the surviving women to construct simple wood furniture for the new little homes and schools we helped rebuild. She was the instructor for many Mayan women in Tioshà, Guatemala, teaching them to make quality bread for their new village cooperative bakery that began to sell delicious products to people who came from all around. Kaye has encouraged me in 30-plus years of church leadership in the Church of Jesus Christ of Latter-day Saints, whether we were living in Utah, Hawaii, or Michigan. In those congregations, I sat near the pulpit on the stand for 22 years while she managed the gang of kids spread over a long bench near the front of those chapels.

I also acknowledge the ten children we raised, either born to us or adopted, American, Mexican, or Brazilian: Erik, Anne, David, Julie, Douglas, Marc, Kevin, Ryan, Kristi, and Micah. I want to also mention the six other young adults who lived with us for a year or more while attending college in Utah or Hawaii. I learned things from each of them. They were amazing kids, getting up five days a week at 6:00 a.m. or earlier, joining us for family scripture and prayer, hiking to their schools, fulfilling their household assignments, and doing community service. Such activities were all important tasks in their learning to become responsible people, not only within our home but also in the larger neighborhood tribe. It also meant a great deal to me that some of our kids lived abroad as missionaries or later in their careers. If my memory is correct, they've lived in Kenya, Brazil, Nicaragua, Kyrgyzstan, Taiwan, Germany, Hong Kong, Chile, France, and probably other places. As important to me have been those of our offspring who learned to become humanitarians, traveling with me to do volunteer work in Guatemala, Mali, Brazil, Poland, Haiti, Thailand, Mexico, Tanzania, Honduras, Lithuania, and Cuba, among other locations.

In addition to the above individuals, I want to acknowledge others who made this book possible. The list would include, first of all, my talented brother, Mark Woodworth of San Francisco, who since earning a master's degree at Columbia University's Graduate School of Journalism has honed his skills on hundreds of published books. For *Radiant Mormonism*, he's provided careful attention to detail and made numerous editorial suggestions. Some years ago, he and I served as volunteers with HELP International in the island nation of Fiji, where he learned more about that wonderful people and culture, along with gaining insights into the "crazy life" of me, his only brother, than ever before. I also want to acknowledge the technical and editorial assistance given this volume by the staff of my publisher, BCC Press. Steve Evans pitched my book proposal to his staff; Michael Austin and Lori Forsyth gave helpful editorial suggestions early on; designer Andrew Heiss did a superb job of designing the book's text and graphics. To each, thank you.

I acknowledge the thousands of my students I have taught at BYU and at such other institutions and locales as Claremont University in Los Angeles, Rio de Janeiro, Lithuania, Hawaii, the University of Utah, and elsewhere. Among my practices was that I always asked my students to address me by my first name and not as Professor Woodworth, Dr. Woodworth, Brother Woodworth, Herr Professor, or other honorifics, because I always felt that I was a student-scholar, just like them, still studying and learning. With them I sought to live a life of authenticity and integrity. In my classes, I emphasized the need to reject greed, as well as high positions of authority and power. Instead, I encouraged such virtues as love, humility, equality, peace, gratitude, and simple living. Without compassion and appreciation for God and our neighbors across the planet, life would be of diminished worth.

Finally, I wish to thank the amazing mentors with whom I've closely worked on our NGO boards, met with at LDS church headquarters, or counseled with face to face over the decades. They must include these, plus many other co-collaborators seeking to change the world, including some now deceased: Duff (Marion D.) Hanks, Chieko Okazaki, Lowell Bennion, Gordon B. Hinckley, Leonard Arrington, Neal Maxwell, T. Edgar Lyon, Dillon Inouye, Truman Madsen, Bob Thomas, Addie Fuhriman, Jeff Holland, Bill Dyer, Gene England, Rex Lee, Mario De Pillis, Armand Mauss, and Bonner Ritchie.

Thank you, everyone.

Preface

This book offers inspiring, highly personal stories of how I and many of my Latter-day Saint friends, students, family members, and other collaborators felt sufficient passion to give of our time, talents, money, and (more importantly) hearts to reduce human suffering around the world. I explore cases of our many initiatives to address crises in Africa, Latin America, South America, the Caribbean, and Asia, growing mostly out of my courses at Brigham Young University, by sharing with readers the needs I saw that grow from extreme poverty, earthquakes, floods, civil conflicts, and much more, to get a vision of how we can individually and collectively help. The results reported herein include the organizing of new start-up nongovernmental organizations (NGOs), mobilizing volunteers, raising funds, and building partnerships with those who joined the cause and assisted. While we were often told our efforts wouldn't succeed, the rollout of these programs, in most cases, still today continue taking practical actions and achieving solid and quite heartwarming results around the world. Each chapter offers analyses of what, why, where, when, and how such interventions were established, and includes LDS prophetic lines as well as scriptural admonitions. The book also features a number of photos of our developing nation collaborators, as well as those working with me in performing such rewarding nonprofit work globally. The book begins with a glossary of terms used and ends with five helpful appendices. Each chapter starts on a hopeful note: with the words of an inspiring, relevant Mormon hymn.

Glossary

Here are a few definitions of methodologies for changing the world and empowering people. They are used in the chapters, case studies, and appendices in this book as innovative ways to help reduce people's suffering:

Civil society   Sectors of a country's social problems and challenges, sometimes referred to as its "social sector" or "third sector," or other terms. In contrast to the traditional arenas of the private sector, such as business and for-profit enterprises, or public sector systems like federal, state, regional, and city governments; schools; and so forth.

Humanitarianism   The belief and practice of benevolent treatment of others, assisting them to improve their living conditions.

International development   Usually implies large-scale government programs focused on alleviating poverty, fostering economic expansion, and improving living conditions in poor nations around the globe.

MFI (microfinance institution)   Term and acronym used herein for all financial services for the poor.

Micro-bank   A village or communal bank group.

Microcredit   Tiny loans or microloans to the very poor.

Microenterprise   A very small income-generating activity or family business.

Microentrepreneur   Recipient of a microloan with which one can start or expand a small business.

Microfinance institution   A more-inclusive term for the above five "micro-" terms, sometimes also including programs such as client savings, health insurance for the poor, education loans, and others.

NGO   A nongovernmental organization or nonprofit that may provide a range of humanitarian and development services, such as literacy, healthcare, education and schooling, crisis response and aid, computer skills, village progress aid, agricultural help, and women's empowerment, as well as microcredit itself.

PVO   Private voluntary organization.

Social entrepreneur   A person who seeks to design programs to improve society, using business methods, not simply charity.

Social impact   The seeking of funding that leads to major economic results, not merely charity but also long-term innovation.

"Because I Have Been Given Much"
LDS Hymns, No. 219

1. Because I have been given much,
   I too must give;
   Because of thy great bounty, Lord,
   Each day I live;
   I shall divide my gifts from thee
   With every brother that I see
   Who has the need of help from me.

2. Because I have been sheltered, fed
   By thy good care;
   I cannot see another's lack and I not share;
   My glowing fire, my loaf of bread,
   My roof's safe shelter overhead
   That he too may be comforted.

3. Because I have been blessed by
   Thy great love, dear Lord,
   I'll share thy love again
   According to thy word;
   I shall give love to those in need,
   I'll show that love by word and deed;
   Thus shall my thanks be thanks in deed.

Text: Grace Noll Crowell (1936-)
Music: Phillip Landgrave (1975-)

1

The Need for Latter-day Saints to Change the World

(November 2020)

Have you ever wondered how you personally could combat human suffering? Empower poor families? Or fight poverty? Four years ago, an eminent professor at Columbia University, Richard Bushman, penned an opinion piece for Salt Lake City's *Deseret News*, titled "Embracing a 'Radiant' Mormonism" (2017), in which he wrote of Latter-day Saint innovators who are impacting societies throughout the world. His argument was that, above and beyond traditional LDS activities long considered the routine actions of the church—such as reading scriptures, performing missionary work, attending and participating in church meetings and other activities, listening to or reading church leaders' formal speeches, tracing one's family history, serving in a temple, and many more—in recent years there has been an explosion of LDS "influencers" reaching out to improve society. Whether they be politicians, insightful authors, creative contributors in the fine arts, or many other kinds of individuals, they are truly making the world a better place, bit by bit, year by year. Bushman cited some of my own

▲ Partners in microcredit: Professor Muhammad Yunus, founder of the Grameen Bank of Bangladesh, 2006 Nobel Peace Prize Laureate, with author Dr. Warner Woodworth, prize-winning academic and founder of 40-plus global NGOs, when both were speaking in New York

▼ A microentrepreneur wood carver in Kenya trying to eke out a living

humble efforts in mobilizing individuals to reach out to reduce human suffering by giving their money, time, spiritual energy, and talents, in ways that go above and beyond traditional church programs:

> They are funding micro-nutrients for starving populations in New Guinea; helping the children of lepers in India; teaching...principles for successful living in inner-city schools; funding an orphanage and school in India again; advancing cancer or other research; and many others. I was vaguely aware of all this activity because of Warner Woodworth's argument that Mormons would bring in the law of consecration individually by creating a multitude of private charities. To prove his point, Woodworth named scores of these enterprises. Through my fundraising, I have learned for myself how accurate Woodworth was. There is no doubt that Latter-day Saints are into philanthropy in a big way.

Bushman creatively labels this new, expanded, and sweeping movement among church members "Radiant Mormonism." He suggests that these examples are "indicators of growing Mormon influence in the world." Although he and I have spoken together at various conferences and seminars, his words struck a chord in my heart as I've searched for ways to explain my life's work in mobilizing church members to reach out and make a difference. Whether I was keynoting a major global conference of LDS international officials from multiple governments, speaking to top executives from major corporations across the U.S. and world, advising LDS Church leaders at Salt Lake City headquarters or internationally, advising and training mission presidents, consulting with area presidencies, working with the church's women's leaders, and advising many other groups, much of my work has been what I consider *a call to social action* and a plea to empower the poor. I've dedicated more than four decades to helping individual Latter-day Saints learn how they can personally become change agents to reduce human suffering. This book brings many of those experiences together and shows how "faith, hope, and charity," combined with gospel-based social innovations and best practices in international development, can generate significant and long-lasting social impacts among the world's poor.

The Plague of Coronavirus/The Pandemic of Poverty

At the worldwide general conference of the LDS Church in October 2020, Apostle Jeffrey R. Holland (2020) lamented the coronavirus pandemic, one of the worst periods of collective suffering globally in a century, with hundreds of millions of people falling ill (more than 222 million as of early September 2021) and the subsequent millions of deaths that have rocked the nations of the world. He raised the ugly specter of individuals feeling deep sorrow, considering that "we are waging an 'all hands on deck' war with COVID-19, a solemn reminder that a virus 1,000 times smaller than a grain of sand can bring entire populations and global economies to their knees. We pray for those who have lost loved ones in this modern plague, as well as for those who are currently infected or at risk. We certainly pray for those who are giving such magnificent healthcare. When we have conquered this—and we will—may we be equally committed to freeing the world from the virus of hunger, freeing neighborhoods and nations from the virus of poverty."

This book is a call to action for Latter-day Saints and friends to work toward freeing the masses from the terrible pandemic suffered by those who are extremely poor. And a call for members of our church to take up the plight of absolute, suffocating human poverty. To lift up our heads, hearts, and hands by responding to church leaders' messages calling for assertive actions. To act, not simply await the "big solutions" of governments, businesses, the Red Cross, the United Nations, and huge healthcare institutions. To serve, not be passive in the face of examples of growing poverty arising from the pandemic's destruction. In sum: to reach out and make a difference.

This volume draws on the work and experience of some of the best and brightest among members of the Church who have given of their time, intellect, spiritual strength, leadership skills, and even personal funds to help improve society, especially in places where hunger, poverty, civil conflicts, oppression of women, and lack of schools and jobs, among other crises, all prevail. Does Mormonism have anything to say about such travails? Equally important, do its adherents play any part in combating such egregious and perplexing human problems? Let us ask ourselves if we are up to the task—not just institutionally through the formal leadership of the LDS Church, with its brainpower and considerable wealth, but also through the hearts and minds of its everyday members, who consider themselves disciples of Christ—the Living Christ who commands us all to "love thy neighbor."

Saving the Living, Not Just the Dead

According to the church's current prophet, President Russell M. Nelson, "Our Heavenly Father is concerned for [the poor and needy]. They are all his children. The poor—especially widows, orphans, and strangers—have long been the concern of God and the godly.... To those who cared for the poor, blessings were promised" (1986, p. 25). Thus, we are called to become "godly" by serving those who suffer. Now more than ever, Latter-day Saints are urged to follow what the church's early leaders, such as Joseph F. Smith (1905), taught: "A religion which has not the power to save people temporally and make them prosperous and happy here, cannot be depended upon to save them spiritually, to exalt them in the life to come." In *The Pearl of Great Price*, originally published in 1851, we read that "the Lord called his people Zion because they were of one heart and one mind and dwelt in righteousness, and there was *no poor among them*" (Moses 7:18). Elsewhere, scriptures contained in the Book of Mormon suggest that to actually create a righteous society, God's people must labor to ensure equality: "And they had all things common among them; therefore there were not rich and poor, bond and free, but they were all made free, and partakers of the heavenly gift" (4 Nephi 1:3).

This new book, *Radiant Mormonism*, shows how thousands of modern Latter-day Saints over the last several decades have awakened to the clarion call of prophets down through the ages to do good, serve the disenfranchised, and consecrate a portion of their own time, talents, and money to "lift the hands which hang down," as then-President Gordon Hinckley once tellingly described it in a church publication (1999). To me, this suggests the need for economic development and humanitarian service in changing the economic misfortunes of those at the "bottom of the pyramid" (Prahalad, 2006) so that we can empower them and enable them to more fully help themselves.

I have always been gratified, even glad, that wherever I've lived around the world, many of my LDS friends, as well as local and general leaders of the church itself, have emphasized the need for us as Christians to give to the poor. Yes, even to the beggars on the street. Some say we shouldn't do so, that beggars might waste our small contributions, using them for alcohol or drugs. Even certain cities in predominantly LDS Utah have passed laws to ban people from assisting those on our streets. I recall one wealthy friend, a former stake and mission president, never giving anyone a handout. In contrast, I always did. One day his wife explained to me his refusal. He had told her his policy was that he would give a couple of dollars to a beggar or "panhandler," as he called them, only if the Spirit prompted him to do so. Yet, having at the time reached his sixties, apparently, he had never been inspired to help. I laughed and asked if he was ever inspired by the Holy Ghost in *any* decision, but she demurred.

In contrast to one person's selfish justification for being stingy, I have often cited the prophet Brigham Young's teaching on this matter—a view that my friend seemingly rejected. In his own words, Young condemned the attitude I hear in church so very often about members being stingy for fear of helping people who don't 'deserve' it. I think it's totally at odds with what it says in Mosiah too. Reason: it does not mince words. Suppose that in this community there are ten beggars who beg from door to door for something to eat, and that nine of them are imposters who beg to escape work, and with an evil heart practice imposition upon the generous and sympathetic, and that only one of the ten who visit your doors is worthy of your bounty; which is best, to give food to the ten, to make sure of helping the truly needy one, or to repulse the ten because you do not know which is the worthy one? You will all say, administer charitable gifts to the ten, rather than turn away the only truly worthy and truly needy person among them. If you do this, it will make no difference in your blessings, whether you administer to worthy or unworthy persons, inasmuch as you give alms with a single eye to assist the truly needy (*Doctrines of Brigham Young*, p. 274).

Likewise, a friend in Okinawa once told me of an incident that occurred when President Howard W. Hunter was speaking at a 1976 district conference in Japan. In his talk, he told the participants that, after he left his hotel that morning to go to the chapel, he was approached by a beggar on the street. He told the audience that he had given the beggar some money from his own wallet and hoped all the Saints would have done the same. I've heard many other Brethren say similar things.

My father, as well as his parents from Ohio and those even further back on my paternal line, were all American Methodists. I appreciated the fact that Brother Brigham himself was Methodist, along with his family. The Prophet Joseph declared that Methodism was the most similar religion to Mormonism of any other faith. So I've always appreciated the ideas of John Wesley, an early advocate of Methodism in the U.K. He occasionally preached sermons that he would end with an old maxim: "Make all you can, save all you can, give all you can." Wesley's counsel, along with similar views about charity by other religious leaders, has served as a hallmark of my expanded view of LDS values about charity and sharing our material resources.

Ways to Donate in Doing Good

Latter-day Saints can do good and provide humanitarian service in a variety of ways:

1. First come the traditional church programs for the Saints, such as paying tithing, making fast offerings, carrying out LDS welfare efforts for our members, donating to the church's Perpetual Education Fund for returned missionaries, and so on. I've come to believe that this kind of service—these LDS offerings, the tithes that we give to bless the Saints, and others—should be our top priority.
2. A second and more recent area of outreach and humanitarian assistance consists of a variety of church programs for our non-Latter-day Saint neighbors. These include the church's Humanitarian Fund, which was established in the 1980s, as well as Latter-day Saint Charities, which began in 2000, and the many efforts of the church to partner with other institutions. The Church partners with other religious groups (like Catholic Relief Services); governments in times of crises (such as the tsunami in Indonesia); other nongovernmental organizations (NGOs) beyond our own, such as the Muslim Relief Society; and businesses and various other LDS-sponsored outreach efforts to bless our nonmember neighbors in need.
3. The third category of doing good while providing humanitarian assistance—and the one this book emphasizes—is our direct engagement in individual acts of consecration and stewardship. These are

what we might refer to as personal initiatives, not prompted by the church's programs, but rather individual acts that often arise after we pray about how we might help those around us, or when we see on network news the devastation affecting a community or a region or a country, even our own neighbors next door, and those we see suffering and struggling in our own community. *I believe it is crucially important that we engage in all three kinds of activities globally.*

This volume emphasizes the third category of actions—those that President Hinckley referred to when he voiced his concern that we not depend solely on large organizations or the institutional service, even of the Church. According to him, "We must take care of [the poor] and we must have the facilities to do so. But we must be careful not to over institutionalize that care. . . . I think there is a tendency among us to say, 'Oh, the church will take care of that. I pay my fast offering. Let the church take care of that.' We need as individuals, I think, to reach down and extend a helping hand without notice . . . to give of that with which the Lord has so generously blessed us" (Hinckley, 2016, p. 459). So he advocated that we also engage in noninstitutionalized acts of service to the poor. On this matter, and following his leadership, I wrote a best-selling LDS book, *Working Toward Zion: Principles of the United Order for the Modern World*, in which my coauthor, James Lucas, and I make the case for practicing principles of consecration and stewardship today, not merely in the coming millennium or in another distant time (Lucas and Woodworth, 1996).

Beyond LDS Institutional Aid to the Poor

Dedicated Latter-day Saints strive to develop the capacity to personally apply the wonderful teachings in the Book of Mormon, in which one humble leader, King Benjamin, clearly affirms that service to others is, in fact, service to heaven. "I tell you these things that ye may learn wisdom; that ye may learn that when ye are in the service of your fellow beings ye are only in the service of your God" (Mosiah 2:17).

As another president of the church, Harold B. Lee, acknowledged, the importance of us members' aiding the poor is critical, going beyond merely carrying out missionary efforts to convert the masses. "I want to say to you that we might just as well throw our hats in the air and scream as to hope to convert spiritually an individual ... whose existence has been reduced to the instincts of animal survival.... We must take care of their material needs and give them a taste of the kind of salvation that they do not have to die to get before we can lift their thinking to a higher plane" (Lee, 1996, 321).

In 1982, President Spencer W. Kimball had articulated three purposes for the church: (1) to proclaim the gospel, (2) to perfect the Saints, and (3) to redeem the dead. These statements guided much of the church's policy-making and practices by providing a framework for emphasizing what we, members and officials alike, should do as a major global religious organization. They were articulated precisely at the time when many corporate consultants and CEOs were attempting to make their organizational purposes explicit so they could achieve maximum results in their work, hit higher outputs, bank larger profits, and reach greater excellence. So the prophet made three such mission statements for LDS members some 40 years ago.

Yet some of us at the time felt that something significant was lacking. Sure, we ought to preach our message to unbelievers and to baptize those seeking the truth who become converted. Clearly, our fellow LDS members needed to grow in truth and light until they became "more holy," as much as is humanly possible. And obviously, performing the sacred work of genealogical research and performing temple ordinances for our ancestors, indeed for the whole world's dead down through history, was a critical goal. But I often wondered about and prayed for an additional driving purpose. While I certainly believed we should work to save the dead, I also deeply felt that we should save the living. Drawing on the marvelous scriptures in the Book of Mormon about Zion and serving others, I have always been inspired by those prophetic teachings that suggest we could build a social utopia as identified in 4th Nephi (Woodworth, 1995).

As the scriptures admonish all true Saints, "after ye have obtained a hope in Christ ye shall obtain riches, if ye seek them; and ye will seek them for the intent to do good—to clothe the naked, and to feed the hungry, and to liberate the captive, and administer relief to the sick and the afflicted" (Jacob 2:19).

The Church's Fourth Mission

Over the years, in conversations with some of the Brethren I knew, I spoke of my sense that we needed to expand the church's mission by considering an emphasis on helping those in poverty. In numerous meetings during my years of serving as an informal adviser on church community outreach and service, I often argued such logic. In hundreds of my fireside presentations, in Utah, throughout the U.S., and even around the globe, I tried to make the case for an additional emphasis. In my writings of conference and Education Week speeches, in the classes I have led at Brigham Young University's Marriott School of Business, as well as in various other settings, I have pled the cause of the poor. Yet, in many cases, my pleas were met with demurrals, denials, and delays. Many people simply dismissed my idea as merely a secondary matter. Some even countered that they thought the essence of their various religious efforts ought to fit neatly within the official threefold missions stated by the Brethren, rather than adding a fourth.

Over time, however, a number of miraculous changes occurred! One of the first ones happened in the mid-1980s, when the church Humanitarian Fund was established. It was, in part, a response to the petitions of many Mormons in America and Europe who called for Church Headquarters to take action to address the massive East African crisis in which millions of children, and even their mothers and fathers, were perishing of starvation because of drought and civil wars. The Brethren felt inspired to take action, and two general fasts were called for, resulting in the collection of more than $10 million from members for relief in 1985 alone. Elder M. Russell Ballard traveled to several refugee camps, his first experience witnessing miseries on that scale, and later said it was a life-changing experience. I wish every Latter-day Saint would seek to have that same experience today by aiding various causes.

While much good was accomplished through the Humanitarian Fund, LDS efforts could not reach certain regions of the world because the church had no official recognition or legal status there. In some cases, we could partner with Catholic Relief Services or other entities. Many of us engaged at the time in working professionally within developing countries wished to establish an LDS nongovernmental organization or nonprofit (an NGO) through which material goods—along with LDS experts in poverty-alleviation, agricultural assistance, and other aid strategies—could provide their expertise to people in those countries.

A second innovation occurred a few years later, with the creation of the church-founded NGO, called Latter-day Saint Charities (LDSC). This happened in 1996 under the direction of the First Presidency. Then-President Gordon B. Hinckley had been keenly aware of the world's suffering masses as he became the most-traveled prophet in the church's history. So he approved the establishment of LDSC. Since then, LDS Charities (to use the shorter name) has been registered as an NGO in a number of nations hard hit by civil unrest, floods, famines, earthquakes, and other disasters. LDSC's many varied activities have enabled the church to channel hundreds of millions of dollars in relief and development around the world.

The next major step in the evolution of service to those in need was to set up the Perpetual Education Fund. This program was announced by President Hinckley at General Conference on March 31, 2001. I began discussing this idea in the late 1980s and had even proposed the creation of a Perpetual Education Fund (PEF), based on the early Mormon pioneer model known as the Perpetual Emigration Fund. In the mid-1800s, the Church brought thousands of converts, mostly from Europe, to settle in Utah and build Zion. Beginning in about 1995, with a few associates, I began to solicit private donations from wealthy Latter-day Saints. We created education funds for returned missionaries (RMs) in such countries as Brazil (where I had served my mission), Chile (where one of my sons served his mission), and Mexico. I called those efforts in Portuguese or Spanish *"fondos perpetuos de educacion"* (perpetual education funds, or "PEFs"). We saw the need and realized we could pull together the necessary funding through our NGOs, though some church officials either did not like the idea or felt it was unnecessary.

Imagine my joy, then, when the church finally announced the creation of the new PEF for returned missionaries in 2001! I dropped to my knees and gave a prayer of thanksgiving because I knew firsthand how such small loans transformed many impoverished Saints—especially those who had returned to their home countries despite lacking jobs. As that church-sponsored fund has since swelled to many hundreds of millions of dollars, I have seen the lives of young adults in developing countries transformed. In fact, the PEF program became so successful—growing to an estimated one billion dollars—that the Church instructed church members to cease donating and give their contributions to other church programs instead. A few colleagues and I, including some of my friends who administered the PEF, eventually received approval from the First Presidency to broaden its agenda to what is now called LDS Self-Reliant Services (SRSS), a program that offers tools and teachings to assist many impoverished LDS members, not only returned missionaries, to improve themselves educationally, financially, professionally, and even socially.

However, I also felt deeply that we, as Mormons, could make a larger difference in society, not just with our own members or missionaries. Back in the 1970s, I was pursuing a Ph.D. in organizational behavior (comprising management, sociology, and psychology) at the University of Michigan. During that time, I sought to combat racism and poverty in inner cities such as those in Detroit, Flint,

Muskegon, and Grand Rapids. I had the opportunity to mobilize a number of LDS members in these projects. Later, I lived as a visiting professor for over a year in Rio de Janeiro, Brazil, where I learned a great deal about hunger and poverty in Latin America. I began to feel that more assistance was needed, and that not only did the United Nations, the World Bank, and the U.S. Government have contributions to make for the poor, the Church did too.

During the 1980s, after the church's threefold mission had been proclaimed, I sensed something was still lacking. We needed a *fourth*. My feelings and prayers for this new emphasis had grown stronger over those several long decades. When President Thomas S. Monson succeeded President Hinckley, I hoped that he would impel another expansion of the Church's focus. After all, President Monson was best known for his personal sensitivity regarding those near death's door, whether in a hospital, a nursing facility, or at home. He was the one admonishing us, by both precept and example, to "visit the fatherless and the widows in their affliction" and to give generously of our time and energy to minister to the "have-nots" in our own community as well as around the world.

President Monson called for a new, fourth purpose of the church—"to care for the poor and needy"—that would raise the prominence of doctrines admonishing us to become more aware of suffering, reach out to others more broadly, and provide community service to the downtrodden. This would be accomplished, not only as a church growing in membership globally, but also by individual members.

We should remember, however, that this new emphasis has actually been among the core elements of church teachings since the early days of the Restoration. Brigham Young argued: "We will take a moral view, a political view, and see the inequality that exists in the human family.... It is an unequal condition to mankind.... What is to be done? The Latter-day Saints will never accomplish their mission until this inequality shall cease on the earth" (*Journal of Discourses*, 19:9).

Adding a new fourth mission helped fulfill a scriptural mandate: "for I will consecrate of the riches of those who embrace my gospel among the Gentiles unto the poor of my people who are of the house of Israel" (*Doctrine and Covenants* 42:39).

Nobody knows why these changes took so long to be institutionalized in Mormonism. Perhaps we as members were not yet ready for them. Many Saints in the United States seemed tired of funding the bulk of donations through their fast offerings. Whether it was a racial issue, or a political agenda, some seemed (and maybe still do) to feel that the poor of our inner cities and the Third World brought their problems on themselves: They were unemployed because they were lazy. They were sick because they were drug or alcohol addicts. They were alone because they simply weren't married in the temple. I disagreed with such assertions, but I have heard such stereotypes often over the years.

A second explanation as to why the fourth mission change took so long to accomplish is that in the early days of the Church, many members seemed shocked by principles of consecration that required care for the poor. This attitude has persisted until today among certain Church members in Deseret's intermountain area. Fully accepting and practicing the laws of selflessness and love were hard back in those pioneer days and are probably much more so now when we are swimming in a flood of materialism and greed. Our society is bombarded by ads that convey the message that "consumption is good, simplicity is bad." Having a bigger home or fancier car seems essential to the public image for many, including LDS families living in expensive condos in Manhattan and Palo Alto or on the foothills of Salt Lake City and Bountiful.

We can also attribute the Church's new emphasis on social justice to the ever-present context of human suffering that we see around us. Statistics from Action Against Hunger (2020) suggest that some 780 million people currently live in "extreme" poverty—that is, those eking out an existence on under $1.90 per person per day. More poor people struggle to live in the world today than ever before. Some 328 million are children under age 18, roughly two million of whom die each year, most from malnutrition. We can add other factors that make these statistics even worse: poverty and preventable diseases. Many families around the globe became richer than ever in recent years, and America has seen a huge jump in the number of billionaires over the past decade. Millions have suffered from the growing gap between haves and have-nots.

The LDS Church worked hard to create a culture of caring for the poor, which took on particular significance during and after the Great Recession of 2008–2010. As of this writing, the COVID-19 pandemic continues to inflict devastating blows on the world's communities, thrusting some 80 million people into worse poverty than they have ever faced (CGAP, 2021). Tens of millions of Americans and hundreds of millions of people globally have become dangerously ill; many millions have suffered and died, seen their jobs disappear, or been denied access to healthcare. Sadly, countless families have also lost their homes because of financial crises.

Meanwhile, the greed and predatory practices of the world's wealthiest and most powerful families have increased their financial holdings, resulting in even greater difficulties for the have-nots. In the United States, for example, during the current pandemic, increasing inequality in wealth distribution and the rise in the number of unbanked people continue. The divide between billionaires and humanity's bottom 50 percent keeps expanding. During the pandemic, which began in March 2020, American billionaires dramatically increased their financial holdings by a *trillion dollars* of new wealth.

Now in 2021, extreme poverty appears to be a never-ending phenomenon that continues to dampen or even tank the national economies of a hundred-plus countries. By 2030, if "business-as-usual" thinking continues to dominate economic policies, hundreds of millions of human beings are projected to be trapped in the ugly realities of extreme poverty. The old folk-adage about "the rich getting richer and the poor poorer" seems to still describe economic reality.

Perhaps the LDS prophets of today sense that neither Big Business nor Big Government will solve society's inequities on their own. It will take a new sector, a social innovation movement in which average folks like you and me begin to assert our agency and act on our own to design new initiatives, not from the top down, but the bottom up.

Many rich Mormons have been (and perhaps still are) offended by the radical idea of a new fourth mission for the church: that of the *redistribution of wealth*. Perhaps some within the church's leadership were themselves not convinced. This may have been why in 2009 there was not a big public announcement about this sea-changing idea. I know many top church officials have debated such policies over the years. Their discussions have included disagreements over having Mormon missionaries spend time each week doing volunteer community service; LDS donations going to Catholics, Muslims, and those of other faiths; and the channeling of church resources to other nations, especially those of leftist or socialist political ideologies. Yet, the cries of the poor have not gone unheard. The suffering of the widow has not been ignored. We must never forget the admonition of the Apostle James: "Pure religion and undefiled before God and the Father is this, "To visit the fatherless and widows in their affliction, and to keep himself unspotted from the world" (James 1:27).

Mormon Means "More Good"

With this overview, I conclude chapter 1 of *Radiant Mormonism* by summarizing the key chapters that follow. I will highlight seven cases of personal initiative shown by Latter-day Saints in reaching out to empower the global poor and to reduce human struggles. Most of these programs occur in other countries where poverty is overwhelming. The bulk of these stories are told from my personal experience as a "Social Entrepreneur"—a Latter-day Saint who has given four decades of my life to reducing people's suffering. I try to spend my days and practice my work by internalizing the meaning of the word *Mormon*. The Prophet Joseph said, "I may safely say that the word *Mormon* means *more good*" as he drew on the original languages of the Book of Mormon in an 1843 edition of a missionary magazine in the U.K. called *Times and Seasons* (4:194; cited in Smith, 2009, pp. 299–300). More recently, in a 1990 general conference address, President Hinckley echoed that when he declared "*Mormon* Should Mean 'More Good'" (1990). The phrase became what he termed his own "personal motto." He went on to affirm that throughout his life, he sought to "make it shine with added luster." Thus, this book—*Radiant Mormonism.*

In the spirit of clarity, this book does not contain the sort of "fluff" sometimes found in LDS books that emphasize "sweetness and light," featuring filler and feel-good stories without bothering to discuss the tough issues or hard facts about the difficulties one encounters when "working to do good." Serving people is always a mosaic of actions that should include the "good, the bad, *and* the ugly," as the title of an old Clint Eastwood movie says. So the following chapters on self-reliance, humanitarianism, and economic assistance in Zion-building do occasionally critique the challenges and occasional conflicts in designing and rolling out social innovations that can actually empower the poor. Readers should consider them both as opportunities to learn in greater depth and as reality checks that, I trust, will inspire us all to do better than we have done in seeking to reduce human suffering.

The following seven mini-cases report on efforts made by me and my far-flung BYU students, neighbors, church leaders, wealthy donors, home-makers, and average Americans as well as international Latter-day Saints to "practice" our religion as the Apostle James declares. None of these initiatives were carried out poorly. In the first several instances, and during the early years when I was starting out on my life's true "mission," I tried to learn deeply, avoid any massive mistakes, keep all our volunteers safe, and do as much good as we collectively could do in designing social innovations while gradually fanning out around the globe. Perhaps we Saints, being "the people of Zion," have not yet achieved a utopia, though doing *more good* is clearly what we should be striving for.

References

Action Against Hunger. (2020). https://www.actionagainsthunger.org/global-poverty-hunger-facts.

Bushman, R. (2017). "Embracing a 'Radiant' Mormonism." *Deseret News.* November 16. https://www.deseret.com/2017/11/16/20623103/richard-bushman-embracing-a-radiant-mormonism

CGAP. 2021. *The State of Economic Inclusion Report 2021: The Potential to Scale.* World Bank.

Hinckley, G. B. (1990). "*Mormon* Should Mean 'More Good.'" *Ensign.* November.

Hinckley, G. B. (1999). "The Work Moves Forward." *Ensign.* April.

Hinckley, G. B. (2016). *Teachings of Gordon B. Hinckley.* Deseret Book, 459.

Holland, J. R. (2020). https://www.churchofjesuschrist.org/study/general-conference/2020/04/43holland. April.

Lee, Harold B. *The Teachings of Harold B. Lee.* Bookcraft, 1996.

Lucas, J. W., and Woodworth, W. P. (1996). *Working Toward Zion: Principles of the United Order for the Modern World.* Aspen Books.

Nelson, R. M. (1986). "In the Lord's Own Way." *Ensign.* May.

Prahalad, C. K. (2006). *The Fortune at the Bottom of the Pyramid: Eradicating Poverty Through Profits.* Dorling Kindersley Pvt.

Smith, J. (2009). From the 1843 *Times and Seasons*, 4:194; cited in *Teachings of the Prophet Joseph Smith.* Deseret Book, 299–300.

Smith, J. F. (1905). "The Truth About Mormonism," *Out West.* Vol. 23, 242.

Woodworth, W. (1995). "The Socioeconomics of Zion." Chapter in *The Book of Mormon: Fourth Nephi Through Moroni: From Zion to Destruction.* (Charles D. Tate, Jr., and Monte S. Nyman, eds.) Religious Studies Center, Brigham Young University.

Young, B. (2013 edition). *Journal of Discourses*, vol. 19, Talk #9, Ogden, Utah, 1977, 19:9.

Young, B. *Doctrines of Brigham Young*, 274.

"Each Life That Touches Ours for Good"
LDS Hymns, No. 293

1. Each life that touches ours for good
   Reflects thine own great mercy, Lord;
   Thou sendest blessings from above
   Through words and deeds of those who love.

2. What greater gift dost thou bestow,
   What greater goodness can we know
   Than Christlike friends, whose gentle ways
   Strengthen our faith, enrich our days.

3. When such a friend from us departs,
   We hold forever in our hearts
   A sweet and hallowed memory,
   Bringing us nearer, Lord, to thee.

4. For worthy friends whose lives proclaim
   Devotion to the Savior's name,
   Who bless our days with peace and love,
   We praise thy goodness, Lord, above.

Text: Karen Lynn Davidson (1943–2019)
Music: A. Laurence Lyon (1934–2006)

2

HELP International

(Honduras and Beyond, 1999–2022)

Have you ever been trapped in a horrific storm while you struggled against winds, floods, and even death growing around you by the hour? Have you experienced something that wreaked havoc during very dark days and darker nights without electricity or communications? Or lived through a crisis that lasted for more than seven days of being whiplashed and you had to endure it for one, two, even ten years afterward? A crisis that made your spouse afraid and your children cry day and night? Think of yourself being in such circumstances back in 1998.

The thrust of this chapter tells of a wild, radical idea that I was inspired to implement in 1999 after Hurricane Mitch slammed into Central America. It's a tale of my and others' designing and carrying out programs that address global problems—poverty, hunger, disease, and other forms of human suffering. It explains principles and values with the ability to reduce suffering, such as consecration, love, self-reliance, poverty alleviation, and to learn that "when ye are in the service of your fellow beings ye are only in the service of your God" (Mosiah 2:17). It featured innovative concepts such as microfinance, disaster recovery, nongovernmental organizations (NGOs), women's empowerment, social and economic impacts, social entrepreneurship, civil society, and much more. This story

▲ HELP International's Nicaraguan women microcredit borrowers

The struggles of the global poor that we are called to help fix, reduce, and eventually eliminate

▼ The challenges of Latin American peasant farmworkers

of Latter-day Saint service to humanity in a time of crisis embodies the teachings of an early Mormon apostle, Parley P. Pratt, who wrote that "I expect the Saints to give money for the support of the poor ... and if they do not do it, their religion is vain.... We preach a religion which very materially affects men's purses; and a religion that does not affect men's purses is worse than none" (Pratt, 1952).

In this chapter, I report on how my numerous program volunteers responded to Hurricane Mitch in Honduras, the earthquakes that hit El Salvador, and other calamities. Together we explored the ways that business schools can transform the world and fight poverty. Which leading-edge tools, I asked, can we apply in new and creative ways to build a more civil society? What learning experiences in institutions such as Brigham Young University could empower my student volunteers and some faculty members to benefit the world by strengthening NGOs, starting new nonprofits, and facilitating microfinance and social entrepreneurship globally? After analyzing these cases, I will explore how other academics may adopt and adapt our cutting-edge approaches to reduce human problems by extending their traditional professional practices into new frontiers for both social and economic justice.

The Launch of HELP International

The nonprofit NGO that we called HELP International was created in a class I taught in 1999 at Brigham Young University's Marriott School of Business during the winter semester. It was a response to the Hurricane Mitch disaster that decimated parts of Central America. HELP began as a course project, yet it has grown in numbers and expanded impacts for over twenty years. Mitch flooded large areas of Central America, leaving some 11,000 people dead, many missing, and a million people homeless. The country of Honduras was hardest hit, with experts declaring it had been set back half a century.

Seeing media reports of the region's devastation brought tears to my eyes as I prayed during the university's holiday break of our Christmas season. I kept wondering what I could do to help. The

LDS values of care, service, and gospel principles peppered my mind and troubled my conscience every day over more than two weeks. What could *I* myself do to help? Donate to the LDS Church humanitarian fund? Yes. Pray more fervently? Certainly. Do more frequent and intense fasting from meals, beyond the typical LDS practice of fasting on the first Sunday of the month? Of course. But what more might be possible?

By early January 1999, I decided that in fact I could boldly create and frame a new course for a fresh semester—out of which HELP International grew. In addition to my regular instruction load, I proposed a new BYU elective course titled Organizational Behavior 490: Becoming a Global Change Agent/Social Entrepreneur. I vividly remember on the first day of class asking students whether a university could be relevant to a societal crisis. Specifically I asked: "Does BYU have the potential to reduce human suffering?" (BYU, 2021). Also: "Is an institution such as the Marriott School able to move beyond corporate power, profits, and economic clout to serve the poor in their tragic struggles?" Most students were shocked at my queries, saying they'd never considered such questions. Nor had their other professors. My response was "Great! You're in for a radically different experience."

Back in those days, there was no online access for students to find new classes to take. Had the internet even been invented by then? So I made a few fliers and taped them up across campus. The course would be an elective option because it was not an official, approved class. But I wanted to find a few venturesome students willing to learn ways to reduce human suffering, take risks with their learning, and show a spirit of adventure. Attendance at the first several meetings was dismal: perhaps a dozen students. So I did more to advertise, even though custodians were removing my forbidden fliers from building entrances and walls. I asked the class to inform their friends and try to recruit more students. After two weeks there were 40 to 50 attending. Even after the university's Add/Drop deadline passed, more kept joining, though they would earn no university credit. The class grew to include students from such programs as Master of Business Administration, Master of Public Administration, and Master of Accountancy, as well as management undergraduates, and others from across campus in the social sciences, engineering, the law school, and so on.

In all my courses I included a number of required readings that were central to an LDS view that the faithful should continually strive to learn about innovative teachings for improving society, reducing hunger and poverty, and living lives of consecration and stewardship in today's challenging world. Thus, the academic focus of the class was on my 498-page volume of teachings and innovations that were designed and carried out by early LDS pioneers in Utah as they practiced the United Order and empowered their poor (Lucas and Woodworth, 1996).

We also required students to engage in a service project of some type so they could learn how to apply concepts they studied, as well as to contribute to some kind of societal improvement, however small. But because of Central America's suffering, I proposed that we design a project to actually provide aid. In other words, I suggested that we collaborate on a plan and then, after the semester ended, a few of us would go down to devastated areas to aid at least some of the hardest-hit people, the worst victims of Hurricane Mitch's destruction. My idea sounded radical to some, probably crazy to others, yet excitement for such a venture began building immediately among my students. I was surprised at the energy and long hours everyone began giving to what some called "Warner's wild idea." (Since I considered those in my classes to be my fellow students/scholars, I always asked them to call me by my first name; this was challenging for students from Asia because of their cultural norms.) I wondered myself if we would succeed! So I gave the project my best thinking and managerial skills, while also spending a great deal of time on my knees asking for heaven's help. I knew I needed spiritual power, in addition to academic prowess, intellectual capital, and high energy.

A few of my students began wondering if I might be "off in the deep end." Others laughingly said, "Warner's a visionary man," drawing on the complaints of certain prophets in the early part of the Book of Mormon. I too wondered! My wife probably worried more. I had done something similar a decade earlier, creating what I intended should be a short-term graduate seminar about starting a limited microcredit project with a BYU-initiated NGO now called Mentors International. Back then my humble little idea took off with just a handful of students and despite the warnings of certain campus administrators who disliked what they called my "radicalness." Yet that simple little NGO not only grew relatively quickly, beginning in 1989–90, but it continues to expand to other countries even today. So I knew then that our HELP International class efforts could also succeed.

Early on there was considerable debate as to what the project should be named. Finally, students selected the name "H.E.L.P. Honduras" for the new NGO (meaning "*H*elp *EL*iminate *P*overty"). The simple organization title evolved as we moved into other nations beyond Honduras. Thus, the expanded organization title, HELP International, became solidified. Within two years, we determined that our small 1999 effort was not simply a semester project, but rather a long-term NGO. It was felt that it should become a 501(c)(3) nonprofit. So the expanded name, denoting more of an international agenda, not merely a Honduras project, was retained and continues today. Short and simple: the universally understood cry "HELP."

BYU Classroom Methodologies

We formed the class as a "self-organizing system" of eight teams to cover various aspects of the project. Each team read my required course materials and developed some of their own. My overview lectures to everyone centered on training them in a few strategies about how to change the world, then organizing teams of practitioners who would help to plan programs or even travel to Honduras during summer 1999 to serve as relief and reconstruction volunteers, as well as creators of new communal banks among the poor. These teams of class members formed specific teams to deal with travel and communications systems we could use out in rural areas, and, most important, to practice in-country safety and health precautions.

Each team did research on their topic, presented to and trained their colleagues during the last weeks of the class, and prepared documentation for a volunteer manual. The strategy was designed so that as soon as the semester ended, the first team of HELP leaders would fly to Honduras to lay the groundwork for other teams that would be established in-country. They would also finalize our incipient partnership with a local microfinance organization that would keep operating the village banks we were going to launch after we returned to college in the fall. Further, they would arrange housing and do other needed logistic tasks.

To my great surprise and pleasure, the course became a dynamic, participatory experience. All told, some 79 individuals either registered for the course or attended twice a week as auditing students. We formed teams to achieve the following: Plan the logistics of going to Honduras, determine where the needs were greatest, explore which microfinance institutions (MFIs), if any, were already in the country and which we could partner with, and determine what kinds of relief and humanitarian aid we might offer to poor families. As well, we organized a Honduras "culture team" to teach volunteers about local norms, values, and technical terms, all in Spanish. Another group was established as a public relations and marketing group to obtain media attention in the area. One of the most important student teams was a fundraising group to help generate monies. Finally, we created a group of microcredit resource people who would train everyone in the class about village banking and how it operates. We put together a packet of the deliverables from each of the OB 490 teams and had it bound and distributed late in the semester as "The Honduras Stewardship Project Handbook." It was a volume of instructions, ground rules, international development theories, and practical advice for each participant going to Central America.

As we initiated our adventure, we heard from university administrators, faculty colleagues of mine, and numerous community professionals who generally opposed the project. They claimed that I would not find more than a half dozen students to go in-country, and that we would not raise sufficient funds, as well as asserting that large relief organizations "would take care of everything," as one told me. They merely assumed the "Big Boys," as I typically called them, would solve life's problems: USAID, the U.N., the World Bank, churches, and the Red Cross. My personal philosophy was—and still is—that we each have responsibilities to improve the world. Even in a huge disaster like the ravages of Hurricane Mitch, *you and I* can always make a difference.

Well, the BYU bureaucrats were wrong. At the end of the semester, 46 students went to Honduras, each committed to volunteering six weeks on site (some worked for 10 or even 20 weeks). We successfully raised a whopping $116,000, while generating contributions from around BYU campus as well as funds from parents and other family members, from a few local businesses, and even from students' neighbors. In Central America, we created no fewer than 46 microcredit organizations, new small communal banks, with our partner, FINCA International (the Foundation for International Community Assistance). We also gave FINCA $40,000 to recapitalize some of its own village bank groups whose microenterprises were destroyed by Hurricane Mitch. Thus, in reality, we had created almost a hundred banks altogether. These young HELP International social entrepreneurs became quite skilled in a multitude of activities, very rapidly.

On the Ground in Honduras

In May 1999, arriving in Central America, we were shocked at the destruction's impacts still evident after only a few months' time. Even though we had seen television footage, read press reports, and searched multiple government resources to gain a comprehensive understanding of the crisis, we were ill prepared for what we encountered in-country. Many hurricane survival victims were cramped in temporary lean-to shelters, makeshift "houses" poorly covered by blue plastic tarps that were gradually being shredded by the strong blasts of evening winds. Dead bodies were still being found under the bushes along the banks of the main river that meandered through the capital, Tegucigalpa. Buzzards high up in the trees lingered, waiting to get at the next torsos of rotting human flesh they knew would soon appear. Bridges and other sections of the great Pan American Highway had been destroyed. Overturned automobiles, trashed downtown buildings that looked as though they had been thrown during a game of pick-up sticks, and other signs of devastation and garbage odors abounded. People especially felt afraid during the night, particularly women and children. Every time a bit of rain began falling, many ran screaming for help and safety. Hundreds of thousands of Mitch survivors struggled as they tried to cope with post-traumatic stress disorders (PTSDs).

In this traumatic environment, we began our labors. While some NGO officials had told us nothing could be done, in fact we accomplished much over the time we were in-country. I hope that, as I relate my and my volunteers' collective learning in the trenches, as well as citing the experience of others, some of this chapter's ideas and suggestions may be useful to other professors and students in the future. Out of the mess and the mud and the homelessness, many insights were acquired. This story is not some theoretical treatise about ethereal concepts. Rather, it arises from the blood and guts of Third World realities.

A summary of all the social and economic impacts of our efforts is beyond the scope of this chapter. Still, a short overview may be descriptive. Our HELP volunteers lived with poor families, paying them a per diem amount for room and board, which aided in the Hondurans' financial recovery. They provided over 20,000 hours of volunteer service, to women and children in refugee camps, to local governments, and to peasant farmers. Volunteers shoveled out mud, washed and disinfected walls, and painted and reopened village schools. They provided manpower to local municipalities by cleaning streets and rebuilding bridges, and assisted groups of peasant farmers who suddenly had neither tools nor seed nor fertilizer. Many volunteers' hours were spent in providing loving aid at orphanages to the children and even the Catholic nuns who were overwhelmed by the growing number of new orphans. HELP also purchased tools for farmers so they could jump-start farm preparations on their tiny plots of land and be ready for the next growing season. We also bought fertilizer and seed to enhance their future recovery.

Multilateral aid institutions declared that Honduras was set back five decades by Hurricane Mitch. Some 70 percent of the country's infrastructure was damaged. Nearly 90 percent of its agricultural produce was obliterated, and the large multinational fruit companies pulled out. Throughout Central America, an estimated 20,000 people had died, an equal number were still missing, and a million were homeless. HELP Honduras's microcredit efforts created some 800 jobs that summer, benefiting nearly 4,000 individuals. Beyond microcredit, we taught computer skills, gathered older street children into care centers, and served in understaffed rural medical clinics. One young BYU student, Vickie, even delivered five babies!

When she returned to campus and told me this, I was stunned. I was glad that her natal work went well, but I worried that Marriott School administrators and other campus bureaucrats, hearing about our efforts, would become angry and make life for students and myself more difficult. So I asked Vickie, "Of the five babies you helped deliver, how many lived?" She laughed and said: "All of them. Everything is good with the infants and their mothers." I felt so relieved. Then I said, "Vickie, I didn't realize you were in pre-med. Or are you studying nursing?" She replied, "Warner, I'm an accounting student." I'm still shocked about this now as I write.

In launching programs to assist Hondurans, we sought donated relief supplies from church groups in Utah, Idaho, Arizona, and California. We took toys to impoverished children in the Hurricane Mitch refugee camps, including lots of soccer balls and air pumps. We delivered quilts and baby blankets lovingly made by the hands of LDS Relief Society women throughout communities in the Rocky Mountain states. We acquired supplies for various needs among the people, families in particular. For instance, we made kits of school supplies and gave them to children after we had hauled the mud out of their schools and had helped to get the classrooms cleaned, painted, and ready for learning. We assembled hundreds of newborn kits for expectant Honduran mothers. We also put together hygiene kits for refugee families—soap, towels, toothpaste and toothbrushes, washcloths, and hair shampoo.

The results? Our social entrepreneurial efforts, new capital, training materials, and organizing skills were supplemented with a host of other humanitarian aid strategies to help the poor get back on their feet. The needs were considerable for the thousands of families that HELP was able to assist. The result for these BYU students was a new perspective gained. I often told my classes that while they cannot do *everything*, they can at least do *something*. They can make a difference, even while young and without decent incomes. They learned the importance of preparation, financing, and skill acquisition. Significantly, they also learned that young college students can become empowered to serve the poor and generate long-term impacts that may eventually become sustainable. By doing so, they can begin to have a life-changing experience that will continue to be played out as other crises occur in the future. Perhaps most important, these Latter-day Saint students understood deeply that we can—and should—consecrate more of our lives to empowering others so they too may become self-reliant, both spiritually and economically. Looking back some two decades now, I believe they can see the ripple effects of HELP Honduras that have continued on into the rest of their lives as social entrepreneurs.

HELP's Initial Outcomes

In contrast to the traditional approach of higher learning conveyed in many college courses, the concepts and strategies that derived from the original course I taught in early 1999 differed from most other experiences, whether at BYU or across the nation. My approach centered on the novel ideas that other global change agents and I were developing. It was a kind of social entrepreneurship that may be considered "action research"—using concepts and tools in hands-on ways, collaborating with indigenous people, developing social experiments, writing up the results, creating case studies, and extending theories in alternative ways. According to one BYU student, Erik Lewis (class of '99), who volunteered in Honduras in May 1999 before launching his career at the prestigious accounting firm Arthur Andersen in Chicago, "Teams of student social entrepreneurs are beginning to span the earth and have an impact for good."

In late April 1999, the first HELP team departed the United States for Central America. By early May almost a dozen student volunteers were there, doing an initial, on-the-ground scan of areas hard-hit by Hurricane Mitch, generating data on families and needs, interviewing LDS Church and community leaders, and meeting with U.S. embassy officials, foreign nonprofit aid groups, and Honduran relief organizations.

Below are a few results of HELP's early efforts:

- Participating students in the project were also recruited from other institutions: BYU, Utah Valley University, Stanford, Colorado State, Washington University of St. Louis, Virginia Tech, University of Utah, and more.
- 79 students were trained as social entrepreneurs in winter semester 1999.
- 46 students served in Honduras between May and September of 1999.
- Fundraising generated over $116,000.
- 47 new village banks were created, and 50 FINCA village banks destroyed by Hurricane Mitch were recapitalized.
- More than 800 jobs were generated that benefited as many as 4,000 victims of Hurricane Mitch.
- More than 20,000 community service hours were given in local governmental projects, refugee camps, schools, rural health clinics, orphanages, and the like.
- Some 20 years later, various innovative social and economic outcomes that grew out of our HELP inaugural effort are still occurring throughout the globe.

A more detailed look below indicates the types of projects implemented in devastated Honduras. They were carried out with careful planning by student leaders on the ground in-country, approved by several of us leaders working to provide guidelines and oversight from campus in Provo, Utah:

- Some 60 school kits assembled by a Provo LDS ward (each containing a small slate board, chalk, paper, pencils and pens, crayons and colored markers, scissors and glue) were given to a small, extremely poor elementary school. Because of Mitch, this school, in rural San Jeronimo, had lost all its supplies and was facing imminent closure, but thanks to these

materials, it reopened to teach peasant children in the region.
- As they collaborated with LDS welfare missionaries serving throughout Honduras, HELP students gave these church representatives entry to numerous village bank meetings so they could teach poor borrowers lessons on health, nutrition, and personal money management.
- Water purification systems, donated by a Seattle company, enabled U.S. volunteers not only to access clean, safe drinking water but also to create new businesses for local people to sell the product to their fellow townfolk.
- Other HELP teams designed and taught nutrition lessons for rural Honduran families.
- On the outskirts of Honduras's capital, Tegucigalpa, stood two huge refugee camps, one with some 500 families, the other with 2,000, victims of Mitch who lost everything. In May I visited the families, nearly all of them headed by single mothers. HELP volunteers became intensely involved in providing encouragement and donating goods to those camps.
- Some eight pickup-truckloads of used clothing were gathered in Utah and delivered to the Honduran poor.
- In Comayagua, the old capital of Honduras, which had been perhaps the most beautiful colonial city in the nation, the HELP team found an orphanage from which street children, all boys, had been rescued. One of the most pathetic outcomes of Hurricane Mitch was the increase in numbers of street children—perhaps as many as 10,000 who had lost their parents in 1998's floods. Without family or shelter, many were forced to survive in the streets by begging for food and sniffing glue. The glue-sniffing was not so much to get "high," but to reduce the gnawing pain

of hunger. With HELP's assistance, the Comayagua orphanage began to operate as a kind of boys' school where young men could learn to read and write, wash their own clothes, and develop woodworking or welding skills so that when they graduated they would have a potential vocation and a better future. Volunteers reported much satisfaction as they served at the school, giving toys, clothing, and other donated goods to these kids.

With respect to microcredit programs, during winter semester 1999 in our BYU planning, HELP first established linkages with other NGOs in Central America to learn their methods and best practices. The group ultimately decided to partner with FINCA (the Foundation for International Community Assistance) so that student volunteers could benefit from their experience, develop skills in organizing new microlending programs, carry out effective training, and add capital to small banks that wanted to offer larger loans to qualified borrowers.

During the first few weeks in Honduras, the HELP volunteers worked closely with officials in the FINCA microcredit program. Students met with their national leader and officers, observed how promoters started new banks, sat in on workshops and new startup meetings, and even followed borrowers back to learn about their businesses, how they worked, and what challenges they faced. HELP also donated tens of thousands of dollars to more than a dozen FINCA banks so that, by recapitalizing existing successful village banks, they could offer larger future loans to microentrepreneurs who had started very small but then paid off earlier loans and were now ready for larger amounts to grow their microenterprises.

Members of the HELP group then began to create brand-new village banks known as ACP groups—for *Acción Contra La Pobreza* (Action Against Poverty)—with training and preparation similar to what FINCA used. HELP volunteers provided the training and formally inaugurated each new bank, drawing on HELP donations raised in the U.S. Each new bank startup required an initial capital pool of at least the local equivalent of $2,500. After launching such a bank, volunteers returned to each weekly meeting to monitor the group's success, as well as to provide further training and consulting.

The wonderful impact of this effort so far can be summarized by several specific cases where lives were changed for the better, children were able to receive more nutritious meals, and families became strengthened.

Members of a new village bank starting up in a rural region called Aldea de Siria had a very positive experience. These women members (called *sócias*) literally became transformed by the group's first experience at borrowing money. As their loans were paid off, interns reported: "They were so excited, so proud of themselves for paying off 100 percent of their loans with interest, as well as having a savings account for the first time in their lives!" One microentrepreneur declared: "We may be poor and humble, but we are responsible and we work hard." The result was not just economic success, but a new, more confident self-image for such impoverished individuals.

Conception Hernandez Martinez, known as "Conchi" to her friends in the town of Danli, began her business with an initial microloan of 400 *lempiras* ($28 U.S.). With that tiny sum she built a simple wooden restaurant that measured 6 by 8 feet—a structure many in the developed world would call a "shack." Gradually, by serving good food and growing her customer base, she qualified for larger loans, and experienced significant improvements. The last time I saw her, Conchi's latest village bank loan totaled over 6,000 *lempiras* (some $420 U.S.) and she had become the proud owner of a large 120-by-75-foot restaurant, the most successful in the region. Her case is but one of hundreds of HELP microenterprises in which just a little capital went a long way. Creating "poverty banks" greatly affected hundreds of Honduran women, as well as thousands of their family members.

The HELP Honduras field director in Honduras that summer was an MBA student from BYU named Lisa Jones, a graduate of University of California–Berkeley. She proved to be a superb leader after completing her first year as a Marriott School MBA student, and is now on the faculty. Among her reports was the following cautionary sentence: "The efforts of our teams have yielded impressive outcomes so far, but our long-term impact and sustainability are yet to be determined." Approximately $116,000 was raised by enterprising volunteers who found generous donors, in many cases including their own families back in the states. A number of students actually paid their own airfare to Tegucigalpa in order to preserve donated funds for microcredit projects. And 47 new village banks were established to empower the poor. According to John Hatch, FINCA's founder, we actually impacted a total of 96 banks because FINCA was able to leverage HELP's monies with other capital.

As with most economic development efforts, several weaknesses became evident in our first HELP year—problems that we decided must be tackled in the future. For instance, in trying to be as inclusive as possible, we included some non-Spanish-speaking student volunteers who did not contribute as much as they, or we, desired. Some of them became extremely frustrated by their inability to communicate what they wanted to say. On a related point, we probably should not have continued to add new volunteers as old ones dropped out, because they were not fully trained or focused on our mission.

Yet, in spite of these first-year difficulties, HELP Honduras as a whole yielded significant results. Many volunteers learned a great deal about the joys of sacrifice and serving those who suffer. They had experiences that not only brought relief to Hondurans, but changed the students themselves. Whatever their eventual futures and professions might be, most achieved greater awareness of the lives of those who struggle—the sick, the weak and vulnerable children, the poor, the widows and orphans. Based on stories we have since learned, many went on to give ongoing service in their careers, families, and communities, full-time or part-time, as they continued to give of themselves.

In addition, our first-year volunteers learned how to offer not merely a handout, but a hand up. By collaborating with FINCA and the Red Cross, they were able to leverage their efforts jointly, to accomplish more than any one nonprofit group could do by itself. Who would have thought that young, middle-class American Mormons could have had such a marvelous impact on over 4,000 poor Hondurans? It was truly a miracle.

From its first year forward, HELP's efforts expanded above and beyond the training and projects emerging from my original BYU course. Additional humanitarian service was also rendered in Honduras through church contacts, such as Catholic Relief programs, and through other LDS efforts, along with other aid organizations such as the Red Cross in various Honduran communities.

Numerous HELP International volunteers found or created new, life-changing experiences in the early years of the program's efforts on returning to the BYU campus after they graduated, assumed new jobs, and went out into the world. Participants began to accelerate their impacts beyond college and built on their typical roles as young adults with new jobs, new families, new residences, and so on. They began going beyond their own summer experiences in Central America to create new follow-on effects, illustrated by the following examples of young people mobilizing other communities to assist those struggling in HELP's first few years of service:

- Several volunteers established a five-year Arizona/Honduras Partnership.
- The power of one: A BYU athlete and swim champion mobilized Americans to volunteer for his medical services project in El Salvador.
- The California Action Group of students raised more funds exclusively for microfinance.
- A Soles for Souls Project was launched to gather good used shoes from America to distribute to scavengers

working in filthy conditions at the metropolitan dump in Tegucigalpa, Honduras.
- The Payson School in another Utah community began an Annual Deliveries to Central America program.
- Finally, some of our HELP alumni took initiatives upon graduating from BYU to create their *own* new nongovernmental organizations in other lands. Their ongoing efforts reflect words of the great playwright George Bernard Shaw, who wrote: "I am of the opinion that my life belongs to the community and as long as I live, it is my privilege to do for it whatever I can."

HELP's Evolution

From that humble beginning in summer 1999, HELP grew into a much-expanded role in venturing beyond Honduras to include other countries in Central America. It also gradually offered a wider range of products and services. The name of our NGO was changed to "HELP International," reflecting an expansion of focus. It grew within BYU to become a sort of business incubator where we had the use of computers and other equipment, as well as meeting facilities for recruiting and training the majority of our volunteers. It eventually became a university spin-off with its own small paid staff, office setup in downtown Provo, along with independence from the Marriott School. This allowed us to take risks, be more innovative, and solicit a growing number of college-age volunteers from other schools. More than 3,200 students have worked with the program for a summer or longer.

Two years after the Honduras startup, further HELP interventions were needed because of a terrible 2001 earthquake next door in the small country of El Salvador. So the team organized a five-person professional team of experts from the Utah community, which traveled with HELP's board of directors on a 10-day site visit to assess quake impacts that destroyed or weakened thousands of office buildings and homes throughout the nation, as well as to plan for the future. Their collective time and expertise was all pro bono. They were mostly BYU alumni who ran their own successful corporate consulting practices. Beyond evaluating and offering microfinance services to the poor, the other goal was to provide professional services such as free consulting to HELP leaders and managers that was typified by the following: action research, process consultation, strategic direction and governance discussions, branding and marketing strategy, individual assessment with feedback and coaching of HELP's country leaders, team building, confrontation and conflict resolution techniques, and more. The resulting sophistication of organizational procedures greatly enhanced how the NGO would operate in the future. New capacities and capabilities emerged, better short- and long-term planning was implemented, and these successes continue even until the present day.

In those early days (2002–2005), HELP's leaders in the U.S. were beginning to design and then implement ever-greater management and organizational competencies. The executive director, a former student, and myself as the faculty founder and chair of the board of trustees, realized that the U.S. office team needed ever-more sophisticated and professional mechanisms, because the demand for our services was quickly growing. That realization was accompanied by ever-expanding numbers of students seeking an international opportunity to learn how to not simply do *well* in their careers with ample incomes and professional opportunities, but also to do *good* in society, developing new personal competencies for blessing others, and much more.

Thus, a two-person Organizational Development consulting team met with the chair of the board and the executive director to further discuss strategy and direction. A clear set of alternative strategic choices was laid out. Ultimately, they presented the information to the rest of the board of directors, after which a major shift in purpose and direction was debated, voted on, and finally adopted. From simply recruiting a few students to help as summer interns after a natural disaster as occurred in 1999's Hurricane Mitch, HELP's primary mission shifted to *"Creating a life-changing experience in the lives of our volunteers as they serve the poor."* It was believed that this opportunity would then lead former HELP volunteers to live lives of service and to make future donations to causes of economic and social justice wherever they could be of assistance. Serving the "poorest of the poor" thus became the secondary, but still vital, purpose of HELP International.

Results of New Strategic Directions

Participating in HELP International clearly accelerated many college students' impacts beyond school and their typical roles as young adults with fresh jobs, young families, new residential locations, and so on. Many have gone beyond their own summer experiences to create new ripple effects and life-changing experiences illustrated by program rollouts and social interventions around the globe.

From the beginning, HELP's work as an NGO continually expanded, attracting students from across the United States from dozens of colleges. In summarizing HELP's two decades of outreach as of 2020, the NGO has mobilized volunteers, each giving three to 12 months of their lives, who have worked in one or more of the following nations:

- Early 2000s – Projects were established in Honduras, Peru, Venezuela, Brazil, and El Salvador.
- Mid-2000s – New projects were added in Bolivia, Uganda, and Guatemala.
- Early 2010s – Additional projects were begun in Fiji, Tanzania, Belize, and India.
- Late 2010s – More projects were initiated in Jordan, the Philippines, Nepal, Thailand, Ecuador, Cambodia, and refugee camps in Greece and Syria.

Looking back over the past 20 years of HELP's efforts in as many countries, I'm reminded of an early LDS prophet, John Taylor, who told the pioneering Saints of his day that they should "unite with [the poor and jobless]... in finding employment for every man and woman and child... that wants to labor" (Taylor, 1878).

The number of countries that HELP serves continues to grow, although the organization has had to discontinue efforts—or at least delay working for a time—in some circumstances of civil war (Syria), earthquakes (Nepal), cyclones (Philippines), gang violence (El Salvador), and, most recently, the widespread suffering from the COVID-19 pandemic (in many nations).

The types of social entrepreneurial projects that HELP has offered have expanded to include microcredit loans, microentrepreneurial training, square-foot gardens, house construction, school teaching, rural health clinics, orphanage and street children care, teaching English, constructing Lorena stoves, building computer skills, starting women's cooperatives, coaching in other appropriate low-tech village technologies, and so forth.

Many of our programs and innovations arose from my decades of partnering with my longtime friend and mentor Dr. Muhammad Yunus, the great Nobel Prize Laureate and founder of Grameen Bank in Bangladesh. He once told me as we dined at a conference in Halifax, Canada: "Warner, credit to the poor must become a fundamental human right." In other words, not merely an option or an opportunity for some who struggle in poverty, but for *all* people in need. Yunus's view fits perfectly with the words of the Prophet Brigham Young on this issue: "We will take a moral view, a political view, and see the inequality that exists in the human family.... It is an unequal condition to mankind.... What is to be done? The Latter-day Saints will never accomplish their mission until this inequality shall cease on the earth" (Young, 2013).

Over the years, HELP International has designed, implemented, and continued to tweak its unique model for change and social innovation. The latest iteration showing the connections between

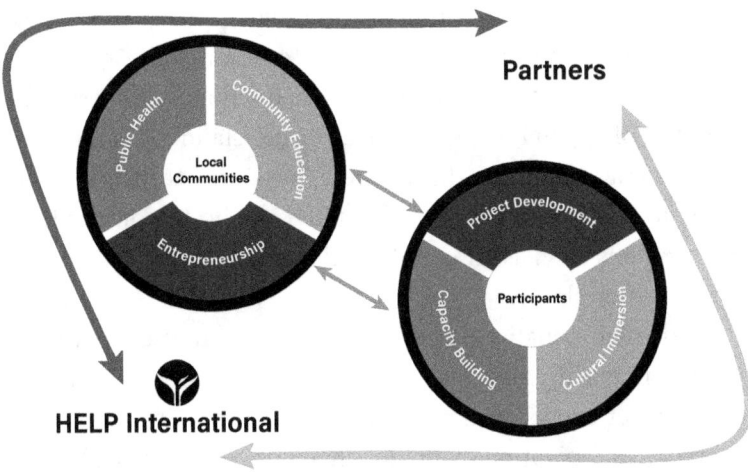

Figure 1: HELP International's model for change and social innovation

our NGO and community partners as well as the synergy within and between local organizations and volunteers is depicted in Figure 1.

Reflections on the Marriott School of Business and the Larger BYU System as an Incubator

One wonders: can campus folks, including administrators, faculty, and students, actually *do good*, above and beyond their studies, social lives, and other school commitments? Even if that requires dealing with resistance from other faculty, department chairs, deans, and top administrators? As discussed throughout this analysis, HELP International was spun off from Brigham Young University and became fully independent in order to be classified as a 501(c)(3) nonprofit social enterprise. The Marriott School was thus a nesting area in which to foster the birth of our efforts to assist the Honduran people after Hurricane Mitch's destruction in Central America, later expanding to the rest of Central America and beyond.

Once independent, HELP could begin to access funding as a stand-alone organization. BYU's business school never provided us money, but acted more as a resource where courses could be taught, where we had venues in which to meet, connections to the internet, open spaces for promoting our work, plenty of access to fellow students in recruiting new volunteers, and more.

This way, donations became tax deductible for those who sought to offer funding, because they could claim a benefit when their own personal federal taxes were due. This became, and continues to be, a useful incentive for the public to contribute to organizations such as HELP International that labor to make the world a better place.

With such donations from a few small businesses, as well as volunteers raising their own $2,800 or so to cover their travel to and summer expenses in a Third World community where they labored, this separation from the official university turned out to be a benefit. HELP started in downtown Provo with an inexpensive, leased office; a one-person staff; and a budget of $200,000. It has grown ever since and today operates on some $400,000 in annual revenue. Today HELP has a small paid staff of three to five persons, most of them part-time college students, in a simple office with only a few overhead expenses such as computers and cell phones. Its goal is to operate as "lean" as possible as a social enterprise while retaining its founding spirit as a spontaneous culture, wild and creative, able to mobilize quickly to fresh innovations or to jump when a crisis occurs anywhere in the world. Whether this informal, self-managing structure can be successfully maintained over the long haul has been a persistent question, but after 20 years, it seems to still be working.

It certainly appears that the rapid growth of social entrepreneurship around the world suggests that such approaches for alleviating human suffering and poverty will require a greater presence on college campuses where global skills can be acquired so as to actually make a difference. Equally vital to me is the fact that not only do the global poor need uplifting, but academia does as well. Courses such as the one that launched HELP International and dozens of additional NGOs and projects have proven to bless the poor globally. Further, this development has also enriched and made college learning more meaningful through action research.

This new social movement within academia will surely expand, and university settings for fostering such innovations are even now accelerating, especially in American business schools, but hopefully in Europe, Latin America, and Africa, as well. The plain fact is this: More and more students believe they can change the world while yet young, relatively poor themselves, and still in college. As I often preached to my thousands of students, "Don't listen to the doubts of other professors. Don't respond to your parents' imaginary fears. Instead, go forward with faith, hard work, and courage."

Why? Because HELP has also motivated multitudes of college students to press forward in their own studies and careers. Past volunteers have not only obtained bachelor's degrees from BYU, Virginia Tech, University of Southern California, University of Utah, Yale, and more. But because of their extraordinary work with HELP International in the trenches with the poor, they were seen as extraordinarily capable of not only earning high grades, but also embracing ethics and values that opened the doors for them to leading graduate schools like Harvard, Cornell, Michigan, Texas, and Stanford. Many of them later secured successful careers as doctors, accountants, biologists, social workers, engineers, schoolteachers, lawyers, entrepreneurs, media experts, professional athletes, and management executives.

Perhaps the reflections from several HELP International students and volunteers capture the personal impacts of some young LDS participants in our work as they reflected on their BYU course and their summer's field work in a HELP country:

> This has been life-changing.... I am new in the social entrepreneurship world, although I feel that I was born for it.

> This course inspires you to help others and become a social entrepreneur. It challenges you to find out what your mission is and then to go and do it.

> HELP International helped me to look at the world differently—and look at myself differently.

The University Context for Combating Poverty

In this section detailing the work of HELP International arising as a spin-off from my own BYU course, I will briefly discuss the role of higher education, and of BYU in particular, as a system for teaching, analyzing, designing, launching, and ultimately moving out from campus into the community, even the whole world.

To me, it's manifestly obvious why academics, especially Latter-day Saint ones, should engage their faculty members and students in their institutions to help reduce human suffering. Worldwide, roughly three billion poor people struggle with challenges of illiteracy, disease, war, natural disasters, hunger, unemployment, droughts, wildfires, inaccessible capital, government corruption, and more. For these people, the world seems immoral and unjust, and lacks equality and opportunity for the masses. Added to these current tragedies is the horrific devastation of the global COVID-19 pandemic that is increasingly shattering the world's economy. It has wrecked economies and afflicted some 245 million people with the disease, resulting in the tragic deaths of over 5 million human beings (Worldometers, 2021).

So my inquiries include these: What can business schools offer to solve problems in the developing world and alleviate human suffering? Do we faculty members possess skills and tools that can make a difference? Perhaps more important, how much do we really care?

Looking at the context of poverty, we see that traditional approaches to international development have had both successes and failures through such institutions as the United Nations, World Bank, Red Cross, Green Revolution, and many more organizations and methodologies. Ample analyses have been conducted by means of books and research articles to explain the complexities, successes, and failures of aid going to needy countries (Allen and Thomas, 2000; Bhaduri, 2005; Fukuyama, 2006; Human Security Trust Fund, 2019; Korten, 1995; Mosse, 2010; Oxford, 2020; USAID, 2020).

During my decades at BYU, and also while serving as a visiting professor at the University of Michigan, the Claremont Graduate School, the University of Utah, and in Brazil, Hawaii, and beyond, I've sought to develop and apply innovative poverty-alleviating tools that utilize concepts and practices such as social entrepreneurship, NGOs, microcredit, microenterprise, microentrepreneurship, microfinance institutions (MFI), and village banking (Yunus, 2009). I'm reminded that BYU, the largest private school in the world, with some 36,000 students today, was founded by Mormon pioneers who were expelled from the United States because of religious persecution, poverty, declaring a prophet, protesting against slavery, founding utopian communities, and other endless struggles. Back then they found themselves in a situation like that of many families in developing nations today. In all my NGO efforts, I often reflect on my pioneer ancestors on my maternal line who, on facing extermination orders, fled from the Midwest to the Utah Territory, which was then part of Mexico, in order to worship, educate their children, live freely, and create communal colonies for their mutual benefit. The Prophet Brigham Young himself, who had led the pioneers west, admonished the university founders to seek the creation of cooperative learning and to apply "United Order" values to business and economics alike. Since its founding and during its miraculous growth over the past century and a half, the university has increasingly emphasized *ethics, community, and caring*, as well as science and all other approaches to higher education.

As a young professor beginning in the mid-1970s, I always sought to raise issues of social and economic justice globally in my work. My research and publications have typically explored successful pathways for employing innovative entrepreneurship processes for fighting global poverty. My work, and that of others of like mind, has fostered new directions at other universities that are also now seeking to create a social entrepreneurial, "pro-poor" track or emphasis. Microfinance has increasingly become a hot issue worldwide. In recent years across the U.S., Pierre Omidyar, the founder of eBay, has donated $100 million for microfinance programs started at his alma mater, Tufts University. Corporate partnerships have been developed by such organizations as Deutsche Bank and MasterCard for hundreds of millions more. The Bill and Melinda Gates Foundation has contributed over $50 million, as yet another example.

At BYU, I and some of my fellow professors have been growing empowerment strategies for the poor for over three decades. I had begun designing new courses in microfinance and social entrepreneurship in the late 1980s, and they became very popular as students realized they could learn new concepts that they could then go on to practice in Asia and Latin America, just as a start. The courses I designed were among the first in the U.S., and today the concepts and methods are being taught at over 600 colleges.

BYU has cautiously increased its interest and has given a degree of support for the kind of work we started by designing and implementing HELP International in 1999. The department in which I taught was housed in the Marriott School of Business, which offers highly ranked programs such as MBA, Accounting, MPA, Marketing, Ethics, Organizational Behavior, Supply Chain, Entrepreneurship, Strategy, and more. After HELP took off, I and a student-turned-colleague named Todd Manwaring sought private funding from several wealthy alumni; they ultimately gave us $3 million to establish a new Center for Economic Self-Reliance (CESR) on campus, now known as the Ballard Center for Social Impact (2019). Over the years, I and faculty colleagues have rolled out new courses on social innovation, microfinance, nonprofit management, and more. We have convened some 11 conferences with well-known speakers such as Muhammad Yunus (founder of Grameen Bank in Bangladesh), John Hatch (founder of FINCA throughout Latin America and Africa), Stephen Covey (author of *The 7 Habits of Highly Successful People*), and many others. We have launched field research supported by the World Bank, CGAP, and FINCA on microcredit impacts, social innovation, and microfranchise; and we launched the first academic research publication on microcredit, called *The Journal of Microfinance*. Our work has led to several pioneering books about these new models for Third World social change, as well as numerous other academic publications (Woodworth, Grenny, and Manwaring, 2000; Woodworth, 2013).

My efforts as an educational innovator and advocate for social innovation have resulted in the design and creation of some 41 NGOs as of today that operate in 62 countries. The NGOs we have founded have received a number of awards from such entities as the LDS First Presidency, Grameen Foundation–USA, the Clinton Global Initiative, *Fast Company Magazine*, Monitor Consulting Group, as well as from political leaders in various countries at the national and regional level, including the presidents of Mali and El Salvador, along with cabinet and ministry members, governors, mayors, and leaders of multiple other nations, such as Brazil, Thailand, Mexico, the Philippines, and Peru.

Collectively in 2019 alone (latest figures available), all our spin-off NGOs achieved the following:

- Raised $28 million
- Trained 347,000 microentrepreneurs in small-business skills worldwide
- Provided microloans to more than 122,000 impoverished families in 58 countries
- Mobilized more than 200 volunteers to raise their own funding and labor in 22 nations to empower the poor through various strategies

The outcomes of our programs show significant change in at least eight broad areas, documented through internal research studies:

- New jobs created through microloans and training
- Rising microentrepreneur household incomes
- Improved food security
- Higher participation of children in school
- Better housing

- Female empowerment
- Increased social capital
- Support services to families in refugee camps

While HELP International's rise from my BYU courses occurred early in my career, it was not the only example of college students fighting poverty. It was not even the only NGO to grow out of the Marriott School. But it did become a model for additional social ventures. To describe them all is beyond the scope of this chapter, but additional NGO spin-offs arose from our efforts and courses covered in other sections of this book, as well as soon-to-be-published additional volumes. Some of these other nonprofits were established by HELP's previous volunteers or by earlier BYU alumni. Most are clearly connected to both institutions. Here are just a few: Empowering Nations (Paraguay, Ghana, Panama); MicroBusiness Mentors (providing microloans and entrepreneurial training to Latino migrants in Utah); Wave of Hope (after the Asian tsunami wrecked Thailand and coastal areas of 11 countries around the Indian Ocean); Care for Life (Mozambique); orphanages (Haiti, Guatemala, and Brazil); PRINCE Cooperative Bakery (Kenya); Sustain Haiti (Haiti); SOAR Microfinance (China); Mussina, a small-scale women's jewelry cooperative (Uganda); Humanitarian Link (Central America); and Casqued Humanitarian (Peru).

HELP International Conclusion

In my work, I always seek to exhort Latter-day Saints everywhere to build community through practicing our faith in fighting poverty, launching new NGOs, carrying out microcredit family impacts, and training future global change agents, among many other actions. To my mind, the most significant questions are these: How can we really be our brother's (and sister's) keepers? For church innovators, how may we generate new conceptual models and systems to assist and serve the world's growing Third Sector? For LDS businesspeople and entrepreneurs, how can we apply proven business models in getting to the next stage of microfinance in order to help others? For LDS neighbors, friends, and extended family members, which scaling-up strategies can be developed to exponentially expand MFI resources to benefit the world's have-nots? For LDS women in particular, moms, and church Relief Society leaders, are there viable, workable social inventions to reduce the gap between available capital and the financial needs of the poor?

I further believe we should marry our precious LDS beliefs and values with international development so as to generate a new synthesis. By so doing, our faith will grow and NGOs can become more effective and more sustainable income-generating social enterprises. Global enterprise at the grassroots offers a new arena for social practice among the world's poor, perhaps creating a kind of Global LDS Peace Corps (a name I rather like). Over the past three decades, HELP International has emerged and continues to grow, still mobilizing college-age students to not stop serving those who suffer, resulting in widely recognized impacts over the years (Ellsworth, 2013).

It may very well be that we are already seeing changes in the lives of LDS professionals. We witness the efforts of schoolteachers, nurses, engineers, former mission presidents, accountants, government employees, doctors, lawyers, and entrepreneurs as they look for ways to "give back." Not just with money, but with their religious faith, career experiences, lifelong insights, people skills, and much more. One of the final articles published by the great management guru Peter Drucker (2005) focused on social entrepreneurship as possibly the next big career for middle-aged Americans who, he argues, will retire early with plenty of money and time to become volunteers in the betterment of society. Likewise, my colleague Stephen Covey's book *The 8th Habit: From Effectiveness to Greatness* (2004) argues the same point: that we need to move from merely being effective to finding our own voice for improving the world, and then to helping others to find their own voices as well.

Older LDS couples can certainly serve as senior missionaries, providing church leadership and perhaps doing proselyting. Later, home from such experiences, they might then consider becoming voluntary social entrepreneurs in the new frontier of strengthening civil society and building socioeconomic justice. Doing so will add meaning to their personal lives as well as to their religious values and faith. Pro bono NGO volunteerism will make their later years more purposeful and help the larger society as well—alleviating poverty, reducing hunger, creating jobs: in short, reinventing the outreach of our entire Church so that it truly becomes an agent for world benefit.

I conclude this chapter with a practical call to action, using the stirring words of one of the world's greatest leaders:

> "You must be the change you wish to see in the world."
> —Mahatma Gandhi

References

Allen, T., and Thomas, A. (2000). *Poverty and Development into the 21st Century*. OUP.

Ballard Center for Social Impact. (2019). https://marriottschool.byu.edu/ballard/.

Bhaduri, A. (2005). *Development with Dignity*. National Book Trust.

BYU. (2021). Brigham Young University. https://www.byu.edu/.

Covey, S. R. (2004). *The 8th Habit: From Effectiveness to Greatness*. Free Press.

Drucker, P. F. (2005). Managing Oneself. *Harvard Business Review*, January. https://hbr.org/2005/01/managing-oneself.

Ellsworth, D. (2013). HELP International has come a long way from a BYU classroom. November 22. https://universe.byu.edu/2013/11/22/help-international-has-come-a-long-way-from-a-byu-classroom/.

Fukuyama, F. (2006). *The End of History and the Last Man*. Free Press.

Human Security Trust Fund. (2019). Human Development Index covering 232 countries. https://www.un.org/humansecurity/.

Korten, D. C. (1995). *When Corporations Rule the World*. Berrett-Koehler.

Lucas, J. W., and Woodworth, W. P. (1996). *Working Toward Zion: Principles of the United Order for the Modern World*. Aspen Books.

Mosse, D. (ed.) (2010). *Adventures in Aid Land: The Anthropology of Professionals in International Development*. Berg Hahn Books.

Oxford Poverty & Human Development Initiative. (2020). Oxford Department of International Development. University of Oxford. https://ophi.org.uk/.

Pratt, P. P. (1952). *Writings of Parley Parker Pratt.* Deseret Book.

Taylor, J. (1878). *Journal of Discourses.* Vol. 20.

USAID. (2020). U.S. Agency for International Development. https://www.usaid.gov/.

Woodworth, W. (2013). Social Business in Times of Crisis: Microcredit Strategies During Social Unrest and/or Natural Disaster. *Journal of Social Business*, Glasgow University, vol. 3, no. 1.

Woodworth, W., Grenny, J., and Manwaring, T. (2000). *United for Zion: Principles for Uniting the Saints to Eliminate Poverty.* Zion's Cooperative Publications.

Worldometers. (2021). Coronavirus Statistics Today. https://www.worldometers.info/coronavirus/. Accessed November 5.

Young, B. (2013 edition). *Journal of Discourses*, 19:9. https://journalofdiscourses.com/19/9, 45–50.

Yunus, M. (2009). *Creating a World Without Poverty: Social Business and the Future of Capitalism.* Public Affairs.

"Love One Another"
LDS Hymns, No. 308

As I have loved you,
Love one another.
This new commandment:
Love one another.
By this shall men know
Ye are my disciples,
If ye have love
One to another.

Text and music: Luacine Clark
Fox (1914–2002)

3

Ouelessebougou Alliance

(From Utah to Mali, West Africa, 1985-2022)

How much human suffering have you personally seen in the developing world? Have you watched in horror the last gasps of breath from a baby in a squalid refugee camp out in an encampment of hundreds of thousands of people squatting in the sand, temperatures above 100 degrees, little food or water, with few resources, medical services, or humanitarian aid? This was the experience in 1985 when a group of Salt Lake City friends felt the desire to reach out and assist the millions of people suffering in a huge crisis in East Africa. The CNN News Channel had just been launched, and folks could sit in their comfortable homes along the Wasatch Front in the Rocky Mountains of Utah, yet be shocked and saddened by the horrific sights and sounds of starving babies and ill mothers trying to simply stay alive. It was heartrending. Some felt tremendous guilt. Others flipped the channel to more pleasant viewing. A few wondered if they could do anything to help. Many perceived themselves as powerless. They knew nothing of countries such as Ethiopia, Kenya, South Sudan, and Somalia where terrible droughts and massive hunger were causing the ugly deaths of more than two million human beings, and knew nothing of the suffering

▲ A 105-year-old village chief (middle), his elderly associate, and the author in a skullcap

▼ Children are Mali's future

of millions more who "survived," not to mention the hundreds of thousands of new orphans, and much worse.

It was with that context that a small group in Utah began exploring what they might do to help Africa. The famine in parts of that enormous continent was seen as too big, too complicated. Trying to work without significant funding and governmental connections and services, as well as knowing little about the region, languages, or culture, seemed an impossible challenge. Yet the group began meeting, reading as much as possible, trying to learn about Africa more broadly so as to perhaps find a specific area where they might be able to make a small difference within the continent. Admitting that East Africa would need the wealth and power of the "Big Boys," such as the International Monetary Fund, the United Nations, and the World Bank, the group assumed that the U.S. and other strong economies would have to address that faraway human crisis. But was there a place of African suffering where a bunch of "regular" Americans might provide tiny solutions?

Thus it was that an amazing nonprofit was born, named the Ouelessebougou–Utah Alliance. Within a few months of exploring potential places, the group determined to launch in Mali, a sub-Saharan region. It's an immense western region bordered on the north by the Sahel, a dry, semiarid area between the Atlantic Ocean and the Red Sea. The Sahel itself consists of over a million square miles, bordered not only by Mali, but also by stressed nations such as Senegal, Niger, and Chad. Mali had suffered from decades of desertification as the Sahara Desert became ever drier, wrecking once-fertile areas in the country's north as its sands blew south across the land. Increasing bloodshed from terror attacks by outside invaders had made matters worse in recent years. Once numbered among the most peaceful of African nations, with decades of experience of democracy, in 1985 Mali was facing growing tensions.

It was and continues to be a region constantly troubled by severe poverty. So several friends from Salt Lake flew to Mali to visit potential regions where they hoped they could make some small differences. They visited with every government official they were permitted to see, talked with a few European business managers there, and did some in-country traveling. They returned to Utah with several attracted to the idea of setting up shop in Timbuktu, the only place anyone in the group had ever heard of. But others felt that the fabled area in the northern part of Mali was extremely poor, so there were numerous foreign aid organizations working up there, and the region also had the only real tourism in the nation. They probed further, looking for an area with greater challenges on which a group of Utahns with a small amount of money could have a noticeable impact.

Finally, they concluded that while people in southern Mali were extremely poor, they had no outside groups assisting them in overcoming that challenge. So the Salt Lakers decided to begin in this region. The group was formed specifically to represent a mix of Utahns from multiple political persuasions and a variety of religious traditions. They included academics from the University of Utah, in Salt Lake City, and Brigham Young University, in Provo. The group expanded to include several well-known LDS leaders as well as Catholics and Muslims. Homemakers, CEOs, attorneys, entrepreneurs, schoolteachers, and many others filled the ranks. They joined forces to create an amazing (and later well-documented) story of love, sacrifice, and humble outreach to people living in circumstances very different from their own.

Founding the Ouelessebougou–Utah Alliance

Drawing on my three decades of action research and academic analysis, the narrative below summarizes my years of work after the founding of the Ouelessebougou–Utah Alliance. I have been involved in several roles, including as chair of the board of trustees, vice chair, board member, consultant, and outside academic researcher, all while laboring within the Koulikoro region of the country. The organization recently altered its official name to the Ouelessebougou Alliance because of a wider involvement of supporters and donors beyond the borders of Utah. It is still registered as a U.S.-based nongovernmental organization (NGO) laboring to raise financial resources and to collaborate with rural villagers in one of the poorest regions within impoverished Mali, West Africa. As U.S. board chair at its founding, I worked with Malian attorneys to also get it legally registered as a Malian nonprofit organization.

I've always loved Nephi's testimony in the Book of Mormon about the fraught word "race." It has guided my efforts to combat injustice and racism across the United States, and in Utah in particular, and even further, to reach out beyond African American travails in my home nation to the struggles of native poverty globally: The Lord "denieth none that come unto him, black and white, bond and free, male and female" (2 Nephi 26:33). This chapter draws not only on LDS values and scriptures to illuminate this case, but on academic disciplines as well, including the social sciences, education, and business. The thrust of it concerning our work in West Africa includes innovations such as microfinance, healthcare, education, agriculture, and literacy, with a degree of emphasis on women's issues. I will explore the country's challenges to our volunteers, their pursuit of several core strategies, and the evolution of building an ecosystem for an improved quality of life and communal sustainability at the grassroots in one of the world's most impoverished nations. My own involvement in this effort was fueled by the great Nelson Mandela's declaration: "*Poverty is not an accident.* Like slavery and apartheid, it is man-made and can be removed by the actions of human beings."

To orient the reader, I'll begin with the fact that Mali has been famous for centuries because of its historic site, Timbuktu, on the edge of the great Sahara Desert north of the landlocked nation's capital. However, it's no easy task to explore, analyze, and summarize the results of 25 years of my work in social entrepreneurship through international development efforts in southern Mali in a region with the challenging name *Ouélessébougou*. My most recent trip to Africa took place in November 2017, when I traveled there to review and assess our progress.

As a bit of background, the cliché word "development" has morphed over the centuries. During the Enlightenment, and into the times of Africa's colonization, many colonial powers saw themselves as the bearers of "development" as they sought to create societies around the world that mimicked their own. In more recent periods, experts have begun to alter this view by moving toward a more participatory process in which poor communities become partners rather than subjects.

Those engaged in development have begun to examine the process on a microlevel. In this readjustment or reassessment, "development" has come to encompass the economist and philosopher Armartya Sen's view that it is "a process of expanding the real freedoms that people enjoy" (Sen, 1999, 3). In addition, other contemporary scholars have begun to foster homegrown development. The renowned economist William Easterly states: "It is a fantasy to think that the West can change complex societies with very different histories and cultures into some image of itself. The main hope for the poor is for them ... to borrow ideas and technology from the West when it suits them to do so" (Easterly, 2006, 28).

The Ouelessebougou Alliance (or simply OA) has utilized the practices of social entrepreneurship for decades (Bornstein 2007; Lewis 2017), by establishing collaborative relationships between and among Utah citizens, academics, and donors with the grateful people of rural Mali. A major goal was that of building innovative partnerships between Utahns and folks in the Ouelessebougou cluster of 40-plus villages that together make up what locals call, in their native French, a *commune* or an *arrondissement*. It's an approach that brings Malian groups together and fosters local councils of indigenous men and women to strengthen one another. This organic, bottom-up approach has been growing in the nonprofit world for decades. The following analysis examines a few of the social and economic impacts within the relationship between this still-Utah-based Ouelessebougou Alliance and the development of the Malian people, and describes some of the organization's successes, failures, and future possibilities for growth. The Alliance is but one of a range of NGOs that I have designed, led, accelerated, or facilitated around the globe, seeking to empower regular American

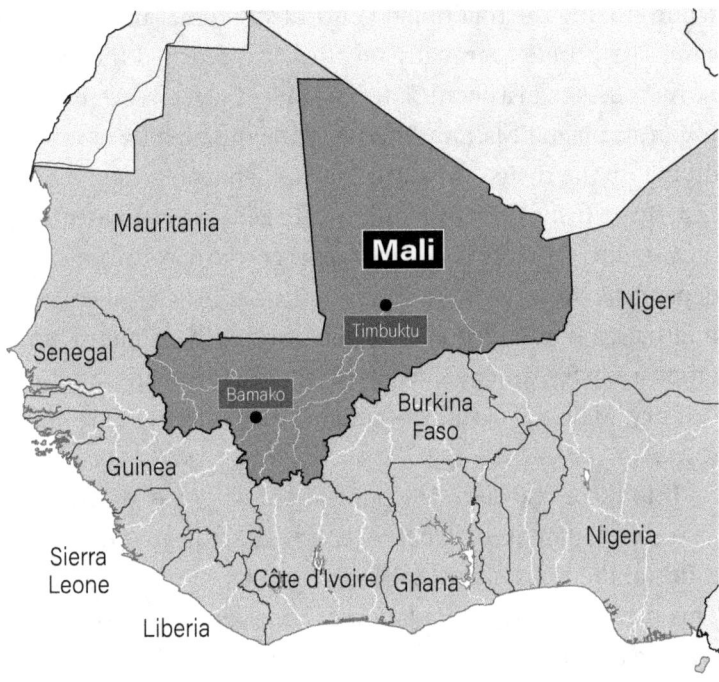

citizens and motivated college students while addressing extreme poverty in countries where oppression occurs (Smith and Woodworth, 2012).

Overview of Mali and the Alliance

The Republic of Mali is a landlocked country in the very heart of West Africa. It shares borders with Mauritania and Senegal to the west, Algeria to the north, Burkina Faso and the Côte d'Ivoire to the south, and Niger in the east. Mali retains many aspects of its legacy of French colonialism. Its 80 million citizens are heirs to a large number of cultural traditions, which in recent decades have been modified by modernization, urbanization, and the gradual conversion of people from indigenous religions to Islam, which now reflects some 98 percent of the region (BBC, 2018; CIA, 2019).

The French began to penetrate the country in the late 1800s, concentrating efforts on occupying the interior of West Africa. As they marched inward, their military forces extracted Mali's resources, while eroding the traditional political structures and local leadership. The people eventually revolted and declared independence in 1960. Less than a decade later, the first of several severe droughts began to plague Mali, interfering with the growth of crops and drying up the rivers—a catastrophe for a people whose diet relies heavily on fishing. From about 1972 to 1984, an estimated 100,000 people died of starvation, and another 750,000 became heavily dependent on foreign aid. Despite the country's leaders seeking international influence and collaborating with a range of humanitarian agencies, droughts returned in 2009, further devastating the country. Mali was—and is—among the poorest countries in the world.

Into these realities, OA continues to promote locally sustainable development in Ouelessebougou, Mali, an *arrondissement* south of the capital city of Bamako that encompasses 72 villages. This region claims a population of approximately 60,000 people, with an agriculture-based economy consisting primarily of millet, sorghum, rice, and corn grown for consumption, as well as cotton for export throughout Africa and to Europe. On average, the Alliance raises between $160,000 and $230,000 per year for its programs.

Over the decades, OA has worked with villagers to address the most basic human needs. Jennifer Beckstead (2018), a former executive director of the Alliance, describes the progression of the organization when she states: "The first projects were to build wells for drinking water. Then, we realized they [residents] had no access to food, so we built irrigation wells. Then, we realized they had to deal with life-threatening yet preventable diseases, so we started vaccinations. We learned there was a strong connection between education and health, and in the 1990s, we started building schools. Later, we noted that if they had access to other resources, *they could find better ways to help themselves* [emphasis added]."

The OA's basic ideas for social entrepreneurship were to identify the people's needs, design new strategies for learning, assist them in becoming healthier, and build local capacity so that further needs could be met. Thus, instead of a handout, OA seeks to offer a hand up as the people gain greater control over their future. One of our board members for many years was Chieko Okazaki, who served as First Counselor in the LDS Church's Relief Society General Presidency, at five million strong the largest women's organization in the world. A Japanese-Hawaiian, she was a bold critic of selfishness and greed, often preaching the need for practicing charity, being tough, and serving the poor. It made her an excellent OA board member because she always "told it like it is." Okazaki helped me raise funds for the Alliance several times, having no fear. In one of her great talks that I have never forgotten, she focused on three words: "Spit, mud, and *Kigatsuku*." She suggested we must be tough, using "spit" and "mud" to pursue our life's work. She defined *Kigatsuku* as having resilience, independence, and laboring to aid others without ever giving up. Her words ring out: It's "an inner spirit to act without being told what to do" (*LDS Ensign*, 1992). Such words are a perfect description of her long life, as well as her years of dedicated service to the poor of West Africa.

Here is only one example of this approach to build resilience. Some years ago, as an OA board member and its vice president, after several trips to Mali I was struck by its massive poverty, and so I began to explore ways we could initiate new programs both to generate family self-reliance and to strengthen the economic grassroots of the region. I argued that we could await help "till kingdom come" from the U.S. federal government, wait for the United Nations' assistance for decades more, and pray for God to send the World Bank to ride to the rescue. Or we could take action from below, there at the grassroots level, amid the ugly realities of suffering and hunger. After some consideration, in response to the ever-present economic struggles faced by villagers, the Alliance's economic development sector was established by me and several students whom I recruited from my own university, BYU, and also from Harvard. I raised money for this new initiative and, after I trained my graduate students in the United States, two of them spent six months in Mali organizing its first village bank.

After they performed a needs assessment, when I arrived there to officially finalize things, I rejoiced to find that we had 162 extremely poor individuals each willing to pay the equivalent of $2 to join the first village bank, or *caisse*, as it was called in French. We held elections to choose the three initial managers of our village microfinance bank, and while having a celebration, even Mali's president—who had warned us the plan would never succeed—suddenly drove into our compound with several jeeps full of rifle-bearing troops to announce he wanted to sign up as a member! The next morning we began training the new leaders and soon after started issuing microloans of $70 each to qualified loan candidates in the new *caisse*. The majority of borrowers were considered to be "microentrepreneurs," "start-up entrepreneurs," or even "necessity entrepreneurs." Most were women, motivated so that they could better feed their humble families. We began to distribute small loans to the villagers of Ouelessebougou, and over time our efforts expanded.

Eventually, OA reconstructed its program to offer revolving loans to entire villages for larger amounts, and the program grew and expanded to 15 villages. Since the *caisse* reorganization, the Alliance has loaned well over $200,000 to various communities. Each village established an Economic Development Committee, formed by the village chief, which was responsible for creating a business plan and then maintaining a payment plan. In addition, these committees participated in an annual business training conference to ensure that their businesses would be successful. In these meetings, knowledge was shared about business plans, loan management, repayment, and other business strategies.

An Alliance assessment later concluded that only 33 percent of the villagers felt that their regular monthly income was sufficient to meet their needs. In order to improve this statistic and help them better deal with the harsh realities of everyday life, the OA provided $16,000 in new village loans. Early on, 91 percent of all loans were repaid or current, which surprised everyone, including Mali's president, but not me. One of the unexpected benefits of our microfinance efforts has been that over time other microfinance institutions (MFIs) have moved into the *arrondissement*. This occurred after we had been warned by various government officials and development experts that the region was "too impoverished," such that the people could not create their own microenterprises and, if imprudently given even tiny loans to start a business, they would never be able to repay such loans. But what happened instead was that OA's economic support succeeded, to such an extent that the villages in Mali became an attractive location for other NGOs to move into the area and set up their own bases of competition.

Below I detail several simple illustrations of the types of microenterprises OA established. Many loan recipients started tiny, open-air "restaurants"—eateries where they would cook simple meals to sell along the single highway passing through the region that took travelers on the 600-mile road from Bamako to Côte d'Ivoire and its capital city, Abidjan, on the Atlantic coast. That was the principal route that conveyed outside traffic through the area, and such traveling customers were generally the only folks with money to spend.

Other microenterprises included women's shared vegetable gardens, for which a group would establish a cooperative to buy seeds and lease small plots of land. After the growing season, the produce was sold in open markets around Ouelessebougou, then the profits were shared collectively and equally. Another venture involved several women who pooled their microloans and bought raw materials and metal vats for the making of soap. Later, after the liquid soap had hardened, they cut it up into large bars to sell to area mothers, who now had hand soap for washing themselves and their families —voilà, a new approach to sanitation and better health!

> "The hyena chasing two antelopes
> at the same time will go to bed hungry."
> —Malian proverb

Here's one further example of entrepreneurial initiative. It was based on a unique business venture that OA supported through microlending. The women in the Ouelessebougou region gathered shea nuts, which are native to and abundant in Mali. They used this crop to extract the oil from the nuts so they could make shea butter, which could then be sold on the international market if the quality met sufficiently high standards. Shea is widely used in cosmetics as a moisturizer, salve, or lotion by millions of people, not only in Mali or Africa but globally. However, a high-quality oil could only be extracted with the proper tools and training. So the Alliance provided training for 30 women to be educated by shea butter experts from the capital city, Bamako. With this knowledge, they improved their butter-making processes and enhanced the packaging, transportation, and marketing of their valuable products.

With respect to how OA actions like the microfinance cases described above occur, strategies and programs have arisen from various approaches. These, in turn, are managed by an Alliance team consisting of a Malian staff of five skilled Africans who operate all programs day-to-day on the ground in the Ouelessebougou area. They have extensive backgrounds in business and development, with three having some college-level education. In the U.S., the Provo OA office is a two-person shop, supervised by a board of trustees with extensive management skills and graduate degrees in social science from major universities, with guidance from attorneys and other volunteers. Altogether they make up a highly committed group that gives of their time, energy, experience, and even family funds to oversee and coach the two Malian staff members, to travel to Mali for occasional oversight trips, and to provide honest and open evaluation of programs and progress. A striking feature of OA to me has always been its members' collective sense of fiscal responsibility and their careful oversight of how they manage its donations from contributors primarily in Utah and also from the western U.S. In 2019, for instance, the organization used an amazing 92 percent of incoming money on its field programs that promote a better quality of life for Africa's poor. A mere

4 percent was spent on management and office overhead, with an additional 4 percent going to fundraising. There's a real sense of stewardship with respect to Alliance finances.

To quote from a recent OA annual report: "The Organization's purpose is two-fold: 1) to work in partnership with village citizens to achieve their economic, healthcare, and education objectives, and 2) to provide the opportunity for both cultures to learn from each other's family and social relationships, in partnership with local villagers to transform the quality of life in the Ouelessebougou region of Mali, West Africa, by delivering sustainable programs in health and education" (OA Annual Report, 2019). Its fundamental design supports development that both originates in and evolves within the existing cultural setting of Mali. As declared by a former program director, Jodi Jensen, "We want to empower them [the people of Ouelessebougou] to take ownership. We need a balance between them coming up with their own ideas and bringing in expertise from the outside" (Wadley, 2009).

With this overview, I turn to consider the two major and most long-lasting programs of the overall Alliance: healthcare and education.

Village Healthcare

Since its inception, Malian well-being has been the primary concern for the Ouelessebougou Alliance. Early on, the U.S. board and Malian in-country staffers together deliberated long and hard about how to improve the physical health of the people in the region's tough climate, where everyone dwells in literal mud huts with thatched roofs, having no electricity, paved roads, schools, or hospitals. Each year, the Mali staff and a Utah-based public health team would meet to strategize and provide a training seminar at the OA compound in Ouelessebougou, where education and instruction is given based on the unique needs of each village. In recent years, OA has emphasized vital efforts like neonatal resuscitation, water purification, and nutrition. In line with the organization's mission to "work in partnership," OA established a "Health Village

Workshop" back in 2005, which still is given today. In addition, early on, the village chiefs formed Village Health Councils, which the Alliance has assisted ever since in planning sessions so as to identify health priorities in the various villages.

When the Alliance began in the mid-1980s, Mali suffered from an infant mortality rate of 145 dead babies per 1,000 live births—the sixth worst in the world. So the Alliance developed, trained, and worked with volunteer village health workers and midwives that it recruited to teach basic hygiene and disease prevention. Currently, OA has provided ongoing training for hundreds of village health agents and midwives. Today the infant mortality rate is effectively down to less than half of what it was in the 1980s: approximately 62 deaths per 1,000 live births (Macrotrends, 2020).

Over the years, the OA has developed a relationship with the Malian government to provide vaccinations to the villages' people throughout the Ouelessebougou region. While the government claims in general to not have the means to provide needed vaccinations, it suggests specifically that it does not have the capacity to treat the most-distant villages in far-off rural communities. So OA has itself committed to assist, and in recent years has provided more than 155,000 vaccinations for a long list of diseases such as polio, yellow fever, measles, tuberculosis, diphtheria, hepatitis A, vitamin A deficiency, influenza, and tetanus. Thus far, OA villages have been able to vaccinate 92.8 percent of the children under five years old, and as a result, less than 1 percent of the children in Alliance villages now die from vaccine-preventable diseases—a remarkable improvement.

The Alliance also works hard to provide mosquito nets, the best-known malaria prevention technique. For several decades, the organization subsidized the cost of the nets by selling them to the village families for $1. Requiring a small fee is important, given OA values that emphasize self-sufficiency. A core principle of our work is that *nothing is free*. We seek not to build dependency or to give "handouts." Rather, we focus on giving a hand up that will help people move toward a more sustainable future that they themselves can control. OA also provides health training with each mosquito net distributed, because data suggest that consistent use decreases without proper education. Approximately half of all OA community adults and children consistently sleep under these treated nets. In 2017 approximately 1,200 new nets were distributed to villagers (OA Annual Report, 2018). Training about mosquito dangers and the need for protective sleeping nets continues to promote villagers' buying about 1,200 new nets annually. Mali is a nation wherein 45 percent of its people receive annual shots in the arm, while 14 percent receive none at all, which deprives them of protection from common childhood illnesses. The Ouelessebougou Alliance continues to work to save lives by providing immunizations in rural communities. In 2019, it vaccinated a total of 4,229 children age five and under against nine life-threatening diseases, with 12,688 total doses being distributed. Importantly, 3,703 expectant mothers received maternal immunizations, an increase of 41 percent from 2018.

Another fundamental health goal of the Alliance is to provide clean-water solutions for the Ouelessebougou region. Since its conception, the OA has dug more than 150 drinking and garden wells, in collaboration with local villagers who perform the labor, assisted by engineers for technical work. It's a social entrepreneurial partnership that yields concrete results. These wells decrease the incidence of diarrhea in children by more than 7 percent, and have been correlated with fewer malaria incidents, as mosquitoes tend to avoid breeding in moving water sources.

For over a decade, OA funded and operated a simple pharmacy in the area's largest village that dispensed medicines, pain pills, health kits for families, and so forth. But in 2014 it was discontinued when the Bamako government declared it had sufficient resources to open its own official "drugstore" in the area.

Another point regarding healthcare was that the Alliance required its health workers to provide the villagers with updated information on preventative disease measures. A study by Brigham Young University researchers found that about half of the OA health workers (47 percent) were trained and offered annual or semiannual seminars on sanitary practices, disease prevention, and nutrition during public gatherings in all villages (BYU, 2009). As of a decade ago, at least, the data indicated that approximately 8 percent of them provided weekly instruction, 10 percent did so monthly, and 18 percent did so bimonthly.

During 2019 the Alliance collaborated with its healthcare workers in 23 of the 25 villages that have active Health Councils that together lead their communities to achieve healthy living goals. They had 24 health agents working to facilitate the Alliance's health programs in their villages, along with 46 village "health matrons" and apprentices who in the past year also received training on COVID-19 health prevention measures as the pandemic erupted. The Ouelessebougou Youth Association distributed over 1,000 facemasks to protect families. In addition, to help battle the pandemic, as well as to assist refugees who were displaced internally because of growing terrorism in northern Mali, OA generated donations from open-hearted Utahns to provide food and comfort to those taken in as refugees in various Alliance villages. It was inspiring to witness families who were already suffering extreme poverty open their arms and hearts to such refugees. For instance, some 30 large bags of corn were distributed as an emergency food relief effort to Internally Displaced Families (IDPs) in the villages of Bassa, Solo, and Famana in January 2020.

During my most recent field trip to Mali at the end of 2017, I felt astounded at the way things were better! As with many aspects of today's world, I suppose, there were clear pluses, as well as some minuses. On that expedition, I was struck by the large new hospital that was built and opened shortly before my arrival. In my mind's eve, I remembered the tiny, unsanitary "clinic" that had provided paltry facilities for delivering a few babies, but little more, for decades. In years past, many people went there only to die, to get away from their humble mud dwelling and far from their families, where they suffered until passing away. With no electricity, it looked dark and dingy, usually having no medical staff except when one might be sent from the capital for several days to attend the most critically ill.

So imagine my great happiness in arriving with a "real" U.S. medical team to be the first visiting specialists to enter and start work in Ouelessebougou's big, new, clean hospital that had recently opened. It came about because of the Alliance and one of our Malian staffers. Years earlier, I had recruited a young Malian named Yeah Samake as a translator on a trip to work in the region. Eventually, with the financial support of my friends, he was able to come to Brigham Young University, be baptized in the LDS Church, and earn a master's degree in public management. Later we hired him for our staff in Mali, and still later for our U.S. management team as well. After marrying and graduating, he returned to Mali and successfully entered politics, hoping to use his Utah education to improve lives in Ouelessebougou. Ultimately, he was elected mayor of the commune and ventured beyond that to campaign for national president. While that effort did not succeed, he attained several offices in the national government and even became Mali's ambassador to India and also to Indonesia.

With his political clout, Samake was able to secure government funding for the building of the big, new medical facility in Ouelessebougou. My colleagues and I were the first foreigners to use its facilities in serving poor villagers pro bono. Years earlier, we had often taken groups of Utah M.D.s to volunteer in Mali for weeklong healthcare ventures. We had even recruited, funded, and flown several Malian doctors from Africa to spend a semester at the University of Utah's highly ranked medical school, with its state-of-the-art facilities and numerous world-class experts and scientists, so that they could return to West Africa with new expertise. On this trip, we had secured some $360,000 worth of high-tech medical equipment for the new Ouelessebougou hospital so that not only could they (and we) do good work during our week in Mali, but they would have considerable new equipment with which to offer better medical care long after we departed. During that trip, our group totaled 22 members, four of them ophthalmologists and the rest opticians, nurses, and technicians. The team performed four corneal transplants with donated eyes we actually flew onboard with us—the first in Mali's history. In addition, the team performed 107 cataract surgeries and did 1,087 eye examinations, as well as distributing over 2,100 new pairs of glasses—all donated from U.S. friends and donors. This illustrates how the Alliance continues to make healthcare a vital element in its services.

An amazing experience on that trip was my being reunited with an old chief of the Keleya village, named Kuntigi Bagayoko, whom I first encountered three decades earlier in about 1990. Back then he was age 75 and, like many Muslim men, had three or four wives. He was blind due to years of cataract problems. I had often tried to convince him to get to the capitol, Bamako, for help, but he always demurred. There were plenty of excuses. He was "too old." Life was "too hard." If one went to a hospital for medical care, one was "likely to die." A decade later, I tried convincing him again, but still to no avail. Another decade went by and I sought to get him help again. By then Kuntigi was 85 and "way too old for surgery." Finally, in 2017, when he was an astonishing 105 years old, I got Dramane, a grandnephew, who was one of 17 children in his father's family, to take me on the three-hour drive over bouncy dirt roads with several Malian friends to again visit him. It was fun to reconnect. I had never chatted with a 105-year-old person. We sat on dusty mats under a palm-leaf-covered shelter and reminisced. Again I pled with him to have the surgery. At that point and with a new Ouelessebougou hospital and a medical team of U.S. experts visiting, I told him that this was indeed "the right time." Thanks also to persuasion by Kuntigi's young relative, this time he finally consented. The next day, cataract surgery was performed on him, and he rested the following four days until our medical team was about to leave the country. He was brought to the hospital where doctors carefully removed the bandages and gauze. Seeing the first bright light in decades, his eyes watered greatly, but the M.D.s slowly wiped his face until dry. The result was shocking, he declared. *He could see!* He didn't recognize people's faces, of course, even his wives and children. Many of his posterity had died much earlier, but he could now view wrinkled faces of his older posterity up through the year 2017. I was overjoyed to see the results. His nephew took him on the slow trip back to his village, where there was great rejoicing. A few months later, he finally died, at age 106. But he'd become a role model encouraging other Malians, including other antiquated village elders and their families, to accept cataract surgery and improve their quality of life, just like their old chief.

I now turn to the use of education as an Alliance tool for humanitarian services—the other primary thrust of our efforts—in Mali.

Education as Social Change

One of the most critical needs for development in many nations is the vital importance of public schools and the education of coming generations. This is particularly the case in West Africa where governments have little money and few schools, especially in rural regions beyond the capital cities. Mali's adult literacy rate as of 2018 was only 35 percent (World Bank, 2019). With such low statistics, OA has made education a priority such that since the formation of the Alliance, there has been a dramatic increase in school enrollment.

The Alliance liked the values of South Africa's great hero Nelson Mandela, who declared, "Education is the most powerful weapon which you can use to change the world" (Mandela, 2017) As a long-term OA board member, I believe those words fit well with the LDS views cited by many Church leaders. For instance, Joseph Smith taught that "no man is saved faster than he gets knowledge" and that "no man can be saved in ignorance" (J. Smith, 2007, p. 266). "The glory of God is intelligence, or, in other words, light and truth" (*Doctrine and Covenants*, 93:36). The Church's first prophet also uttered many more words to encourage both spiritual and secular learning. I have always felt these ideas clearly applied to West Africa.

So once the Alliance fixed on its goals for Mali, one of its earliest tasks was to actually build schools there so education could grow. Since 1985, some 42 schools have been constructed with Alliance funding and engineering expertise to ensure that the buildings would last. In the first decade (1985–95), the few schools built were not well designed. They were made of adobe bricks that villagers would prepare, after which Alliance volunteers would arrive from America to help erect the buildings, put up thatched roofing, and make them the schools that we considered viable, yet as inexpensive as possible. However, seeing the gradual disintegration of those early structures due to heat, rain, and faulty materials, as well as children's necessary wear and tear, we determined that better solutions were needed. Over time, construction experts helped design and then manage teams of villagers in the erection of new schools using cinder block with cement floorings poured, metal roofing, and (for protection) thick tin or steel doors and windows.

The national government had informed the communities that it did not have funding for impoverished Ouelessebougou. Instead, its money went toward supporting public schools in far-off Bamako. So our organization not only erected the schools, but also convinced local chiefs and families that they should raise their own funding to educate the next generation. Our objective was to ultimately have at least a single, one-room schoolhouse in each village that would be accessible to even the poorest families. Ignorance and illiteracy, we felt, were too costly to ignore. So OA helped fund teachers using a simple formula that would gradually shift responsibilities from the NGO to the community. It would start with the time, energy, and muscle of villagers to build their own humble school. Then the OA would fund the cost of supplies and 100 percent of a teacher's salary for the first school year. He or she would relocate from Bamako to Ouelessebougou. For the second year, the Alliance would pay two-thirds of the cost and the village one-third as their little microenterprises began to grow and to generate more disposable income among the locals. In the third year, the formula was to supply two-thirds of the revenue from villagers, and one-third from OA. Finally, in the fourth year, local people were to finance 100 percent of a school's operation so that the Alliance could withdraw and shift its school construction money and energy to other villages that still lacked classrooms for children. This procedure worked very well as our strategy grew and became both institutionalized and adequately funded.

In addition, after a school's completion, we sought to provide textbooks and decent furnishings for the buildings, with benches and roughhewn "desks" handmade by men of each village. These material necessities were funded at 100 percent to begin with, and then funding tapered off as villages became more sustainable over time. In 2018 approximately 2,230 students attended schools at which in prior times no formal education at all had been available. Another educational intervention by OA was that it has become receptive to community requests to install solar panels atop the buildings of the elementary schools, to generate electricity and lighting for adults taking night classes.

These education strategies have worked very well over the years. After some two decades-plus, the organization stated that "since the inception of an Alliance education program . . . school enrollment has risen dramatically" (OA Annual Report, 2010). It has continued unabated ever since. The Alliance has been particularly pleased about the enrollment of females, which is 21 percent higher than that of national school enrollment in Mali generally. As one villager stated, "Education is the key to success; it doesn't fix everything, but it gives you access to things and ability to progress" (OA Annual Report, 2010.). The Alliance has always been strongly committed to balanced gender issues, seeking to ensure that women and girls are primary beneficiaries of social innovation, which stresses education and health for females in their striving for empowerment and support for their families.

In 2005, the Malian government adjusted the national curriculum for first and second grades in order to require that teachers teach in Bambara, the nation's indigenous language. After that, beginning in third grade, French, Mali's official language, would start being taught. The national government asked the Alliance to pilot this program. Some 23 teachers participated in training sessions organized by the Alliance to help assist with the difficult transition from the indigenous language (in first and second grades) so that students could be completely French-speaking by fifth grade as the new curriculum policies required.

It should be mentioned that OA's education programs have long valued involvement from parents and the larger local community. Thus, parents from the villages in Mali attend training sessions to learn how to become more active in their own children's education. Often, these parents become inspired to make sure that teachers support the education of their daughters as well as their sons, ensuring that female enrollment continues to grow in the region. In 2019–2020, to enhance nutrition, some 300 Alliance school kids and their mothers created educational gardens adjacent to buildings to grow nutritious produce that improves diets and enhances everyone's health.

Unfortunately, Mali has often neglected its girls, with remote government officials usually explaining that they are needed to help mothers at home with chores, cooking, cleaning, and tending the younger kids of a family. This attitude reflects the centuries-old attitudes of chauvinism in many places of the world still today. In contrast, the Alliance seeks to gradually counter the oppression of females at all ages, and strives to create new opportunities not only for girls but also for their mothers and single women in general.

Approximately a decade ago, the Alliance initiated a "sister-school" program that addressed an additional part of the organization's mission statement: "To provide the opportunity for both cultures (American and Malian) to learn from the other's family and social relationships" (OA, Mission Statement 2010) Since then, 11 schools throughout Utah have been selected to partner with the same number of schools in the Ouelessebougou region to exchange cultural experiences. A few American teachers have traveled annually to Mali to meet with teachers there, observe local customs, and record music and stories that they then take home to teach and inspire their Utah students while building global appreciation and mutual understanding.

One further aspect of this NGO's educational development strategy is that of creating a "Lead Teachers" program. This aspect of the OA education process is quite unique. The organization has established and funded Lead Teachers on the ground in Mali, selected because of their excellent teaching skills, who receive yearly training and a small stipend to coach other teachers in certain schools within the region. These Lead Teachers are required to make monthly visits to each school to follow up on training and to provide constructive feedback for future program improvements.

Current Ouelessebougou Challenges and Changes

Unfortunately, the Ouelessebougou Alliance has not created a utopia in Mali. The country still experiences far too much poverty and malnourishment, even though people's diets and nutrition are improving somewhat. While more schools are being built, education is woefully underfunded, and improving the quality of learning will require both many more francs and dollars.

As I write in 2020, people around the globe are embroiled in the horrific devastation of the coronavirus pandemic. Worldwide there are 16,418,867 coronavirus cases globally and 652,256 deaths (Worldometers, 2020), and the worst is probably still to come. The crisis has been hitting the United States hard, resulting in some 32 million cases and 576,000 deaths (as of April 2021). In Mali, as of mid-2020, there were 2,500 cases of the disease with only 123 deaths. But, of course, each one is tragic—each individual, each family, each village, each region. As for the Alliance, the U.S. toll is shaking the American economy which means, if the pandemic continues much longer, OA supporters will not be traveling to volunteer in Mali for the foreseeable future, nor will donations to the NGO's operations continue at recent levels to support the people of Ouelessebougou in the future like they have in past decades. What this means for the long term is unclear. However, Mali's coronavirus impacts—including border shutdowns, in-country road closures, and with local market curfews—have blocked many entrepreneurial efforts and disrupted trade routes throughout West Africa.

In summing up the social impacts of the Ouelessebougou Alliance and the people it serves, I recall the insight of the Prophet Joseph F. Smith (1902), who declared that, as Latter-day Saints, "we depend on mutual helpfulness." We see that development through social entrepreneurship is a multifaceted process of working together that incorporates all aspects of human well-being. Perhaps the words of the Malian managing director of the Alliance, Anounou Sissoko, offered a holistic vision a few years ago when he commented: "Development is a multi-aspect. It is the human being complete" (Ward, et al., 2008, 475). When he and I jointly presented the NGO work of the Alliance to an LDS crowd in Provo when he was in town for a board meeting recently, he affirmed this, telling people that without a holistic methodology, development will only be a piecemeal process when what is required is *evolution toward comprehensiveness* (Sissoko and Woodworth, 2018).

The narrative of the Alliance is not one about top-down control, as is the case with many NGOs and development institutions. In this instance, it's more of a reciprocal relationship in which African needs are identified, Utah resources are found to be available, and mutual exchanges are made. Both groups, the Utahns and the Malians, have established innovative networks using social entrepreneurial values such as shared passion, inventing new methods, exercise of cooperation, and joint problem-solving. Expertise is shared, mutual respect and love develop, and lives are enriched on both sides of the world.

For example, on my most recent trip to Mali in 2017, I was one of 22 U.S. experts with various health and development backgrounds, all committed to reduce African suffering. Most of the other members of the tour were trained in medicine, the majority being ophthalmologists who do surgery, or optometrists who diagnose vision problems and prescribe and fit new eyeglasses. With each member paying their own expenses, our group tested the vision of some 2,100 villagers and gave them new glasses. The team examined 600-plus patients and performed 162 cataract surgeries, restoring the ability to see for many individuals, from age 23 to 105 (as described in an earlier section). The top M.D.s also transported corneas in our carry-on bags and performed four corneal implants, the first in Mali's history—an accomplishment heralded by the country's Minister of Health, leading to a banquet of appreciation at the end of our work, one of a few formal signs of appreciation in Alliance history.

In field interviews during those weeks in Ouelessebougou in November 2017, the general consensus I heard from the Malians was one of appreciation for what Utahns have done to design and execute a long-term development model that stays focused in this one area, the villages of the Ouelessebougou *arrondissement*. On the other side, from the American visitors, the feeling was similar in that they expressed how much they learned from the women and men of Ouelessebougou. As one doctor told me, seeing the people's strength despite their abject poverty and their dignity in gradually overcoming hardships, was inspiring. He saw much improvement since his previous trip four years earlier. OA has stayed grounded in the belief that collaboration and joint decision-making are effective methods for gradual improvement in a village's quality of life, even in faraway Mali.

During my last work there, a group of old village elders in a rural cluster of mud homes with their thatched roofs told me that they have witnessed incremental improvements in the lives of themselves, their children, and their grandchildren during more than three decades of visits from Americans of the Alliance In comparison with other areas of Mali, Ouelessebougou is gaining in better education and improved health as it facilitates an ever-expanding social ecosystem. While several other NGOs over the years had their groups go into Mali and soon move on elsewhere, OA has stayed focused on achieving long-term, in-depth impacts in that area. The elders saw that the Alliance believes in a concept of development as one that includes growth and progress, accomplished through the realization of individual potential, along with building and strengthening of social relationships. In another village, one person in a group of women leaders suggested that, to her, "development" means that health and literacy improve so that self-sufficiency is strengthened. "Then I think that this country is developed," she remarked.

Unfortunately, Mali struggles today in coping with multiple political issues. In 2020 its military carried out a "bloodless coup" because of what were perceived as growing political instabilities. Top officials were replaced by a military junta that promised major reforms. Throughout the previous decade, multiple movements had been increasing after the U.S. invaded Afghanistan, such as the "Arab Spring Uprising" in Libya. Many al-Qaeda followers fled Libya, heading south from that nation into northern Mali. Islamists were soon pushing into the Timbuktu region to impose sharia law. Ultimately, many gained control over Timbuktu and Gao, destroying ancient shrines and imposing a harsh interpretation of Islamic rule. At Mali's request, France sent a few thousand troops to advise the Malian military and lead the fight to protect civilians and aid the efforts of local militaries. Soon, more than 13,000 U.N. peacekeepers were deployed, and their efforts in Mali have been called that venerable institution's "most dangerous mission" ever because of the high number of attacks on peacekeepers. American troops have also been deployed, with results both positive and questionable. The recent crisis is both a humanitarian and security concern as militant groups in the Sahel region often "tax" trafficking and smuggling routes to fund their campaigns.

While our work with OA has been in the southern region of Mali, we have dealt with continuing concerns about terrorism. During my last trip to volunteer there a few years ago, some 500 schools were shuttered because of terror threats in the capitol, Bamako. As our medical team provided care and as we traveled out to observe women's co-op agriculture and garden projects, tree planting by village youths, new water wells, school programs, and more, the Malian Army accompanied our every move with adequate military protection. I felt quite secure, but while having meetings in the capitol, visiting old friends, and traveling on dirt roads to observe some of the villages and catch up with old chiefs I had met there, I felt a degree of concern I'd never experienced previously. Still today I continually pray for my Muslim sisters and brothers in that far-off and beleaguered nation.

Mali's challenges continue. And the work of the Ouelessebougou Alliance seeks to consistently facilitate a better quality of life there, lower infant mortality rates, improved nutrition, more jobs, clean drinking water, expanded schools with good teachers, higher literacy rates, minimally adequate healthcare, and a stronger economy that will provide electricity and other services. Of course, I should mention that from the amazing successes of the Ouelessebougou Alliance, two other Utah NGOs were eventually established: Mali Rising, which has now built some two dozen additional rural schools, and another, called Empower Mali. Both of those organizations were launched by former OA staff in the U.S. or in Mali. Their work is primarily focused on developing wider and better education in the area, building schools, raising monies for hiring teachers, and so forth.

In writing of these Africa experiences, I recall laboring with my old Malian warrior friend Modibo Diarra, who was the first Malian to join the LDS Church. It took three decades before the Church became willing to send its first missionaries to the nation—all four of them—in 2018! Throughout his life in Bamako, Modibo had been a committed Muslim, a trade union leader, and a person who'd had the opportunity to get an education and eventually become a school teacher. He helped lead the 1960 revolution that eventually overthrew the French colonizers, after which he become a fairly prominent Malian. Upon learning of Mormonism's arrival in the capitol from an American LDS veterinarian, he received a testimony and joined the Church. As his children grew up, they not only were baptized, but even served LDS missions; two eventually studied at BYU Idaho (Diarra, 1993). Modibo was not merely beloved and respected by only the people of southern Mali, but also by all our Alliance staff in Utah. One of my favorite General Authorities, Elder Marion D. Hanks, at times referred to him as the "Malian Moses." Elder Hanks and our mutual Salt Lake friend Elder Robert Garff—one-time Salt Lake Temple President, London Mission President, and CEO of Garff Motors—served together for years on the OA board, where we enjoyed sharing stories of interactions with Modibo and valued his spirituality as well as his humor.

In the 1990s, we hired Modibo as our Field Director for the Ouelessebougou Alliance in Africa, and I've been blessed to have him and his brother Mohammed stay in our Provo home. I have also visited him in Africa on many occasions while we collaborated on complex problems facing his people. One evening, as I sat with him under a tall mango tree in a village, he declared:

> "We have learned much from the outside world, including ideas from Europe and America. But to fully develop Mali, we must walk our own pathway through the villages of Africa."
> —Modibo Diarra

References

BBC. (2019). Mali country profile. http://www.bbc.com/news/world-africa-13881370. Feb. 19.

Beckstead, J. (2018). Author's interview notes. May 7.

Bornstein, D. (2007). *How to Change the World: Social Entrepreneurs and the Power of New Ideas.* Oxford University Press.

BYU. (2009). Field Study of Ouelessebougou Impacts in Mali, West Africa. Unpublished report.

CIA. (2018). *World Factbook.* https://www.cia.gov/library/publications/the-world-factbook/geos/ml.html.

Diarra, M. "After My Trial Came Blessings." *Liahona,* August 1993.

Easterly, W. (2006). *The White Man's Burden: Why the West's Efforts to Aid the Rest Have Done So Much Ill and So Little Good.* Oxford University Press.

Lewis, J. (2017). *The Unfinished Social Entrepreneur.* Red Press.

Macrotrends. (2020). Mali Infant Mortality Rate 1950–2020. https://www.macrotrends.net/countries/MLI/mali/infant-mortality-rate.

Mandela, N. (2017). *Oxford Essential Quotations* (5th ed.). Ed. Susan Ratcliffe. Oxford University Press.

Okazaki, C. N. (1992). Spit and Mud and Kigatsuku. LDS Relief Society Sesquicentennial, General Conference, *Ensign*, May. https://www.churchofjesuschrist.org/study/general-conference/1992/04/spit-and-mud-and-kigatsuku.

Ouelessebougou Alliance. (2010, 2018, 2019). *Annual Reports*. https://www.lifteachother.org/about-us/.

Sen, A. (1999). *Development as Freedom*. Alfred A. Knopf.

Sissoko, A., and Woodworth, W. (2018). The Vibrant Ecosystem of Social and Economic Development in West Africa. A social entrepreneurship seminar to the Provo, Utah, community, May 7.

Smith, I. H., and Woodworth, W. P. (2012). Developing Social Entrepreneurs and Social Innovators: A Social Identity and Self-Efficacy Approach. *Academy of Management Learning and Education* (AMLE). Vol. 11, no. 3, 390–407.

Smith, J. (2007). *Teachings of Presidents of the Church: Joseph Smith*. Intellectual Reserve, 266.

Smith, J. F. (1902). Editor's Table, *Improvement Era*. December.

Wadley, C. (2009). Journey of Hope. *Deseret News*. Quote by OA staffer Jodi Jensen. http://www.deseretnews.com/article/705288344/Journey-of-hope.html, March 3.

Ward, C. et al. (2008). BYU Mali Study. Women's Research Institute.

Woodworth, W. (2018). Seminar discussion at the Association for Research on Civil Society in Africa (AROCSA). Cairo, Egypt, July 26–28.

World Bank. (2020). Literacy rate, adult total for Mali. https://data.worldbank.org/indicator/SE.ADT.

Worldometers. (2021). COVID-19 Coronavirus Pandemic. https://www.worldometers.info/coronavirus/. Accessed November 5.

"Hark, All Ye Nations!"
LDS Hymns, No. 264

1. Hark, all ye nations! Hear heaven's voice
   Thru ev'ry land that all may rejoice!
   Angels of glory shout the refrain:
   Truth is restored again!

   [Chorus] Oh, how glorious from the throne above
   Shines the gospel light of truth and love!
   Bright as the sun, this heavenly ray
   Lights ev'ry land today.

2. Searching in darkness, nations have wept;
   Watching for dawn, their vigil they've kept.
   All now rejoice; the long night is o'er.
   Truth is on earth once more!

3. Chosen by God to serve him below,
   To ev'ry land and people we'll go,
   Standing for truth with fervent accord,
   Teaching his holy word.

   Text: Based on German text by Louis F. Mönch (1847–1916)
   Music: George F. Root (1820–1895)

4
Sustain Haiti

(Post-Haiti's Earthquake, 2010–2020)

Have you ever dreamed about wanting to change the world? Or sometimes felt powerless as you witness or hear about massive human suffering around the world? At times, have tears filled your eyes as your television displays children's broken or dead bodies on the nightly news? Then this story from Haiti following the terrible earthquake and destruction of 2010, which basically flattened the island nation, is intended for you. It's a tale of my class of Latter-day Saint millennials joining with me to take action, reduce human suffering, and lift the poor who survived in the Caribbean that year. It was then that we designed and implemented our humble "class project" that became known as Sustain Haiti.

As Latter-day Saints, we have a rich legacy of Mormon humanitarian outreach to respond with emergency aid to those in need. Throughout the past couple of decades, some of us have been blessed to help develop such programs as the Church's Humanitarian Services in the 1980s, which grew out of the suffering of millions of Ethiopians in East Africa. In the late 1990s, Latter-day Saint Charities was formed as a nongovernmental organization to assist impoverished families around the globe even though they were not of our faith. In 2000, the Perpetual Education Fund became official, thereby enabling returned missionaries and college-age

▲ Sustain Haiti board members at the "Mormon Orphanage" for survivors of massive 2010 earthquake that killed some 250,000

▼ Volunteers from BYU teaching kids in a cow pasture after their rural school was destroyed

church members in the developing world to begin a better life. In addition, private and family-initiated nonprofit projects have likewise grown. From only a couple of Mormon-based NGOs started in the 1980s, today there are at least 200 such social enterprises incorporated just in Utah, with many more in Idaho, Arizona, and elsewhere across the United States.

However, the heritage of LDS humanitarianism goes back over a century and a half. Do you recall hearing of the pioneer travelers buried in the Wyoming blizzards of the 1850s? I want to draw a parallel between the long-ago suffering and death they experienced and the plight of today's earthquake victims in Haiti.

The tragedy of both the Martin and Willie handcart companies, trapped by fierce, early winter storms in the 1850s, is one of the most painful episodes in Mormon history. Some of my ancestors were victims of the growing disaster. They were unexpectedly caught in early deep snow, and subsequently became exhausted. With hundreds of miles yet to travel, their meager supplies dwindled rapidly. Provisions that had been expected along the way were nonexistent, and desperation settled in. The remaining amount of daily flour to be consumed was cut from a pound per person to a mere three-quarters of a pound, and then to only 10 ounces.

As our LDS pioneer predecessors faced the challenge of struggling up and over the Rocky Mountains in freezing snow, severe concerns increasingly weighed them down as they attempted to survive. Bitter cold seeped through their few layers of worn-out clothing. Wet items became harder to dry, even at night around a campfire. Overexertion, fatigue, and gnawing hunger began to take their deadly toll. First the elderly and some of the infirm began dying—along the trail or during the freezing night. Then the young, and even some of the strong, started to die. Fathers who had pulled their little ones through snow drifts one day would die during the evening while their children slept. Family members would go to bed huddling together in a tent, then awake in the morning having to check to see who had died during the night. Snow, mud, frostbite, starvation, bleeding feet—all were accompanied by the tragic demise of many souls. While some succumbed to the ravages of the early ferocious Wyoming winter, survivors lacked the strength to even bury the deceased. Instead, the two, five, or 13 bodies of the dead during a single night would simply be piled together and covered with snow to await the resurrection. I believe the graphic story of their rescue has implications for those of us who have resources to help suffering people across the globe in 2021.

As the handcart pioneers were being brutalized by these extreme conditions, word of their imminent demise reached Salt Lake City. At the General Conference of the LDS Church on October 5, 1856, President Brigham Young stood before thousands in the newly built tabernacle and announced: "Many of our brethren and sisters are on the plains with handcarts, and probably many are now seven hundred miles from this place, and they must be brought here, we must send assistance to them...

> I shall call upon the Bishops of this day. I shall not wait until tomorrow, nor until the next day, for 60 good mule teams and 12 or 15 wagons. I do not want to send oxen. I want good horses and mules. They are in this Territory, and we must have them. Also 12 tons of flour and 40 good teamsters, besides those that drive the teams.... First, 40 good young men who know how to drive teams, to take charge of the teams that are now managed by men, women and children who know nothing about driving them. Second, 60 or 65 good spans of mules, or horses, with harness, whipple trees, neck-yokes, stretchers, lead chains, &c. And thirdly, 24 thousand pounds of flour, which we have on hand....
>
> I will tell you all that your faith, religion, and profession of religion, will never save one soul of you in the Celestial Kingdom of our God, unless you carry out just such principles as I am now teaching you. *Go and bring in those people now on the plains.* And attend strictly to those things which we call temporal, or temporal duties. Otherwise, your faith will be in vain. The preaching you have

heard will be in vain to you, and you will sink to *Hell,* unless you attend to the things we tell you.

Brigham the Prophet then counseled church members about how to treat the survivors who would be rescued and brought into the Salt Lake Valley:

> I want to have them distributed in the city among the families that have good and comfortable houses; and I wish all the sisters now before me, and all who know how and can, to nurse and wait upon the new comers and prudently administer medicine and food to them. To speak upon these things is a part of my religion, for it pertains to taking care of the Saints....
>
> The afternoon meeting will be omitted, for I wish the sisters to go home and prepare to give those who have just arrived a mouthful of something to eat, and to wash them and nurse them up. You know that I would give more for a dish of pudding and milk, or a baked potato and salt, were I in the situation of those persons who have just come in, than I would for all your prayers, though you were to stay here all the afternoon and pray. Prayer is good, but when baked potatoes and pudding and milk are needed, prayer will not supply their place on this occasion; give every duty its proper time and place....
>
> Some you will find with their feet frozen to their ankles; some are frozen to their knees and some have their hands frosted.... We want you to receive them as your own children, and to have the same feeling for them. We are their temporal saviors, for we have saved them from death (Hafen and Hafen, 1960, pp. 120–21, 139).

Of this poignant story of poverty-stricken pioneers suffering, death, and survival, James E. Faust (1997) of the First Presidency declared: "Now I think our prophet today is telling all of us, in this day and time, to go and bring in those people who are out on the plains. I am impressed with what President Gordon B. Hinckley said about this event in the previous October 1996 general conference: 'Wonderful sermons have been preached from this pulpit, my brethren and sisters. But none has been more eloquent than that spoken by President Young in those circumstances'" (Hinckley, 1996, p. 7).

President Hinckley had asserted such in our day: "There are people, not a few, whose circumstances are desperate and who cry out for help and relief. There are so many who are hungry and destitute across this world who need help.... My brethren and sisters, I would hope, I would pray that each of us... would resolve to seek those who need help, who are in desperate and difficult circumstances, and lift them in the spirit of love" (Hinckley, 1996, p. 86).

These words, too, gave my BYU class and me a sense of calling and caring. In 2010, some of our Sustain Haiti volunteers began to build models of post-earthquake service as well as to gather useful tools so they could rescue some of the contemporary poor among the island's many victims. We realized that the people might not require teams of horses, but they *were* desperate for shelter. Instead of "pudding and milk," they needed an income sufficient to buy corn, beans, rice, and chicken. They also needed education for their children, and to have their schools rebuilt or reopened.

Clearly, the situation for most Latter-day Saints along the Wasatch Front today is a far cry from that of the pioneers over a century ago. Many LDS Utahns dwell in luxurious homes up on the East Bench with ample garages to hold their various automobiles such as expensive Teslas, Mercedes Benzes, or BMWs, along with snowmobiles, dune buggies, and even boats. Some folks stand in church testimony meetings to express gratitude for all the "comforts" of life, glad they do not have to make the sacrifices and endure the hardships that their ancestors suffered. However, much more is needed to lift the poor today, including sharing our financial resources. Writing a check to assist devastated people of the island of Haiti, we felt, was a *good* thing. But some Latter-day Saints were able to even do more.

A few years ago, President Hinckley told newly called mission presidents at the Missionary Training Center in Provo, "The day of sacrifice is not over." Some of those in attendance wondered what he meant, as have others who heard the prophet's message secondhand. But to me the implications were clear: It is not enough to merely donate 10 percent as a tithe to God and assume everything is all right. Nor is it sufficient to pray for the "poor and needy" every morning and later to engage in conspicuous consumption patterns. We must give of our time and resources—including our financial means—as instruments for personal and family consecration. By taking such action, not only are the world's poor blessed and lifted up, but those of us who truly give also enjoy greater joy and spiritual purpose in our lives. This is the legacy of Mormon humanitarianism.

The Launch of Sustain Haiti in 2010

Over the decades, I have labored to mobilize my BYU students, as well as alumni and faculty from the social sciences and Utah's business community, in empowering the poor around the world. I have always sought to inspire students both at BYU, where I taught most of my career, or at other institutions where I served as a visiting professor, including the University of Michigan in Ann Arbor, Claremont University in Southern California, the University of Utah, or in Brazil and Hawaii and even Lithuania. We used social change models and concepts such as entrepreneurship, financial inclusion, cross-cultural management, international development, economic self-reliance, and organizational change tools to design projects that are sustainable over the long term.

In exploring how college students and professors could come together to address the suffering of the global poor, a paper I've drawn on for this book applies "base-of-the-pyramid" (BOP) logic to address demands of the Caribbean poor—in this case, the struggling nation of Haiti (Woodworth, 2010). According to BOP theory, several developing countries can take advantage of opportunities for helping their people and accelerating societal potential, even in times of abject poverty, disaster, and the simple struggle to survive. This was the case in Haiti after it suffered a massive crisis following the 2010 earthquake. With my associates, we sought to build people's capacity through the creation of a new development ecosystem that would give voice to the poor. It helped heighten survivors' ability to analyze their predicament and begin to dig their way out of the disaster. It happened from the low and miserable base of the economic and political pyramid in Haiti, as people began to take control of their own futures. By linking paradigms from social science, business, and development practices, my BYU students connected with Haitian stakeholders from decimated communities so as to begin new lives (London, Sateen, and Hart, 2014).

In my 2010 paper I took both a descriptive and a normative approach, which together governed our application of social entrepreneurship in Haiti. My work on it began in 2010, and summarized efforts into 2020 with several teams and multiple evaluation trips. Clearly it is still a work in progress. This chapter in *Radiant Mormonism*, then, presents an analysis of social action, of a project that is yet emerging—not a final assessment. The flavor is one of advocacy and passion, not theory and conceptual reasoning. My hope is to explicate the potential power that business school faculty as well as students possess in improving society beyond the traditional corporate paradigm.

Social Entrepreneurship, Passion, and Compassion

Management and organizational behavior fields have long been in flux. One of the exciting developments has been the fact that the Academy of Management (AOM) has held some of its annual meetings in recent years with themes such as "Capitalism in Question," "The Informal Economy," "Dare to Care: Passion and Compassion in Management Practice and Research," and even "Doing Well by Doing Good." The academy's leaders articulated their vision of the rolling conferences as an opportunity to "consider whether our research and the knowledge we produce contribute to the well-being of the larger society in which we live and work" (AOM, 2010).

The goal of the 2010 event was "to dare managers and management scholars to care more deeply about our roles—to have passion about what we do and compassion for the people for whom we do our work. 'Dare to care' orients managers to a focus on enabling others to create, produce, and deliver goods and services that enhance the well-being of, and generate value for, all the stakeholders involved (notably customers, employees, investors, and the public). Daring to care encourages management scholars to expand their focus toward an understanding of how solving organizational problems might ensure a sustainable future" (AOM). I believe this to be an exciting and even pathbreaking new agenda for management scholars and practitioners alike, as well as for Latter-day Saints seeking to use their academic skills while integrating them with the gospel.

A number of sessions and papers at recent management conferences have emphasized using business schools and research to understand and practice the values of caring in our disciplines. Titles included phrases like "Navigating the Tensions in Poverty Alleviation Research: Scholarly Rigor vs. Practical Relevance"; "Base-of-the-Pyramid Interventions"; "Social Capital and Social Exchange"; "Ten Years of Daring to Care: The U.N. Global Compact (2000-2010)—What Has Been Achieved"; "Daring to Measure Social Impact: Performance Management in the Social Sector"; "Sustainable Global Enterprise: Building Research on Caring and Daring MNEs"; and "Social Repair Through Micro-Business."

This chapter attempts to build off the mission and agenda of both social science and these AOM trends, doing so by describing and capturing the spirit of social entrepreneurship in my labors primarily with LDS students at BYU and also with my colleagues in accelerating the next generation of changemakers and advancing the well-being of society.

A Personal Context: Past Academic Incubator Experience

It has been suggested that real insights about social innovations come from one's own experience. This certainly seems to be the case when one talks of trying to "change the world." Thus, I will speak from my own life, my personal practice, and my commitments to practice gospel principles. LDS values have been the foundation of what I do and how I live, drawing in my family, friends, and neighbors as we seek to strengthen Zion by serving the poor globally. But I do these things while acknowledging my many limitations and being painfully aware that we must all continue to learn, to question, and to critique our own life's work. I hope these personal illustrations will show the tremendous possibilities of generating action-based learning and research, not only for academic purposes, but also for engaging Latter-day Saints in reducing human suffering and building civil society around the globe.

While my BYU students and I have launched many other social entrepreneurship start-ups through the years, the story I relate here about Haiti is extremely powerful. Let me clarify that when I discuss "social entrepreneurship," I seek to take a broad perspective. Essentially, I mean the mix of individuals who see social problems that may not be being addressed by either government or business. Thus, such individuals question "Why?" and begin to take action. At times they are referred to as change agents, "movers and shakers," radicals, social innovators, positive deviants, the "crazy ones," and so on. Often, they see a societal need, collect some initial data, try to understand the causes of social problems, and then design new institutions to respond. Such new entities may be referred to as nongovernment organizations (NGOs), private voluntary organizations (PVOs), social enterprises, nonprofit organizations, or other terms, depending on the country or culture. In some instances, such entities may seek a financial return, as well as having not-for-profit characteristics that seek to do good. For purposes of this chapter, though, I will generally use the term NGO to characterize my cases that have grown out of an academic context.

This emerging field of social entrepreneurship has evolved in the management literature gradually over the years, but is currently accelerating dramatically. Some four decades ago, William Foote Whyte (1982) called for the creation of new "social inventions" to address societal problems—perhaps one of the earliest articulations of the need for social innovation. Whyte was widely recognized for his classic research and his being elected president of the Industrial Relations Research Association, as well as of the American Sociological Association. By the mid-1990s, no less a figure than Peter Drucker argued in the *Harvard Business Review* that social entrepreneurship would become the second careers of masses of professional or knowledge workers (1999). This literature has exploded ever since those days (Aldrich and Zimmer, 1986; Bornstein, 2004; Dees, 1998 and 2007; Light, 2006; Mair and Marti, 2006).

The essence of my argument is that LDS college students, along with faculty members, can literally become radical social innovators by inventing new courses and projects that adapt entrepreneurship to empower the world's poor by harnessing *sustainable strategies that last*. In several instances, spinoffs from my courses have led to collaboration and involvement with students from other universities who joined our on-the-ground summers of volunteering in the field. They include students from Portland State University, Stanford, VA Tech, Colorado State, University of Washington, University of North Carolina, and so forth.

With this context, I turn to the case profiled in this chapter—Haiti, where 10 years ago a number of LDS donors, local Church leaders in Utah and Haiti, BYU students, and others established programs of action learning and the practice of social entrepreneurship.

The Case of Sustain Haiti

Our mission-driven learning effort became one of a number of my platforms for action from BYU's base. It was a program in which I worked with students in my MBA 632 Social Entrepreneurship course through winter semester in 2010 to design a classroom project to fight poverty, implement the project in Haiti, and eventually spin it off as an independent NGO—that is, a social enterprise. It grew out of the design and implementation of a social entrepreneurial strategy to mobilize, train, and send MBA students and others to help to rebuild Haiti after the 2010 earthquake. That program proved that Latter-day Saint students as well as action-minded business executives can come together and share how their best practices may be integrated in reducing human suffering in a nearby island nation.

In the summer of 2010 I began working with a team of college students and others in Haiti, where we were rolling out a new project in response to the devastating earthquake that had hit the country in January. My notes from August 22, 2010, suggest the sweat, smells, and noises in that setting. I wrote: "Clouds were beginning to cluster above the silhouettes of banana trees, palms, and huge mango trees. Below, where I sat in the growing darkness, was a beehive of activity: All kinds of Caribbean music blasting out of every conceivable technology, huge trucks laden with tons of earthquake debris rumbling down the street, small motorcycles with multiple passengers crowded on a one-person vehicle. People were sauntering along through the intersection where our house was located, not only city dwellers, but peasants herding a cow or two along the 'roads.' These streets had actually become jumbles of dirt, rock, and potholes. The temperature was around 95 degrees, accompanied by approximately 94 percent humidity" (Woodworth, 2010, p. 21).

I was there in one Haitian town, sweltering in the heat, with a number of young BYU social entrepreneurs out to change the world. We had formed a project called "Sustain Haiti" in which we had recruited and trained volunteers and raised money to assist the people of that impoverished nation. Haiti was already the poorest nation in the Western Hemisphere. Then, on January 12, 2010, a horrific 7.0 earthquake destroyed much of the country. When the quake struck, I wondered, as a professor in BYU's Marriott School of Business, what *could* I or *should* I do about this tragedy of such

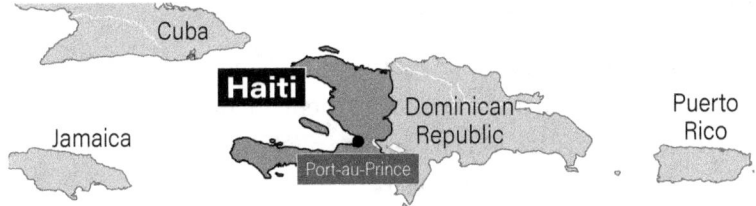

epic proportions? The idea came deep in my heart: I felt the Spirit of God tell me that my friends and I should take action.

Over the next several days, I began to talk with campus associates, neighbors, church members, and professional colleagues about the growing crisis. The capital city of Port-au-Prince and surrounding towns were largely demolished. More than three million people were affected by the disaster. The Haitian government and U.S. officials reported that an estimated 250,000-plus people died (BBC, 2010). In the months following the destruction, various statistics emerged that some 300,000 had been injured and one million were made homeless. It was truly catastrophic. The Haitian people needed help from numerous sources. I knew that what I called the "Big Boys" (the Red Cross, large churches, USAID, the World Bank, and governments around the globe) would rush in money, food, water, and medical care. Our team began to consider what would happen after they all dropped off their supplies, spent a few weeks on the ground, and then left. I realized, as I have so many times before in crises like this one, that the hard work really begins after the initial shock wears off and the early emergency aid has been delivered.

In our case, we looked at the disaster and determined that our model for helping Haiti would be different from that of the Big Boys. In previous years, with colleagues and earlier students, we drew on several commonly used conceptual stages for successfully helping communities after disasters, described next.

Stages of Crisis Assistance

1. *Rescue*, in which the goal is to find those who survived the earthquake and get them out of the rubble
2. *Relief*, in which food, water, and medical attention are given to everyone in need
3. *Recovery*, in which the bodies of the dead are located and buried or disposed of
4. *Rebuilding*, in which homes, businesses, schools, and other institutions are rebuilt in order to reestablish society

Within a week after January 12, in my home community of Provo, Utah, I began gathering a group of friends, colleagues, and neighbors, meeting together to explore how we might proceed. We decided to call ourselves Sustain Haiti, and we wanted to generate a long-term commitment to those who were suffering. With ideas from campus and community volunteers, we identified key tasks and formed teams around those tasks. They included a needs assessment of the Haiti situation, logistics for how to get people to that country, fundraising, recruiting of volunteers, lessons in Haitian culture and the local Creole language, where we could best labor in Haiti, and which skills we could offer the survivors. We knew that large aid organizations could give billions of dollars, but they would not solve the problems of Haiti *after* the quake. Only the Haitians themselves would ultimately be able to solve their problems. Our objective was to empower them to do so.

Students from my BYU class and beyond were formed into action committees to determine needs in Haiti, where we should labor, what the realities were regarding our own health, security, and safety on the ground. We also established a public relations group as well as a fundraising team. Graduate students led each group—as they tended to be more mature and experienced, and to have more-advanced education. Day after day we secured as many as 60 volunteers for our adventure, eventually recruiting individuals from coast to coast, ranging from an LDS mother in Virginia to a student at Mesa Community College in Arizona. And we raised more than $300,000.

For this project we were *not* looking for volunteers who lacked real-world knowledge or who seemed to merely want to be "humanitarian tourists." In particular, we sought to recruit older graduate students. Other preferences were for students who had experience living abroad in developing countries, especially returned LDS missionaries. A few volunteers we found were already fluent in Creole, some spoke excellent French, and still others had some foreign language speaking competencies that enabled them to quickly learn the basics of Creole so as to communicate with Haitians, at least in rudimentary ways. These volunteers, I found, were uniquely qualified individuals who knew the challenges of living and working among the poor around the globe. They were aware that they would be required to work hard from 6:00 a.m. until dark six days a week. They knew how to cope with ambiguity and change, possessing a deep commitment to love and serve the local people. Many also possessed the ability to be cautious and smart in cases of potential danger, and to be cognizant of other demands for not only surviving, but thriving.

Our BYU teams met at times other than the regular class period because some students joined the cause, but had other commitments at the appointed hour. So we gathered during afternoon breaks and evenings, planning our strategy in the early weeks. We invited and heard from a number of resource people who shared their knowledge of post-quake Haiti, including women who assisted at orphanages in Port-au-Prince, an M.D. who had just returned from giving medical assistance to those injured in the earthquake, a team of regional volunteers who went down to help during the initial shock period, and others. A dozen or so local NGOs had already made quick relief trips to Port-au-Prince to assess initial damage and provide emergency medical assistance, so we tapped into their experience as we began planning. As reported in the *Deseret News*, the overall objective was to aid Haitians in their recovery from a devastating national crisis (Romboy, 2010).

Because classes were packed with theories and debates and discussions of each day's assigned readings on Third World development, disaster relief strategies, and more, our team had to meet outside of class time. BYU administrators had told us we were not a "legitimate" organization and sought to block our efforts to design a new NGO and go help the earthquake victims that spring. This meant that we did not have access to regular classrooms for our planning sessions. So team leaders and members would show up at 5:00 p.m. outside my office door in the Tanner Building as campus offices were closing, then we would find an empty classroom and meet anyway. I hung a small sign above my office door that read "*Niatsus Itiah Headquarters.*" The sneaky reverse spelling for "Sustain Haiti" seemed to work. Eventually we regularly gathered in classroom 374 every other evening. I posted a large sign with our headquarters' name on it high above the chalkboard, and it remained there for months. Apparently it went unnoticed by the custodians, other professors, and their classes of students. It was but one of various "subversive" initiatives that Dr. Woodworth carried out over his 40-plus years as a BYU professor!

Within two months, we began designing and conducting training sessions for all potential participants who would travel to Haiti. Those beyond the local area viewed online training and YouTube video clips about skills required for the various projects. Eventually we produced a training manual filled with educational materials, to be used not only in preparation for traveling to Haiti to labor but also to have available later in-country so that as volunteers' assignments changed from time to time they could be better utilized on the ground in serving those in need.

We dispatched a student who had lived in Haiti a few years previously to fly down and get a hands-on sense of the situation, then return to Utah and report. We also searched for Haitians living or attending college in our region who could advise or join us, teach us some basic Creole, and provide cultural training. We dug through extensive reports from the U.N., USAID, Red Cross, and other organizations to learn as much about the deaths, destruction, and areas where we could make an impact.

The more we discovered about Haiti and its disaster, the clearer it became that we needed to focus on capacity-building. To do that, we decided to emphasize four primary areas of intervention: (1) to provide hands-on education in square-foot-gardening, which would give a family fresh produce for its own nutrition, plus generate a surplus to sell in the street markets; (2) to provide sanitation, hygiene, and health education to help survivors cope with dangerous new diseases that would emerge post-earthquake; (3) to provide clean-water technology for families and neighbors so as to avoid water-borne illnesses; (4) through our own efforts, as well as those of existing Haitian microfinance institutions, to provide training opportunities, loans, and other services for income-generation activities.

Some administrators and individual students at BYU and beyond laughed at our vision. They said we were too optimistic and naïve. Others were downright critical, warning us that Haiti was too dangerous, that its poverty was too great, and that the destruction would overwhelm us Americans. Furthermore, they claimed that Haiti would never recover, making our efforts futile. I wondered what they were thinking.... Were they just willing to cross Haiti off the list as a failed state? Should we simply wait for the Big Boys to work some kind of miracle? As members of Christ's church, would it be best to sit home and only passively change the TV channel whenever coverage of Haiti's tragedy appeared? Should we have bought into their passivity and waited for *others* to act?

My feeling was that while we were merely a group of average people, our gospel was clear: we had opportunities and social responsibilities to try to make a difference where we saw a need. We realized we could not do *everything*, but we could each do *something*. And this is what inspired Sustain Haiti. We became committed to improving the lives of the Haitian people, whether others agreed or supported us or not.

What was and is that thing called "Sustain Haiti"? We are a group of independent Haitians, Americans, and people of other nations as well: development specialists, homemakers, executives, students, social entrepreneurs, and concerned citizens from all across America. Beginning in late April 2010, we started sending teams of five to seven volunteers almost every Monday to the Haiti headquarters (a house we had rented) in the town of Leogane, the very epicenter of the quake. It was among the hardest-hit communities, a town that had boasted about 140,000 people before the earthquake, and where an estimated 20,000 to 30,000 individuals had been killed. Nearly all of its buildings were made of concrete but no steel infrastructure so some 90 percent of them were either severely damaged or destroyed (Millar, 2010).

Official statistics at the time were woefully lacking. We assumed early on that perhaps several hundred thousand Haitians had been killed in the earthquake and its aftershocks, making it one of the worst disasters in human history. Years later, people claimed that there were bodies disintegrating under the rubble.

Haiti was already the poorest country in the Western Hemisphere, and had been so for decades. Now with the grinding poverty exacerbated by this new crisis, everything became far worse. The gap between the United States and Haiti had never been greater. For instance, during 2009, New York City alone had gained 105,400 new millionaires. That made a total of 667,200 throughout just the Big Apple itself (Smith, 2011). In contrast, the few lucky Haitians who actually had jobs made only about $5 a day. That means they were trying to care for themselves and their families with a mere $1,500 to $1,800 per year. To me, something about that was just terribly wrong.

Sustain Haiti Values

For our new NGO, we based our work on several main values. The first principle that inspired our effort (most volunteers being LDS) was the gospel of the Savior. Next was a requirement that whatever we did in Haiti would be done with local partners—nongovernmental organizations that would keep our efforts going when our teams returned to the U.S. Long-term sustainability was essential to our mission. Over the summer of 2010 we collaborated with more than a dozen NGOs to ensure that by meeting some Haitians' needs, we would be helping to leverage their own impacts. By providing them with a portion of our remaining funds after we were to leave Haiti, we felt confident our programs would be maintained. We also hired several local LDS Haitians whom we got to know, who labored with us, whose work ethic was strong, and who were 100 percent responsible and trustworthy. These actions guaranteed that our projects would continue until we could return the following summer.

Another of our core values was the notion of giving of our own means on behalf of the people of the affected community. Virtually every one of our volunteers was willing to offer their time, money, and energy to the cause. We discussed consecration principles during the semester, which became a great motivating factor. Everyone raised their own funds to work in Haiti. We each spent at least two weeks in-country; a number of us spent a month or two, even up to four months, on the ground in Haiti. Some left husbands, wives, or children to labor in the Caribbean right down in the trenches alongside the poor. Every volunteer had to come up with a minimum of $2,000 in order to serve. For many, that sum would have paid for tuition the next semester at BYU, bought a better used car, or covered the cost of doing an internship with corporate America.

An additional value of Sustain Haiti was that of job creation through microenterprise. Basically, this consisted of giving tiny loans to poor Haitians so they could lift themselves out of poverty. One MBA student who had taken my Social Entrepreneurship course from January to April during the time of the earthquake took the initiative to explore NGOs in Haiti that offered microcredit services. Other volunteers worked to prepare to offer microcredit for a small, extremely poor village up in the mountains, which had received no post-quake aid. I had the privilege of conducting a final training session in that village with two groups of men and one group of women, whom we organized into "solidarity groups." We then gave each member of each group the equivalent of a U.S. $70 microloan that they were to pay back, in full, with 5 percent interest, after four months.

They used these monies for various family income-generating efforts, and when the first loans were paid off, they qualified for other loans that doubled the first, growing to $140 and so on. Ultimately, those peasants were able to literally work themselves out of the "poorest of the poor" class—and perhaps even up into the Haitian middle-class in future years. In doing so, they would be able to educate their children as the first of their generation from their village to go to school. They would also have the funds they needed to get medical care when a child was sick or injured.

A related thrust of Sustain Haiti was to train young, budding entrepreneurs who already had businesses going as to how they could increase revenues, market their products and services, and learn other management tools to enhance their enterprises. For some of them and their friends, we held a Haiti Business Plan Competition activity—the first of its kind in that nation. We gave prizes to those with the best ideas for how to start or accelerate their firms. Amazingly, over a hundred Haitians participated in the venture! A number even established their own small enterprises in the following months. We were able to assess the results in the summers that followed, including a field study later done by students and faculty at another school, Indiana University.

Sustainability and stewardship were other core elements of our program. We and our partners taught classes on community development and social support. In a coastal fishing village called Destra, we collaborated with an NGO called G.O.A.L.S., named for a small soccer program created to help youth after the 2010 destruction. Together, we sought to enhance the quality of life for some 1,500 rural villagers living in plastic tents because virtually all their homes had been destroyed. The young people were trained in ecological principles and the need to not deforest their environment more than had already been done, using their favorite game—soccer—as a motivation tool. We also sought to be good stewards of the earth and nature in our core town where we were based, Leogane. We worked with Haitians to establish innovative and highly sustainable square-foot gardens. The local LDS Church gave us permission to plow up the lawns on church property to make such gardens for our members. The result was the creation of some 300 garden plots growing tomatoes, peppers, squash, beans, onions, carrots, and so forth. Over the decade since, many families have been able to draw on fresh, nutritious produce, not only in the harvest season each fall, but also in the cooler winter growing season that follows.

In addition to these four guiding principles, we later offered several other services, in response to many requests from Haitians in the communities of our focus. They consisted of teaching English classes, a competence people sought in the hope that, as foreign aid grew, a number of U.S. firms would begin investing and building factories in the area. Hence, English skills would give individuals a big advantage in obtaining employment. We also offered support for the staff and children at five area orphanages, each of which was caring for more children than before as a result of parental deaths, while also suffering structural damage from the earthquake.

At the end of summer 2010, we returned home to our jobs and studies at BYU and other universities, but continued to move Sustain Haiti forward in pursuit of a better future. In the first year, we raised over $100,000 for helping Haiti. While in-country we also trained several Haitian leaders to keep our efforts at microenterprise, water purification, and square-foot-gardens going, and growing, in the months to follow. Back on campus during fall semester we reviewed the various project reports, assessed our strengths and weaknesses, and began to plan for the future.

As with most of our other initiatives, new strategies became additional phases of our work in subsequent years. We continued to design innovations and recruit new volunteer managers, as well as others who went to Haiti for at least a month during each summer. We spent considerable time and energy designing a formal website that offered much more than the previous blog we used.

We also formed a board of trustees to establish overall planning and policies. This allowed us to finish the final steps of incorporating as a 501(c)(3) nonprofit organization with the U.S. Internal Revenue Service. I was grateful that my students and I could be joined on the board by Paul Thompson, a good friend of mine, and the former department head; he was dean of the Marriott School, eventually was named president of Weber State University, and later served as mission president in Boston. Another new board member, Roger Williams, was a favorite former student of mine who went on to be named a top executive at Bell Helicopter. He traveled with me to Haiti over many years, helping, advising, and even donating large sums of money to expand our services. More than money, though, I appreciated his thinking, analysis, and good heart. Sadly, he passed away while too young, leaving a wife and new baby girl.

During the past 12 summers since the earthquake, there have been 140-plus volunteers in Haiti, including a student from there who attended college in the U.S. He willingly gave up his studies, and his precious visa status, to return to Haiti as our in-country leader for the first several years. He coordinated all our projects with NGO partners, as well as managed up to 21 volunteers on the ground at one time. In addition, there were another two dozen or more individuals who volunteered back home in the U.S. They assisted with recruiting, fundraising, teaching Haitian culture, and many other initiatives. More individuals donated money, including some who could only afford to give $5 or $10. Thus far, we have generated some $570,000 since the launch of Sustain Haiti.

To lay out a bird's-eye view of Sustain Haiti's achievements, Table 1 summarizes the extent of our first years of services in key areas, though growth continues and the data continued to be collected through 2019.

During the past decade, from 2010 to 2020, our efforts in Haiti have encountered a number of new challenges, generally much more fraught than in other projects that my students and I had carried out in earlier years with other countries. In the first year of the earthquake, we experienced almost daily aftershocks, which

Table 1: Project results (*continued on next page*)

English classes	Over the summers, Sustain Haiti volunteers taught approximately 225 English classes. Although this project was not originally in our plans, on arrival in the country leaders and volunteers realized that there was a significant demand. So the leadership determined that teaching English would be a worthwhile project that fell within the scope of the organization's mission. News of the free English classes spread via radio and word of mouth. The classes, which were usually held at local schools and churches, were taught every weekday starting at 6:30 a.m. The classes were eventually split into beginner and intermediate levels, and more than 300 Haitians attended regularly.
Hygiene education and clean water	Hygiene education and purified water were some of the original planned projects of Sustain Haiti. Volunteers began devising hygiene lesson plans in the U.S. before any went to Haiti. Once there, volunteers teaching the main lesson—about malaria—realized that many Haitians already knew what they had planned to teach. So the volunteers shifted their focus and developed lessons on other subjects, such as wound care, washing hands, and so on. Over time, other projects were implemented that fell under the umbrella of "hygiene." Water purification systems were set up at various locations around the city. Volunteers helped clean and reorganize a local hospital in a town. Feminine hygiene lessons were taught and donated kits were distributed. Volunteers also traveled to various tent cities with other NGOs to distribute medical and hygiene supplies. Eventually, government organizations were able to install access to new, clean, water sources, so that effort ended.
Microfinance	Business education was one of the primary goals of Sustain Haiti. Over the years, that aspiration gave rise to the establishment of a community microcredit bank. Our team leaders held business skills training sessions in several villages for almost a decade. They eventually ran business plan competitions and partnered with other microfinance institutions to distribute loans. Over time, reported repayment rates have ranged from an astonishing 100 percent down to about 80 percent, but many new jobs emerged.

Table 1: Project results (*continued*)	
Orphanage support	Sustain Haiti volunteers routinely worked closely with seven orphanages, visiting more than 160 children each month. Our NGO leadership partnered with a local organization, *Ayuda à Haiti*, to help distribute donated clothing, food, and medicine to orphanages.
Square-foot gardening	A gardening initiative was one of Sustain Haiti's earliest projects. One of our main objectives, as outlined in the mission statement, was to provide hands-on education in square-foot gardening techniques. The goal of this project was to give Haitians a chance to grow nutritious vegetables themselves, for a fraction of the price they would pay at the market. It would also give them a chance to put organic waste to use by creating compost. Over many summers, more than 410 gardens were planted in surrounding communities.

frightened the Haitian people (as well as our volunteers!). The sweltering heat was almost unbearable each summer. For the first few years, we lived in a house without electricity (hence no fans or lights). The only way to shower was for us to fill large buckets with cold water downstairs and lug them up to the second floor where a person would then stand in a bathtub and pour the water over oneself. We needed assistance in living, and wanted to create a few jobs ourselves. So we hired several local Haitian women to do the cooking and house cleaning, as well as a man to guard the house while we were out working all day. The results? Nearly all volunteers had a bit of sickness, mostly consisting of the usual Third World bodily adjustments to different climate, meals, hygiene, and so forth. With respect to crime, we were robbed of a few cameras and cell phones taken while we were out of the house doing service projects among the poor. As people in French-speaking Haiti say: *C'est la vie!* (That's life!)

Even though I was the founder of Sustain Haiti, as well as its lead researcher and professor, I became ill with dengue fever on one of my summer volunteer trips on the island. Dengue is a mosquito-borne viral disease occurring in tropical areas. I had taken the requisite meds to protect me from malaria and more, but somehow got sick anyway. Returning to the U.S. for my fall university responsibilities, I soon became extremely ill. I had to cancel my BYU teaching load and stay in bed for several months while dealing with symptoms of high fever, rash, and muscle and joint pain. The only treatments were fluids and pain-relievers.

Over the past decade, our team and I have collected considerable data from Sustain Haiti's programs, including a 102-page report prepared by an independent team of graduate students who did not go to Haiti but instead acted as third-party researchers. The diagnosis of our years reveals both significant positives and negatives. This outside group used "Program Theory Assessment" methods, specifically a *logic model*, which lays out the expected sequence of steps, going from program services to client outcomes. They assessed each of our NGO's projects by asking guiding questions such as these to develop the evaluation:

Key Evaluation Questions
- *Inputs:* What are the resources or investments that go into the program?
- *Activities:* What actions, processes, events, services, products, technologies, or other elements will be used to implement your project?
- *Outputs:* What are the activities, services, events, and products that reach people who participate or who are targeted?
- *Outcomes:* What initial and later changes or improvements in learning, awareness, knowledge, and attitudes will have occurred under direct influence of the activities?

After each summer's intervention, we would return home to our jobs and studies, but continue endeavoring to move Sustain Haiti forward toward a better future for the country's people.

Unfortunately, in recent years Haiti has still suffered (Oxfam, 2019). Many families were broken up during the destructive earthquake, and there were a number of attempts by foreigners to take some of the 750,000 children affected by the disaster away from parents and out of the country. More than half a million people continued to be displaced, living in crowded camps under plastic tarps that were disintegrating. Shelter, schools, and other services were lacking for the masses. The government itself was crushed structurally when its office buildings were destroyed, and still today some of its operations occur in temporary facilities. As always, most Haitians lack opportunities for education. Nor do they have access to safe water, sanitation, and hygiene. Cleaning up the massive amounts of debris is painstakingly slow (or nonexistent). But rebuilding has continued, and it is wonderful to see the progress over the last decade.

A series of other unfortunate events have made things difficult over that time period. Powerful hurricanes flooded parts of the country and exacerbated conditions of those in tent cities. Then a plague of cholera broke out in Haiti, and the disease quickly spread everywhere, resulting in some 100,000 ill and 2,500 more deaths. Huge political crises have arisen after various presidential elections, which included politicians distributing hundreds of thousands of guns and machetes to supporters, as well as spewing acrimonious accusations and spreading blame for Haiti's misfortunes to others. In 2016 Haiti was struck by Hurricane Matthew, which leveled entire communities and caused an upsurge in the ongoing cholera epidemic that had earlier been introduced to the island. By 2017, around 7 percent of Haiti's population (some 800,000 people at the time) had been infected with cholera, and more than 9,000 Haitians had died. Collectively, such difficulties made aid and rebuilding activities either slow down terribly or grind to a halt.

Making things more complicated in 2018, a new 6.0 earthquake hit the island, damaging or destroying some 17,000 homes, as well as schools, businesses, and churches. Unfortunately at the time, the government announced it would eliminate subsidies, allowing fuel prices to increase by up to 50 percent. This led to widespread protests and the worst civil unrest the country had seen in years. A resurgence of gang violence also led to further instability (Human Rights Watch, 2018). During that same year, then-U.S. President Donald Trump criticized immigrants from what he condescendingly called "S✳✳✳-hole countries," which included Haiti, adding to the mental and emotional suffering of Haitians in the United States as well as the country of Haiti. That verbal attack caused days of rioting across the island nation (Dawsey, 2018).

In the time since the disasters of 2010, numerous aid projects have been initiated from the U.N., the governments of France and Canada, USAID, and many more. Big-name "do-gooders" have spent time and money declaring their personal concerns and help; to name only a few, Bill and Hillary Clinton, actor Sean Penn (who established his own NGO and lived there for months), actor Matt Damon (who invested in creating large new garment factories to produce apparel for world markets), and others. On the downside, thousands of Haitians ultimately fled to Latin America, and many now eke out an existence along the Tijuana, Mexico, border with the hope of eventually gaining entrance to the U.S. for a better future. I've met with and interviewed Haitians from the caravans of 2018–19 arriving in Mexico, and felt disappointed that their suffering is still so great. Late that same year, a federal judge blocked President Trump's decision to terminate Temporary Protected Status (TPS) for Haitians beginning in 2019, which would affect an estimated 60,000 Haitians who had been permitted after the 2010 earthquake to stay in the U.S. (Human Rights Watch, 2018).

Since the 2010 earthquake, Haiti's politics have been increasingly roiled with conflict and disruption. There have been eight different prime ministers in the decade, as well as four presidents, in an era of competing campaigns, fights, riots, and even handguns distributed to secure people's votes for various candidates. Such crises and physical dangers were not only extremely troubling to the Haitian people, as they damaged the fragile economy and created numerous crises for potential outside investors, but they also slowed the efforts of *all* NGOs, including Sustain Haiti, to help build capacity in the towns in which we labored to reestablish improvements.

Thankfully, the LDS Church has been committed to shipping large containers of supplies to assist Haiti's church members and their neighbors. In my discussions with our church's humanitarian program managers in the capital of Port-au-Prince, I learned of the good they were doing, as well as heard their appreciation for the humble efforts of our work at Sustain Haiti. Happily, the church rushed to build its first temple on the island—a fact that was perceived as a great blessing to the Haitian Saints, as well as a sign that the church will continue to bless the people for the long term.

As Sustain Haiti, we have labored on, remaining committed to our efforts to help the island's people. We have strived to dig deeper and spread our impacts more broadly each summer. Then, during each academic year at BYU when our U.S. team is back at school in Provo, our Haitian staffers have kept our programs operating in Leogane. Of course, the challenges are still enormous, and we know full well that nothing about this massive tragedy will be easily fixed.

Challenges and Weaknesses

As I end this chapter, I want to add several caveats regarding Sustain Haiti and the briefly mentioned earlier social ventures highlighted above. Lest this case appear to all be "sweetness and light," I should acknowledge that we have faced numerous problems.

First, certain difficulties came down from "above," as university administrators tried to block our efforts, or at least diminish them. They issued uninformed bureaucratic policies with virtually no understanding about our mission, work, or safety protocols. They heavy-handedly ruled that no faculty or students were to raise money for Haiti on campus, start any programs, or even travel to Haiti. As a result, many recruiting ads and posters across campus were torn down due to rigid decrees in an apparent attempt to block students' getting involved in Haiti's troubles. In response, we simply functioned increasingly underground.

Second, Sustain Haiti's recruiting of more volunteers was not hugely successful. We have operated at about the same level each summer, with a mix of new volunteers and a few returnees from previous summers. As near as we can figure, the widespread national media coverage of the Haiti crisis has gradually diminished the amount of energy and interest in LDS or other volunteers going to serve Haiti in our rebuilding programs each season. Like most Americans, some college students may be quite fickle regarding helping those who suffer in a crisis. Also, the improving U.S. economy appears to have attracted more students to seek corporate internships while out of school or in jobs as they graduate. Over time, less news coverage has also led to fewer donors to Sustain Haiti's programs.

A third challenge has to do with physical dangers of this kind of work. Although safety abroad has always been my No. 1 priority among the many social enterprises we have launched, several of them in various nations have had incidents that resulted in robbery. For example, with an older NGO, we were forced to pull out of Guatemala when that country became increasingly beset by crime and *narcotrafficante* violence. Over the decade in Haiti, we were robbed at gunpoint several times after withdrawing hundreds of dollars from our bank account. Likewise, we had to delay our return to Haiti for a short period during its presidential elections because of political violence in the streets.

Other facets of our "dark side" regarding social entrepreneurship include difficult struggles to raise donations in the context of the U.S. economic recession of 2010–11. Also, using college students meant that we would have a high degree of turnover, as volunteers returned to summer school or jobs. Thus, we were always adjusting for new participants with different skill sets. At times we may have been our own worst enemy, since even though we tried to be selective, some of these university-age social entrepreneurs seemed naïve, lacking the management skills that only come with years of experience. In addition, the realities of initiating social innovations as a response to a crisis, such as Hurricane Mitch in Central America, as detailed in chapter 2, or the Haitian earthquake, involve their own unique difficulties in terms of such things as road conditions to get around in-country, crime, and political unrest, not to mention witnessing the emotional pain of those who survive disasters.

I have always sought to create a climate of experimentation in my various NGO start-ups. My basic idea, born of long experience, has often been to begin by generating multiple tactics and solutions. Then, they can be attempted and tested, one at a time, little by little. But I always seek to avoid getting overly invested in any single tool or method. Thus, if the first thing does not work, fine. We just toss it aside and try the next one.

Another weakness of our Haiti programs was that at times our strategizing may have overlooked a vital point or two, led to groupthink, interfered with our ability to manage our time effectively, or ignored subtle data we should have seen. Indeed, the practice of social entrepreneurship needs a good deal of critical analysis so that we as its practitioners can achieve better results in the future than we have in the past.

In spite of our valiant efforts, Haiti continues to suffer from multiple disasters and events—not only the hundreds of thousands of people lost in its 2010 earthquake and later in its 2021 quake, but also the assassination of the country's president, the kidnapping-for-ransom of Christian missionaries, and recent violence raging throughout the country. Add to such crises the prevailing political corruption and frequent hurricane devastation, which have kept much of the country in a terrible state.

Conclusion

In spite of Sustain Haiti's weaknesses, however, I believe we achieved significant successes, some of which have been maintained. I hope that this case indicates that social innovations *can* succeed and *do* have genuine impacts, even those designed and implemented by sometimes-beleaguered university professors and overly busy students. I think they suggest mechanisms for taking leading-edge managerial principles and concepts from academic university environments and applying them to current, outside societal ills. Yet these social entrepreneurial models need to be integrated with new visions, radical interventions, and best practices from the sectors of business and social science, so as to generate innovative methodologies for fighting poverty at the "bottom-of-the-pyramid" and toward building sustainable communities. Fusing the best societal innovations with practical LDS values and beliefs, I believe, can provide amazing ways to improve the world. This was a major aspect of my speech at the World Parliament of Religions (founded in 1893), which for the first time was conducted in Utah in 2015 with some 9,000 participants coming to Salt Lake City. I gave a presentation to representatives of various spiritual traditions—Sikh gurus, Buddhist monks, Jewish rabbis, Muslim imams, Hindu swamis, and even indigenous shamans—on how the faith of Latter-day Saints blesses the entire world. I emphasized Sustain Haiti as a mini-case of several ways in which our faithful people labor to build civil society, especially following disasters (Johnson, 2015).

Through more such processes, I am convinced that "pro-poor" applications of social entrepreneurship may transform academia into more relevant and real-world approaches to education, including at BYU and other LDS universities. I've been amazed that Sustain Haiti and some of my other NGO start-ups originating on campus have finally inspired other departments to "Go Forth to Serve," as the campus motto has called us to do. Now, other programs train students to at least offer their services abroad. For instance, the College of Nursing sends some students to volunteer in Jordan. The BYU Accounting School allows a group to assist small businesses in Ghana. From the Kennedy Center for International Studies, students travel out to volunteer in multiple countries of Asia. By cooperating among multiple disciplines and with private-sector companies, I am confident we will see more ethical and socially responsible firms begin to benefit society's have-nots. At the same time, nongovernmental institutions harnessing the efforts of MBAs and social science students may benefit by more rapidly achieving scale, by collaborating with other organizations to accelerate their efforts, and also by developing enterprise cultures of problem-solving. The resulting synergies from such innovations and partnerships have the potential for producing transformative processes for organizational design and the strategic implementation of a great many social enterprises.

Lastly, my hope is that this chapter has practical impacts as a form of invitation or call to action not only for LDS university professors and students, but also for church members throughout the world, as they strive to accelerate the social entrepreneurship movement. Although students may seem young and somewhat naïve, they are becoming the next wave of genuine changemakers. Today's LDS millennials are accelerating their impacts as social entrepreneurs who actually "walk the talk." I hope this book becomes an inspiring story of how for 30-plus years LDS students from a range of disciplines have designed and launched social enterprises, primarily utilizing the university as an incubator, that have spread around the Third World. If we can do this at BYU, I imagine a number of other schools with more sophistication, larger numbers, more money, and greater global perspectives can do even more. My ultimate objective in this chapter is to inform and perhaps even inspire additional Latter-day Saint individuals, whether in school or not, to see new possibilities for launching their own unique approaches to the growing social entrepreneurship movement around the globe.

I conclude this amazing story of Sustain Haiti with several stirring quotes from LDS theology. Remembering the deep problems inflicted on most Haitians that inspired us to establish an NGO to help, I love the Lord's call to action through a revelation to Joseph Smith in *Doctrine and Covenants* 58:26–28 wherein he declares: "It is not meet that I should command in all things.... Verily I say, men should be anxiously engaged in a good cause, and do many things of their own free will, and bring to pass much righteousness; for the power is in them, wherein they are agents unto themselves." Apparently, bemoaning the problems of the world and merely responding with fasting and prayer is simply not sufficient. We must have the faith to take action. We ourselves must do so. Not the church nor the government alone.

As I reflect on the suffering of Haiti's many victims over the decades, I draw on Jesus' *New Testament* teachings when he walked among people in crisis and reminded us: "For I was an hungered, and ye gave me meat: I was thirsty, and ye gave me drink: I was a stranger, and ye took me in. . . . Inasmuch as ye have done it unto one of the least of these my brethren, ye have done it unto me" (Matthew 25:35–40).

References

Aldrich, H. E., and Zimmer, C. (1986). Entrepreneurship Through Social Networks, SSRN: http://ssrn.com/abstract=1497761.

AOM. (2010). http://meetings.aomonline.org/2010.

BBC. (2010). Haiti Quake Toll 'May Be 200,000.' January 18. http://news.bbc.co.uk/2/hi/8465137.stm.

Bornstein, D. (2004). *How to Change the World: Social Entrepreneurs and the Power of New Ideas.* Oxford University Press.

Dawsey, J. (2018). Trump derides protections for immigrants from 'shithole' countries. *Washington Post*, January 12.

Dees, J. G. (1998). The Meaning of Social Entrepreneurship. October 31. http://www.caseatduke.org/knowledge/seprocess/index.html.

Dees, J. G. (2007). Taking Social Entrepreneurship Seriously: Uncertainty, Innovation, and Social Problem Solving. *Society*, vol. 44, no. 3, 24–31.

Doctrine and Covenants 58:26–28.

Drucker, P. F. (1999). Managing Oneself. *Harvard Business Review*, January–February, 100–109.

Faust, J. E. (1997). "Go Bring Them in from the Plains." *Ensign*, July, 2–7.

Hafen, L. R., and Hafen, A. W. (1960). *Handcarts to Zion.* Arthur H. Clark Company, Pioneers Edition.

Hinckley, G. B. (1996). Reach with a Rescuing Hand. *Ensign*, November, 85–86.

Human Rights Watch. (2018). https://www.hrw.org/world-report/2019/country-chapters/haiti.

Johnson, K. (2015). Parliament of the World's Religions: Creatively doing good, both locally and globally. October 18. https://universe.byu.edu/2015/10/18/parliament-of-the-worlds-religions-creatively-doing-good-both-locally-and-globally/.

Light. P. C. (2006). Reshaping Social Entrepreneurship, *Stanford Social Innovation Review*, Fall, 45–51.

London, T., Sateen, S., and Hart, S. (2014). *A Roadmap for the Base of the Pyramid Domain: Re-Energizing for the Next Decade*. William Davidson Institute at the University of Michigan.

Mair, J., and Marti, I. (2006). Social Entrepreneurship Research: A Source of Explanation, Prediction, and Delight, *Journal of World Business*, 41, 36–44.

Matthew 25:35–40.

Millar, L. (2010). Tens of Thousands Isolated at Quake Epicenter. ABC News, Australia, January 17. http://www.abc.net.au/news/stories/2010/01/17/2794190.htm.

Oxfam. (2019). An overview of Oxfam's Humanitarian Response to the Haitian earthquake. January 6. http://www.oxfam.org/en/policy/haiti-progress-report.

Romboy, D. (2010). BYU Volunteers Trying to Sow Hope in Haiti, *Deseret News*, May 24.

Smith, A. (2011). Millionaires on the Rebound. *CNNMoney*, March 16. http://money.cnn.com/2011/03/16/news/economy/millionaires/index.htm.

Whyte, W. F. (1982). Social Inventions for Solving Human Problems. *American Sociological Review*, vol. 47, no. 1, 1–13.

Woodworth, W. (2010). Laboring in the Trenches with the Poor of Haiti: Practicing the New Fourth-Fold Mission. *Meridian Magazine*, December 28, 1–10.

"Have I Done Any Good"
LDS Hymns, No. 223

1. Have I done any good in the world today?
   Have I helped anyone in need?
   Have I cheered up the sad and made someone feel glad?
   If not, I have failed indeed.
   Has anyone's burden been lighter today
   Because I was willing to share?
   Have the sick and the weary been helped on their way?
   When they needed my help was I there?

[Chorus] Then wake up and do something more
   Than dream of your mansion above.
   Doing good is a pleasure, a joy beyond measure,
   A blessing of duty and love.

2. There are chances for work all around just now,
   Opportunities right in our way.
   Do not let them pass by, saying, "Sometime I'll try,"
   But go and do something today.
   'Tis noble of man to work and to give;
   Love's labor has merit alone.
   Only he who does something helps others to live.
   To God each good work will be known.

Text and music: Will L. Thompson (1847–1909)

5
Philippines Enterprise Development Foundation

(Mentors International, 1990–2022)

Have you ever heard about *"Tsang dakot na bigas"*—a handful of rice? Years ago, I visited the Pasay First Ward in the Philippines where, as a result of members' extreme poverty, they had created a program to organize a resource committee to serve their welfare needs. All the saints with jobs were asked to bring a handful of rice to church each Sunday, or to buy an extra can of goods to donate as they entered the chapel for sacrament meeting. The unemployed were also invited to sacrifice by bringing items such as old clothes and toys to church meetings—anything they no longer used. Those without jobs on Saturdays would go to the ward to repair and paint the used items, and would keep a record of time spent. With earned credits they qualified to take things they needed from this "ward storehouse." The outcome was significant. Within one year, fast offering monies were no longer necessary. Members who had no jobs became able to start their own microenterprises. This simple initiative idea went on to spread to other wards. At first I was in sorrow about the plight of our LDS members. But I was later happy to learn of the success of this program.

▲ Mentors International staff and loan recipients at their offices

The Filipino people are of great promise but have many hardships. However, these days Mentors offers microfinance and new business training, which is helping a great deal.

▼ *Sari-sari* shops (street vendors) in Manila

That experience occurred as a great and meaningful joy in my life to establish a humble little project to help Latter-day Saints in the Philippines. It gradually grew to educate members, fund tiny family enterprises, and mentor over a million impoverished LDS folks and their neighbors throughout the past three decades—a total of 32 long years of empowering families in their hand-to-mouth struggles. This chapter describes what, how, and why I and others established a nongovernmental organization in the Philippines—an organization we established in Manila called Philippines Enterprise Development Foundation (PEDF)—with additional offices gradually spreading to other regions to empower Filipinos. A U.S. NGO partner was incorporated in St. Louis, Missouri, to generate funding and provide expert technical assistance to the Filipino leaders.

The story begins in the late 1980s when I took my family to live for a year in Hawaii, away from Brigham Young University, where I had carried a busy teaching load, done extensive research, and offered management consulting to firms across the U.S. I decided to move us to BYU Hawaii, on the north shore of Oahu, so I could spend a year writing a book. I also did some university teaching, as well as hitting the beaches and relishing the deep blue water with 11 of us body surfing regularly. In our courses, I and my fellow professors studied worker ownership and rural cooperatives as organizations that give people power over the means of production. The case of egalitarian co-ops known as Mondragon in Northern Spain seemed to especially catch the interest of students in the Philippines. They liked the concepts, along with cases of microlending and women's entrepreneurship. Some of these Filipinos asked if we could establish a co-op project for their relatives in Hawaii. When I asked why, they explained that Filipino immigrants went to Oahu to work so they could send money to the families, because there were so few jobs back home. I assumed many were employees in the pineapple and sugarcane fields and orchid nurseries, which turned out to be correct. But as I dug into the matter, I discovered those huge, successful businesses were all owned by wealthy Japanese, Chinese, and American *haoles*. Filipinos were merely exploited peasants, and they had to deal with the exorbitant cost of living in Hawaii.

So we held some community meetings with their relatives and friends, and learned that the groups wanted to join together. If I could help them obtain land and start-up capital, we could organize several co-ops, elect managers, and help move toward a degree of financial self-reliance. I explored perhaps getting some LDS Church or even BYU Hawaii funding to lease small tracts of agricultural land up toward the northern part of the island. We'd start small and would learn as we experimented, as they did in the co-ops in Mondragon, and we would see where it might go. The response from the church and the university was, "No thanks."

Eventually, we met with Catholic Church leaders in Honolulu, as well as with staff at the Philippines embassy. From them we secured a few thousand dollars, leased some small agricultural plots, and began tiny vegetable and fruit enterprises and farming. A year later, when I announced that our family was returning to work as a BYU professor in Provo, Utah, the Filipino students begged me instead to go to the Philippines and start projects there to assist their relatives, some of whom were LDS, some members of other faiths. I agreed. After settling back in Utah and starting a new semester of teaching, I received several letters and phone calls reminding me of my commitment. My former students on Oahu said they were praying for me to move forward. I felt overwhelmed getting my family readjusted to life in the states, my kids all in school, my office organized, my courses up and going, and more. But I decided to start a new little course, giving it a title about using our skills to solve global problems. To my dismay, only six grad students registered. I explained to them I wanted to fulfill a promise to and prayers from my new Filipino friends, but confessed that I knew nothing about that Asian nation. So I suggested that some of us learn about the country, its culture, history, and challenges. If we attained a good grasp of their economic challenges, maybe some of us could spend the summer doing field research and planning to start a new nonprofit to help the masses in faraway Philippines.

The Marriott School dean at the time, Dr. Paul Thompson, had switched academic positions, moving to BYU from the Harvard Business School. He had helped recruit me to BYU from Michigan and Brazil, and I liked him a great deal. He was open to change, he liked innovations, and when I explained what I wanted to do, he felt supportive. So the winter semester of 1989 became a fun-filled search for all the Philippines information we could find. Eventually, we began planning the work of three Masters of Organizational Behavior students who would head to Manila. I would travel with them to set things up, get everything started, and return to my university job in Utah, but I would later go back to Manila where we'd hold a seminar to report what was learned and prepare to launch a new nonprofit to assist Latter-day Saint Filipinos in improving their well-being.

Throughout the start-up process, I met two people who wanted to help. One was a fellow named Steve who'd graduated from our program before I arrived at BYU. We met serendipitously, but when he asked what work I was doing, I told him I did action research and was launching a project in Manila. He asked more questions, and after I explained a bit, he wondered what I needed. I told him we needed money because this was not a BYU project. He asked, "How much?" I told him "$10,000." He reached into a suit pocket and wrote out a check for the full amount! That was the day I discovered I could raise money—from strangers! That amount would give the students $3,000 each for airfare, living and other expenses, as they lived, researched, communicated with us back in the states, met with experts, and so forth.

Later I met a wealthy former mission president who'd spent three years in the Philippines, and together we moved forward with the project. The following section describes the what, where, when, and why of our launching the Philippines Enterprise Development Foundation, which has made important impacts in the Philippines and several other nations since 1990.

A Typical Case of Filipino Poverty

Let me create the setting and personalize this story by conveying the exuberance of Alisa, a young girl in Davao, the large, southern island of the Philippines. Alisa Alan and her parents appeared to enjoy a good quality of life, but that was not always the case. Her mother and father, Van and Virginia Alag, struggled on a daily income of just a few pesos, usually allowing only one small bowl of rice per day for each of their six children. Alisa's father purchased an old bicycle, known as a "pedicab," and he would pedal passengers around town, dodging cars and buses, bouncing over potholes, sweating profusely in the 90-degree heat and humidity. By night he would stagger into bed in their small shanty, too exhausted to eat, even if there was sufficient food.

In subsequent years, PEDF was replicated with different names in other areas of the Philippines. One was called the Mindanao Enterprise Development Foundation (MEDF), which Van and Virginia signed up for in order to learn basic business competencies. After completing the course, Van was eligible to receive a microloan so he could purchase a motor to power his pedicab, enabling him to double the number of passengers from before—more customers, speedier service, an easier job, and a bit more in fares. Now, at the end of the day, Alisa's father is in a better mood and has greater energy to play with his offspring. More food and better nutrition are also now available to the family daily. The Alags have fully paid off their loan at market interest rates, so that other microloans can be channeled to additional poor Filipinos. They feel pride in their success and experience new dignity as small-business people.

Over the years, the experience of a single family—the Alags, in Davao—gradually expanded exponentially throughout the Philippines. Branches and sister nongovernmental organizations (NGOs) of Mentors were established in Davao (Mindanao), Cebu, and Manila as partner organizations to a U.S. NGO—Enterprise Mentors, as it was called, or EMI. We started out with a few dozen microenterprises and grew gradually. With newly acquired skills, growing capital, and increased confidence, many client

Table 2: EMI's growth, 1996-1997

	Manila	Cebu	Davao	Totals
Existing consulting contracts	346	316	265	927
New contracts	260	313	292	865
Loans accessed	1,084	281	456	1,821
Training seminars held	186	91	33	310
Seminar attendees	2,384	742	164	3,290
New jobs created	131	171	633	935
Businesses represented	84	80	118	282

entrepreneurs created new jobs as they grew. Between 1991 and 1996, a total of 2,281 new jobs were established. The number of loans accessed by EMI clients continued to increase over the next several years. In 1996 EMI partner foundations provided 1,284 loans to growing micro and small businesses. Over $450,000 had been granted in small loans.

The statistics in Table 2 spell out the nitty-gritty of EMI's early growth, which convey a sense of its trajectory from 1996 through 1997.

As I reflect on this project today, the work I launched in the Philippines really took off because, to my mind, God's purpose has always been clear: "To provide for my saints, that the poor shall be exalted and that the rich be made low. For the earth is full, and there is enough and to spare; yea, I prepared all things, and have given unto the children of men to be agents unto themselves" (*Doctrine and Covenants* 104:15, 17). Apparently, the problem with poverty versus wealth has been one of distribution of economic resources, not simple production or the amount of capital. The methods advocated in this chapter suggest new mechanisms for reallocating financial power so that all persons, even the "poorest of the poor," may access economic resources and thereby *lift themselves.* Such a philosophy is based not on a handout, but on a hand up. Instead of giving one fish, or even teaching one person how to fish, the underlying premise of village banking is that of giving a person a loan. I've often cited the admonition of LDS Church President John Taylor to pioneers of his day, to "unite with (the unemployed and poor)...in finding employment for every man and woman and child...that wants to labor" (Taylor, 1879).

Ultimately, in January 1990, our NGO was incorporated in the U.S. as Enterprise Mentors International (EMI). Simultaneously an indigenous NGO was launched in Manila, the Philippines Enterprise Development Foundation (PEDF). Each had its own board, staff members, offices, and ongoing projects. A second foundation, the Visayas Enterprise Foundation (VEF), was established two years later in Cebu, the central island of the Philippines. The Mindanao Enterprise Development Foundation (MEDF) began a year afterward.

Establishing a Board of Trustees

A major objective early on was to assemble EMI's board. I hope to show that establishing an organization, even one with noble motives like empowering the poor, is never easy. The simple act of creating a board of trustees may be fraught with difficulty, as an organizer must seek out and recruit capable individuals who can offer wisdom, energy, and either some funds of their own or at least connections to raise money from their social circles. I often used the following three qualities as my criteria for selecting board members. I called them the "Three W's"— Wisdom, Wealth, and Wit. In other words, I always wanted EMI trustees to add expertise and insights from their own successes. And they needed to be able to help build capital resources, either making their own donations to combat poverty or being able to secure or solicit financial contributions from their associates. The final criteria is Wit. I found that having members with a sense of humor and who really enjoy life can sometimes make all the difference in tough board decisions and occasional setbacks. Being able to have fun, especially when times are tough and the NGO lacks much of what it needs to continue forward, can make all the difference in finding the strength to keep going. These key words were my philosophy throughout the EMI experience and ever since that time (around 1990) through dozens of other NGOs boards I've created.

Among the EMI group that I organized were myself as an academic activist, plus a California consultant friend who donated the first monies so I could take my students to do field research in the Philippines in 1989. Also in the group was a wonderful LDS Filipino, formerly a church leader, who had moved to Utah, who gave the rest of us useful cultural understanding. Another was a former USAID official who had worked for years advising the U.S. Government on policies and practices to help the global poor, drawing on good research and his Latter-day Saint values. I soon invited the former Marriott School dean, a wise and effective professor in BYU's Department of Organizational Behavior. In addition, we hired one of my favorite grad students as EMI's staff expert on microfinance and social innovation, as he had lived in Bolivia for years and had absorbed many important development theories. As the board rolled out programs over time, we collectively learned the following lessons in challenging and sometimes conflicting ways.

Filipino Challenges of Poverty

Among EMI's founders and initial board members was one person who held a lot of sway with the more conservative members. That person assumed that the big problem with the Philippine economy was that the masses were "lazy," were "uneducated," and "wanted something for nothing." The few of us at the other end of the table knew better. We knew that the Philippines had long been corrupt because of dictators like Ferdinand Marcos, who stole billions of dollars and was thrown out of office just before EMI was beginning. When the LDS Church was established in the country in 1961, the Philippines was the Number 2 economy in Asia. By 1991 it had sunk to Number 2 from the bottom. Greed, a dictatorship, and the power of corrupt businessmen had exploited the working-class poor, driving the people into abject poverty. Volcanoes and cyclones around the various islands made everything worse.

Our research team also discovered another factor: the increasing poverty of Filipino Latter-day Saints. Each decade of church member growth had brought more and more poverty. When I took this to the attention of the Brethren at church headquarters in Salt Lake City, they didn't understand. I explained that most missionaries serving there were Filipinos. As a former colony of Spain, the country had had social class embedded in every facet of its culture for some 400 years. When our church launched, the elders and sisters called to serve were mostly among the poor to begin with, because of course the gospel appeals to the weak and hungry. Then when lower-class members begin missions, they don't try to teach the people in nice, big, comfortable homes. Instead, they go "downstream" to try to teach and baptize Filipinos even more humble than themselves. They would never dream of trying to teach a business leader, a doctor, or a professional person such as a lawyer. So each cadre of new LDS missionaries there baptized ever-more-poverty-stricken generations, and as a result the church became poorer and poorer. This fact was a shock to the General Authorities in Salt Lake. They assumed that if people simply joined the church, the Lord would bless them and they would move up the food chain.

I suggested that the best solution would be to start calling many more *American* missionaries to serve in the Philippines, because young white First World missionaries are perceived as assertive, a bit egotistical, and full of confidence. They'll approach *anyone* about the gospel, and often achieve a fair amount of success. Converting many already successful Filipinos to the Church, in turn, raises the perceived social class of the church itself. So church leaders eventually made an adjustment in the makeup of missionaries they called to that country, and that has helped its Filipino members ever since.

Now, what does this have to do with EMI's growth? Simply that its conservative board members, who assumed that they understood poverty generally and the Philippines in particular, felt that EMI should mostly promote "morality" and LDS principles. On the other side of the board table, I and my like-minded associates argued that, no, Filipinos needed capital in the form of microfinance so as to dig themselves out of the ugly poverty in which they were trapped. The wealthy board members felt confident the "lazy" Filipino people just needed to be trained and educated like white Americans—in other words, given more schooling. Again, some of us pushed back, arguing that the poor can do a great deal for themselves if given an opportunity and a bit of money. On occasion, I enjoyed countering our more-rigid board associates by quoting the great conservative economist Milton Friedman to our conservative Mentors board members. The quote is one of the few things I ever agreed on with that Nobel Laureate. He is supposed to have said, "The poor stay poor, not because they are lazy but because they have no access to capital." I wanted EMI to primarily offer capital to the extremely poor through microloans. I don't know if Friedman ever supported microfinance, but I hoped he would have done.

I used that quote many times over the decades with EMI as well as with leaders of other NGOs. Regarding the struggles of Filipinos, my associates and I would say: "Impoverished Filipinos primarily needed a hand up, not a handout." They don't need religious ethics, though I'm all for that, but mostly they need a small amount of capital and an opportunity.

The two EMI strategies of training members of the public who were poor, then consulting over time with specific microentrepreneurs, led to the creation of nearly 1,000 jobs over the first few years, laying the groundwork for more numbers subsequently. That early growth in capital to improve or expand those businesses was channeled through some 2,000 loans. Based on Philippine government projections, each new job benefited a family of five. So the total impact of EMI's initial work benefited roughly 5,000 Filipinos whose lives were improving. The additional income from microbusiness expansion and access to credit led to more family revenue for food, as well as a reduction in malnutrition; more pesos for education and thus a better future; savings for future medical emergencies arising from accident or illness; and, overall, greater economic self-determination. Importantly, from an LDS perspective, well over half of all beneficiaries of these programs were Church members. They were among the "poorest of the poor." I learned that a few dollars can go a long way in empowering them with new skills and jobs.

The importance of the Philippines is key to understanding the growth of the LDS Church worldwide. In recent years, that island nation has averaged about 10 percent of all converts to Mormonism around the globe. Yet while LDS membership was expanding, LDS Filipino families had become more and more poor. The country's fortunes were declining even as those of Japan, South Korea, Taiwan, and Hong Kong were ascending.

Unfortunately, over recent decades, Latter-day Saints in the Philippines have tended to be worse off than the typical nonmember Filipino—with lower household income, higher unemployment, greater percentages of squatters, shanties lacking plumbing, and so on. While pinpointing the causes of economic decline is beyond the scope of this chapter, a brief history of the origins of LDS strategies to start and to expand Filipino microenterprises may be useful.

Combating Economic Travail

In early 1989, I traveled to the Philippines with Ruben Lacanienta, a native Latter-day Saint who had immigrated to America, but wanted to help his people. We met with government officials in the top echelons of the Manila government—cabinet members such as the Secretary of the Treasury, the Minister of Trade and Industry, officials of the Asian Development Bank, economists in academia, LDS General Authorities, and others.

Meanwhile, at Brigham Young University, during the following winter, I put together a team of graduate students to study the culture and socioeconomic conditions of the Philippines. Over time, our team began to design the setting up of a nonprofit foundation for job creation.

The plan was to create an organization based in the U.S, and then launch affiliates in the Philippines. NGO programs stood as a stark contrast from typical development institutions such as U.S. AID, the World Bank, and other huge, government-based efforts. After months of literature-based research and planning, the four of us from BYU traveled to Manila and began surveying LDS wards and stakes, interviewing members and leaders. We also met with business executives, NGOs, and government experts in development. Needs were assessed, problems identified, and change strategies formulated.

The BYU team organized a two-day working conference in Manila in August 1989 to report results of our research and to propose the creation of a new LDS-related NGO for livelihood and technical assistance. The meetings were attended by General Authorities of the Philippines Area Presidency, key local Filipino church leaders, several mission presidents, stake officials, regional representatives, and Relief Society leaders, as well as several professionals in business. We also included several Filipino non-LDS academics and development experts, as well as a couple of U.S. executives and presiding officials from church headquarters in Salt Lake City, including the first counselor in the Church's Presiding Bishopric.

The study team proposed focusing on methods for creating jobs and businesses among the Filipino poor, both LDS and others. Developing business skills through competent training would provide personal growth for such individuals and enable them to move toward self-reliance—an objective congruent with the church's purposes for earthly happiness. Over the two days of discussion and debates, a mission statement was defined, objectives became spelled out, and services and programs were established for target populations. A pilot program was proposed for the Metro Manila region and staffing needs were designed, along with an initial budget and funding sources. Projections for management-training participants and creating new jobs and other services were targeted for the first two years, and a timeline for official start-up was established. Other components and considerations were identified, including legal requirements for incorporation and makeup of governing boards, as well as cultural issues such as dependency, diversity, local community involvement, and ethics.

Ultimately, in January 1990, our NGO was incorporated in the U.S. as Enterprise Mentors International (EMI). Simultaneously an indigenous NGO was launched in Manila, the Philippines Enterprise Development Foundation (PEDF). Each had its own board, staff members, offices, and ongoing projects. A second foundation, the Visayas Enterprise Foundation (VEF), was established two years later in Cebu. The Mindanao Enterprise Development Foundation (MEDF) began a year afterward.

At the time, the primary role of the U.S. NGO (that is, EMI) was fundraising, communicating with groups in the Philippines, creating policy, and evaluating foundation progress. Enterprise Mentors started with a small board of eight but grew to over 20 directors, consisting mostly of LDS executives. For years, its chair was Marion D. Hanks, a much-beloved General Authority who had served in the Presidency of the Seventy.

Enterprise Mentors' mission was stated as follows: "To build self-reliance and entrepreneurial spirit within those who struggle for sufficiency in developing countries. We do this through the principle of a 'hand up, not a handout,' for those who are committed to building their livelihood, their families and community through micro and small-scale enterprises."

Rather than becoming spread too thin, or trying to assist everyone regardless of their values or capacity to succeed, EMI's change efforts focused on certain targets, outlined in an early brochure: "Enterprise Mentors is founded upon the fundamental premise that meaningful, long-term success for an entrepreneur is unlikely unless he or she personally subscribes to and lives by sound moral principles." The following qualities were requisite for each client: (1) morality—a commitment to ethical behavior; (2) mentality—the ability to grasp and apply basic business concepts; and (3) motivation—a genuine desire for entrepreneurial accomplishment.

Table 3: Connections beween resource and user systems

Resource System	User System
Enterprise Mentors International	PEDF, MEDF, and VEF
Raised Money	Received Funds for Projects
Knowledge Acquisition	Application of Knowledge
Business Skills Training Materials	Skill Training Implementation
NGO Management/Administration	Consulting with Poor Clients in the Philippines
Board Oversight and Policy	Staff Implementation of Policy
Research and Development	Local Problem Solving

Connections Between Groups

The basic structure of the relationship between Enterprise Mentors and its partner NGOs in Asia was one of building connections and relationships. The U.S. organization functioned as a resource system of capital, equipment, expertise, and legitimacy. Simultaneously, the Filipino NGOs functioned as the users of such resources—the consumers, the doers, the implementers. PEDF, VEF, and MEDF collected data, defined problems, developed action steps, and carried them out. Strategic plans were formulated and proposed to EMI in the U.S., whose board then reviewed and analyzed the feasibility of such plans. If and when the two parties agreed on a budget, funds were dispensed to the Philippines for the coming year.

Drawing on the research models of my colleague Ronald Havelock (1969) and others at the University of Michigan's Institute for Social Research, where I earned my Ph.D., the diagram in Table 3 depicts the connections.

It should be pointed out that each EMI partner group in the Philippines also had its own indigenous staff and a local board of directors that acted as an intermediary with the American EMI.

The latter had ultimate fiduciary responsibility over the Filipino programs and projects.

Another way to view the connections is as follows:

| **EMI** | → | **Filipino** | → | **Indigenous** |
| Resource System | | Area Boards | | NGO Staffs |

The Asian boards typically consisted of Filipino executives, bankers, government officials, academics, and leaders of humanitarian groups. Each professional staff offered training, consulting, and access to credit through microlending methods. In Manila's PEDF, the executive director was Tony San Gabriel, a returned native missionary and a young LDS bishop who had earned a master's degree in International Development from the Asian Institute of Management, the premier graduate school for a Pacific education. Thelma Caparas, a CPA and attorney, with considerable experience in LDS women's leadership, directed the MEDF, created in 1993. The head of VEF, Gomez "Ed" Siady, initially ran the program in Cebu. He was a successful Chinese-Filipino entrepreneur who did a good deal of foreign trade in Japan and other countries, as well as having served as a stake president.

I myself carried out several action research programs, integrating my academic work as a professor in the Marriott School of Business, while also traveling to the Philippines to help design, launch, train, and evaluate Mentors' programs there. Serving in multiple roles—as a cofounder, a board member, and the lead officer—offered me the opportunity to conduct interviews, observe microfinance clients, train staff and groups of Filipinos, and more. My writings and publications detailing that early research have appeared in academic as well as Latter-day Saint sources, including such articles as "Philippines Indigenous Management" in the Marriott School's *Exchange Magazine* (Woodworth, 1996); an article in the prestigious *Journal of Managerial Finance* by Brau, Hiatt, and Woodworth (2009); and my book *Small Really Is Beautiful: Micro Approaches to Third World Development—Microentrepreneurship, Microenterprise, and Microfinance* (Woodworth, 2000), among others.

As EMI became established and began hiring additional managers, securing able staff and board members, these three NGOs almost immediately made a significant impact for good among the LDS communities of the Philippines, and beyond. As the word spread about positive results, media awareness grew, giving the efforts the ability to recruit more clients. For instance, PEDF's director was interviewed on a one-hour national talk show, ZNN Radio Veritas. Six PEDF micro entrepreneurs offered firsthand testimonials about how PEDF had improved their living, and the program was such a hit that call-in phone lines were jammed with reactions and requests for more information. The response was so positive from listeners across the islands that another hour-long broadcast about PEDF occurred a month later (*Philippine News*, 1995).

PEDF was awarded several contracts to train displaced workers from large Filipino corporations, including San Miguel Corporation, the largest company in the Philippines. This gave us additional revenue to expand our MFI programs to more locations. The same NGO was also recognized with a major award from the International Labour Organization (ILO) in Geneva, Switzerland, a global agency of the United Nations that promotes international labor standards and cooperation between countries. By being so lauded, PEDF increasingly earned its reputation for value-based training and consulting. It was selected by the ILO over a number of other prestigious institutions, including the Filipino federal government's Department of Trade and Industry, the Institute for Small-Scale Industries, and the University of the Philippines (*Philippine News*, 1996).

The indigenous NGOs were impacting not only the Filipino society at large, but Latter-day Saints in particular. To some extent, EMI and its parties operate in tandem with LDS Church efforts to improve people's lives. "A church-commissioned study indicated that 68 percent of Church members in the Philippines live below the official poverty levels in areas of income, housing and nutrition. This is substantially higher than the national poverty rate of 49.5 percent" (Anderson, 1992).

In providing microloans and economic training, money management, personal savings, and additional services, Latter-day Saint Filipinos were slowly but surely improving their quality of living and becoming more self-sufficient.

Even while combating poverty and alleviating its painful results, EMI also sought to complement the ecclesiastical activities of the church. As featured in my book *Working Toward Zion: Principles of the United Order for the Modern World*, on building a better life for church members in poor nations in modern times, Mormonism has some of its most compelling tenets in the importance of temporal as well as spiritual well-being (Lucas and Woodworth, 1996).

Such principles include that the spiritual and the temporal are one; that a church that lacks the power to save its people in mortality cannot be depended on to save them in eternity; that socioeconomic equality is a core value of the good society on earth as it is in heaven; that true followers of Christ consecrate what they have to lifting the poor and building Zion; that work is noble and labor is essential—making idleness among the poor and the rich unacceptable; and that each person has a sacred stewardship to be accountable to God for how they use their talents, skills, and resources to expand their capacity and bless the lives of others. Rather than accumulating wealth and engaging in conspicuous consumption, individuals and families need moral motivation—improving the world rather than profit-maximization, valuing cooperation over conflict and self-aggrandizement, building community rather than individual achievement (Lucas and Woodworth, 1996).

Yet in developing cultures right up till the late-1980s, there was no program to offer all the traditional LDS welfare services to poor, struggling saints. "The Church resources cannot offer programs to directly assist businesses or entrepreneurs, and the difficulties inherent in too much dependency and elevated expectations are very real" (Woodworth, quoted in Anderson, 1992). So rather than the Church's directly channeling money to sponsor new LDS-based microenterprise start-ups or village banking, EMI and its partners, operating at arms' length, were able to do so. To clarify, the management training of EMI was not tied to a bishop's stewardship. One's assigned client or consultant may or may not have been LDS, or even Catholic, in the preponderantly Christian Philippines. And microloans were processed by a credit cooperative or other such entity, not as LDS ward fast offerings or tithing funds. They required a signed, legal agreement and the payment of interest and principle until all monies had been repaid.

It should be pointed out that the church looked favorably on these efforts, to the extent that some of EMI's initial capital was essentially a grant from LDS Humanitarian Services, now known as Latter-day Saint Charities. But Filipino clients were not informed of the source of such funding, because of worries that it might be construed or viewed as a church handout, thus not necessitating repayment. Rather, PEDF and its sister NGOs operated as what were considered "professional partners."

Several cases of our Filipino microenterprise clients below summarize EMI's efforts through the years:

- *Allan Tereno*   He used to sell fish balls from a pushcart on the city streets. With microenterprise consulting assistance, he was able to hire four additional employees besides himself. They operated three additional pushcarts, adding fresh fruits and other products as street vendors.
- *David deLara*   Having started a business in 1989, he collected used cooking oil from Filipino restaurants and processed it into large slabs of soap for use by industry. He needed more capital to expand, but could not qualify for a bank loan. With help from PEDF, he received a microloan and began to sell soap as an equipment lubricant to many Filipino companies, as well as giants like PepsiCo.
- *Anita Bernales*   After years of laboring for other bosses, she sought technical assistance from MEDF in the southern city of Davao. Consulting advice and

access to microcredit enabled her to buy equipment, hire several shoemakers with good experience, and begin production of shoes on the patio outside her little house.

By 1996, private donations to EMI had totaled $728,475, a little over half of which was derived from individuals, 38 percent from foundations and churches, and 8 percent from corporations. Results of that year's microenterprise and credit programs in the Philippines revealed that the monthly income of microentrepreneurs who received consulting, training, and a small loan afterward increased their income by an average of 56 percent—a wonderful outcome!

EMI's operational budget for 1997 grew to $900,000. By far the vast majority of EMI's donors were successful Latter-day Saints who wanted to make a difference in the world. Later, EMI and its global partners began applying for and receiving grants from U.S. nonprofit foundations. For example, Levi Strauss contributed thousands of dollars for microcredit financing efforts of PEDF in Manila. EMI received a donation and recognition from the Lord Acton Institution foundation. And grants from Kiwanis Clubs and Rotary International also enhanced EMI's early efforts to increase the impacts of microentrepreneurial and credit programs.

Since those early years, beginning in 1990, there has been a steady stream of ever-increasing contributions through 2020. As of the last report, what is now Mentors International had generated a total of some $160 million for loans, training, and mentoring of clients over three decades. An additional $22 million was donated by its board of trustees to cover various overhead costs, such as international travel expenses, certain overhead costs, and other purposes to keep the organization operating.

The genius of microcredit, sometimes called poverty-based lending, lies in its simplicity and capacity to empower the poor. Without a microloan, poor rural or urban Filipinos were unable to successfully manage and grow their tiny, vulnerable businesses.

Regular banks refused to help because often the loan amount needed was a mere $80 or so—too small for commercial banks to even justify doing the paperwork to process such a loan. There were other concerns, also, such as a person's lack of collateral or documented credit history. Of course, the poor had no credit report, because they had never qualified for a Visa or MasterCard. Some were illiterate. And since many were squatters, their family shack of cardboard or plywood would never qualify as collateral. Furthermore, most of these people would never own their own land, never receive a paycheck from a corporation, never enjoy health insurance, and never receive a pension or social security.

So in general, for a truly enterprising Filipino, the only path to lift oneself or a family was to subject oneself to the depredations of a local "loan shark." Assume, for instance, that a small loan were needed in order to purchase handicraft supplies. Say that Luisa had no capital, but she possessed expert basket-weaving skills learned from her youth. Now a single mother with four children, she lives in a shanty by the side of the road, having been abandoned by her husband. To generate an income, she is often forced to seek financing from a "5/6th lender." This person agrees to loan Luisa 50 pesos in the morning with which to buy reeds and other materials for her basket-weaving crafts. She works rapidly and skillfully, completing seven baskets, which she is able to sell in the market by 6:00 p.m. Charging 12 pesos for each basket, she generates revenues of 84 pesos by nightfall. With her hard-earned money from a long day's work, Luisa must then go back to pay off the loan shark. For the 50-peso loan at 7:00 a.m., she might have to pay him 60 pesos with interest by evening. This would amount to a simple interest rate of 20 percent per day! Thus, we see the realities that hard-working individuals confront each day in attempting to survive, feed their family, and live a hard life in a shack.

With such a painful penalty, it is no wonder that millions of the world's poorest people are trapped in a vicious, never-ending cycle of painful poverty. The loan sharks of the developing world (at every level) become rich, while the poor drop ever deeper into a destructive, economic black hole. These 5/6th lenders in the Philippines make American "Quick Loan" finance companies appear as charitable humanitarians with their daily interest rates of "a mere one percent."

The village banking approach of microcredit, in contrast, enables people like Luisa to break the cycle of poverty. She can access a loan along with her peers, even though she has no collateral or credit history. She works with people whom she can trust in her lending group, each of whom has their own microbusiness. They pay interest and principle daily, but not at exorbitant rates. After the first round of paying back her small loan, Luisa qualifies for a larger loan, and this is repeated each successive time. With increasing profits, she is able to better feed her children, provide medical care for her family when injury or illness occurs, and ensure that her children will have an education in the future. In the case of Enterprise Mentors, being mutually responsible for the total amount of the loan ensures an astonishing payback rate of 99 percent. This is coupled with microenterprise training and hands-on consulting programs through EMI and its NGO partner groups.

This strategy to lift poor Filipinos became extremely important, not because of the aggregate statistics summarized at the outset of this chapter. More impressive is the tangible experience of each individual microentrepreneur—the single woman and her children, the poor LDS bishop with his little family business, the group of Relief Society sisters who collectively borrow to establish a women's co-op as a group, thereby leveraging their collective skills and energy.

A number of key features underlie the work and tactics of EMI and its affiliates:

- Objectives include helping the poor achieve self-sufficiency through self-help, mentoring, and training.

- Programs offer business training such as simple bookkeeping, marketing, and management, as well as microcredit.
- The emphasis is not on creating a short-term project, but instead on building a long-term program that is truly sustainable.
- Participants are not viewed as mere pawns in an economic game, but as intelligent, creative individuals who may simply lack entrepreneurial skills or access to funding.
- The strategy is to develop those poor who are committed to building their livelihood, their families, and their communities through micro and small-scale enterprises.
- The methodology used is that of working through indigenous staffers and local NGOs, rather than sending in U.S. experts at great expense to administer programs in the Philippines or other countries.
- A basic premise is that consulting and training should not be a gift and that financial assistance ought not be merely a free grant. In other words, there is no "something for nothing."
- Rather, all transactions are to be exchanged in order to reinforce a sense of responsibility. This means that usually small fees are charged to clients for attending a workshop. Likewise, a reasonable amount of interest is paid on each loan, thereby ensuring that participants feel accountable for what they receive.
- Finally, beneficiaries must commit that down the road, after they have greater success, they will also teach others. Each client agrees to consult and help the less fortunate who may need assistance in the future, thereby giving back to the program.

Mentors' Continual Growth

While the Philippines has been the major thrust of this chapter, continual growth has occurred as EMI gradually expanded to other nations. Although some of the board sought to focus our work solely on the Philippines, others of us argued the need to spread the Mentors model elsewhere so that Latter-day Saints and their neighbors of other faiths could benefit from its programs. Over the past decade, starting in Guatemala (Hiatt and Woodworth, 2006). EMI has expanded its services, funding, training, mentoring, and more to poor communities, both LDS and others, in additional Latin American nations, such as Nicaragua, Honduras, Mexico, Venezuela, Peru, and the Dominican Republic. Other Mentors operations are based in countries as far-flung as Cambodia, Ghana, and Nepal, each starting small and slowly but gradually expanding to build self-reliance.

Over the decades, the Mentors program has had continual growth. To illustrate, here are only a few trends. In 2007 it had 256 employees, working from its various offices. Among other things, this means that over a thousand of their family members enjoy decent housing, three meals per day, and the chance to learn new skills and competencies, so as be able to teach or train others, while enjoying professional jobs and more. Among the poorest, at the time, there were some 20,000 active Mentors clients. By 2012 the total had more than doubled to serving 52,000-plus. During that five-year period, the default rate on its microcredit loans dropped from over 8.3 percent to 4.9 percent—a solid sign of success.

So by 2012, Mentors had successfully given out more than 350,000 microloans, a far cry from its humble beginnings in 1990 when just a few dozen were made. Equally important, the financial self-sufficiency of the NGO offices in five nations grew from a mere 66 percent and exceeded that level 22 years later. That means that the organizations could sustain themselves with their own country's revenues rather than being dependent on Mentors' U.S. funding. The total Mentors loan portfolio for granting microloans had expanded to over $3.7 million, clearly evidence that its "pro-poor" business model was becoming scalable. Its overall impact on people—meaning its communal bank clients and their family members—rose from just over a million of the poor in 2007 up to benefiting over 2.5 million in 2012 (Peterson, 2012).

Mentors survived several destructive natural disasters in the Philippines, although the results were at least short-term catastrophes. For instance, in the mid-1990s, Typhoon Angela caused deaths of thousands and damages totaling some $240 million. Then in late 2010, Typhoon Megi brought similar devastation. In both instances, not only were towns destroyed, but also schools and churches closed, government operations diminished, and more. Unfortunately, tens of thousands of tiny microenterprises went bankrupt each time. Thankfully, top managers of PEDF decided to offer loan forgiveness to thousands of its clients, helping them with fresh microloans to begin anew. Still, the experience was a severe setback for many of the Filipino poor.

Slow but deep EMI expansion continued until several challenges in 2020. That year was tough for millions of people around the globe. Yet in spite of many challenges, Mentors continued its forward trajectory, as illustrated with the numbers below from its Annual Report (2020). The worst crisis grew out of the coronavirus pandemic that made tens of millions suffer, and has killed millions of people globally. The world's economy shrank significantly, as well, making the poor more vulnerable than ever. In the Philippines there was the eruption of the huge Taal Volcano near Manila that forced a million Filipinos from their homes. More typhoons and earthquakes followed. In other locations like Nepal and Ghana, Mentors launched healthcare training to help people learn the importance of wearing a mask, washing their hands frequently, and social distancing. In Cambodia, a relatively new Mentors start-up emphasized education and training, though it gave few microloans because of COVID-19's dangers. There and in other Mentors countries like Ghana, a good deal of the work shifted from microcredit to sheer survival. In Peru, a nation extremely hard hit, Mentors had to halt one-on-one mentoring of clients, and conduct small-business trainings using the internet. Only some 500 clients received a microloan to launch a tiny new business.

Yet there were shining moments for Mentors and its many clients, too. For example, in Nicaragua, 2020 was disrupted by political conflicts and social unrest over the nation's future. Natural disasters exacerbated the problems, including rainstorms and mass flooding, along with the coronavirus pandemic. Yet 2,020 individuals and families were served in Nicaragua during those 12 months. Many of Mentors' students went above and beyond the 40 hours of required community service for their education. The results were a total of 56,854 service hours performed in multiple towns and *barrios*. Also, that year, Mentors launched its new Global Technology Center in Managua that will operate as a technology and tech-support hub for the entire Mentors global organization. Staffed by volunteers, it is beginning to provide technical support to the growing numbers of online vocational students that Mentors will train globally, and, in the process, the volunteers will gain valuable career experience for future private employment opportunities. Due to Nicaraguan government policies and laws, Mentors is not yet able to offer microcredit loans, but the licenses should be approved in 2021.

Next door to Nicaragua, the unemployment rate in Guatemala is 45 percent, threatening most aspects of living or simply existing. Yet approximately 5,160 Guatemalan clients continued to benefit from loans and mentoring so as to launch or retain their microenterprises. More students earned their self-reliance and other business certificates than ever before. In the Dominican Republic, additional clients received mentoring and microloans. And in Honduras, there were many microloans as well as training and funding. The Mentors Center for Education and Mentoring in San Pedro Sula was forced to close its doors, but clients and students kept moving forward. Nearly 600 individuals completed vocational training certificates that year.

Generally, governments sought to protect their citizenry with pandemic lockdowns, business closings, and smart hygienic practices. These resulted in seriously curtailing most microenterprise efforts. Yet, amazingly, Mentors students in many of the above countries channeled their time and person-power to volunteer in serving their communities. In Honduras, for instance, the country suffered large disasters from the destruction of Hurricanes Eta and Iota. The result? Altogether, Mentors' students donated more than 40,000 service hours in 2020 alone to clean up communities, repair damaged buildings, and provide a variety of other community services.

While Mentors International faced enormous challenges in recent times, especially during the world crisis of 2020, it has continued its forward progression. In terms of sheer numbers, more than 4.9 million entrepreneurs have now benefited from training, loans, and job-creating strategies. Many more families in many parts of the globe have benefited from education and other services. In spite of ongoing challenges, Mentors in the United States, as well as its entities in other nations, will continue to thrive by empowering the poor among God's Third World children.

To conclude this chapter, I recall the long-ago 1995 trip that our board chair, Elder Marion D. Hanks, made to the Philippines. He wrote a touching report that graphically describes a colorful picture of the kind of microenterprise success he witnessed. He spent a week in-country, and his notes were later transcribed and reported in the Salt Lake City *Deseret News* as follows:

> We walked out about a half mile and up steps carved in a muddy hillside. This little person lived in a hut with no electricity. On an ancient treadle sewing machine she made shoe coverings, packed them in attractive packages and put them on her back. She would take a 'Jeepney,' then cross the River Negros to sell her backpack full of materials. She would pay some guy '6 for 5' or worse and have nothing left when she was finished. On Monday she would have to borrow money again. She had six or eight little children. [After a microloan] she now pays a rational market rate and is feeding her children. She is able

to pay two helpers and her children help, too. This really made a convert of me (Boren, 1995).

"It is a very great poverty to decide that a child must die that you might live as you wish."
—Mother Teresa

References

Anderson, L. (1992). Foundation Helping Filipinos Establish Small Businesses. *Deseret News*, September 9.

Boren, K. (1995). Foundation Gives Hand Up, Not Handout. *Deseret News*, June 1.

Brau, J. C., Hiatt, S., and Woodworth, W. (2009). Evaluating Impacts of Microfinance Institutions Using Guatemalan Data, *Journal of Managerial Finance*, vol. 35, no. 12, pp. 953–74. (Emerald Publishing.) doi: 10.1108/03074350911000025.

Doctrine and Covenants 104:15, 17.

Havelock, R. (1969). *Planning for Innovation: A Comparative Study of the Literature on the Dissemination and Utilization of Scientific Knowledge*. University of Michigan.

Hiatt, S., and Woodworth, W. (2006). Alleviating poverty through microfinance: Village banking outcomes in Central America. *The Social Science Journal*, vol. 43, 471–77. doi: 10.1016/j.soscij.2006.04.017.

Lucas, J. W., and Woodworth, W. (1996). *Working Toward Zion: Principles of the United Order for the Modern World*. Aspen Books.

Mentors International. (2020). Annual Report. https://mentorsinternational.org/wp-content/uploads/2021/02/2020-Annual-Report-Web.pdf.

Peterson, M. (2012). PowerPoint presentation in W. Woodworth's Social Entrepreneurship course, BYU, Utah.

Philippine News. (1995). October 4–8.

Philippine News. (1996). January 10–16.

Taylor, J. (1879). *Journal of Discourses*. Vol. 20.

Woodworth, W. (1996). Inventing the Future: LDS Self Reliance in the Philippines. *This People Magazine*, 20–26. https://warnerwoodworth.files.wordpress.com/2020/06/philippines-enterprise-development-foundation.pdf.

Woodworth, W. (1996). Philippines Indigenous Management. Marriott School's *Exchange Magazine*.

Woodworth, W. (2000). *Small Really Is Beautiful: Micro Approaches to Third World Development—Microentrepreneurship, Microenterprise, and Microfinance.* Third World Think Tank.

"They, the Builders of the Nation"
LDS Hymns, No. 36

1. They, the builders of the nation,
   Blazing trails along the way;
   Stepping-stones for generations
   Were their deeds of ev'ry day.
   Building new and firm foundations,
   Pushing on the wild frontier,
   Forging onward, ever onward,
   Blessed, honored Pioneer!

2. Service ever was their watchcry;
   Love became their guiding star;
   Courage, their unfailing beacon,
   Radiating near and far.
   Ev'ry day some burden lifted,
   Ev'ry day some heart to cheer,
   Ev'ry day some hope the brighter,
   Blessed, honored Pioneer!

3. As an ensign to the nation,
   They unfurled the flag of truth,
   Pillar, guide, and inspiration
   To the hosts of waiting youth.
   Honor, praise, and veneration
   To the founders we revere!
   List our song of adoration,
   Blessed, honored Pioneer!

   Text: Ida R. Alldredge (1892–1943)
   Music: Alfred M. Durham (1871–1957)

6

MicroBusiness Mentors

(Utah Latino Immigrants and Refugees, 2003–2022)

The pioneering hymn "They, the Builders of the Nation" captures the pioneering spirit of MicroBusiness Mentors (MBM), a small, innovative nongovernmental organization that today continues helping to build a better future for Utah residents, especially immigrants. In Spanish, of course, it became known as *Mentores para la Microempresa*. It offers microlending services based in Provo, Utah, to poor families as a student-run nonprofit that in 2003 grew out of a Social Entrepreneurship practicum course I taught at the Romney Institute in the Marriott School of Business, Brigham Young University (BYU, 2021). This chapter reports how student innovators designed a social enterprise in their graduate course while earning a Master's of Public Administration (MPA) degree. Begun as a semester practicum, the group's humble efforts have continued to show success and staying power, as well as evolutionary growth, despite limited resources and volunteers. The course, "Becoming a Global Change Agent," encouraged students in the class to tackle international projects, seeking ways to reduce poverty in far-off locales such as India or South America. One group decided to apply course innovations in the community adjacent to campus.

▲ Argentine parents who graduated from MBM training and mentoring as a client family

▼ One-on-one mentoring process with clients as we worked from Utah Valley University's center as microfinance spread throughout Utah Valley

The relevance of this chapter in *Radiant Mormonism*, given our present circumstances with the COVID-19 pandemic, cannot be overstated, as people seek to answer questions about jobs, justice, and their health. Thus, I will explore ways in which academics, students, and entrepreneurs can design their business and professional impacts so that they may survive and maybe even thrive in challenging times. What is increasingly important and required these days is the ability of experts, governments, universities, and nonprofits to generate capacity-building outcomes for those who struggle economically, even in large well-developed nations like the U.S. As we and the rest of the world cope, in a variety of fashions, with the unprecedented disaster of the coronavirus pandemic, worries have been expanding. By the time of this writing, approximately 773,000 Americans were dead and over 47 million had contracted the disease (Worldometers 2021). The explosion of suffering across the entire planet is, of course, much worse.

Among those who battle the deleterious effects of mass pandemics globally, poor families face the largest challenges. But for those in America from other countries, whether legal immigrants or undocumented workers, barriers to survival are often complex and even seemingly insurmountable. Thus, this chapter documents innovative ways in which people can use microcredit to manage their small business while continuing to face economic uncertainty and the pressures of illness, closed businesses, school cancellations, and the worries of both children and parents in their daily lives.

For many Utahns, the notion of creating and lending money to risky, tiny businesses has been a common practice since the early Mormon pioneers began settling what was then called the "Utah Territory." Under the leadership of Brigham Young and the early apostles, much emphasis was placed on building a sense of community, helping everyone to have a job, and extolling the importance of hard work and the dignity that would follow. A primary motivation driving my own desire to build better lives for the poor—including the establishment of MicroBusiness

Mentors—has been the teachings of modern prophets who have declared that both Latter-day Saints and the larger masses of oppressed people need and deserve economic justice. In General Conference in 1854 John Taylor saw something like microfinance as a critical need in his day and age, even as we do today:

> Talk about financiering! [sic] Financier for the poor, for the working man, who requires labor and is willing to do it, and act in the interest of the community for the welfare of Zion, and the building up of the kingdom of God upon the earth. This is your calling; it is not to build up yourselves, but to build up the Church and kingdom of God. . . . Do not let us have anybody crying for bread, or suffering, for want of employment. Let us furnish employment for all (Taylor, 187).

Just as the people of God were described in the Book of Mormon, the Latter-day Saints "began to have success among the poor class of people" (Alma 32:2). As we remember the Tenth Article of Faith penned by the Prophet Joseph Smith: "We believe in the literal gathering of Israel and in the restoration of the Ten Tribes; that Zion (the New Jerusalem) will be built upon the American continent; that Christ will reign personally upon the earth; and that the earth will be renewed and receive its paradisiacal glory" (Articles of Faith, 2020).

While such a utopia seems promising, my understanding of the Gospel is that the so-called Zion to be established will require the elimination of extreme poverty. Thus we read that such a Zion will require us to replicate or otherwise build a higher order society per the *Pearl of Great Price:* "The Lord called his people Zion because they were of one heart and one mind and dwelt in righteousness, and there was no poor among them" (Moses 7:18). The people of Enoch consecrated all they possessed to building their Zion. But Utah with its strong LDS presence seems to be a far cry from ancient righteousness. Instead, we often see inequality, homelessness, greed, crime, selfishness, racial injustice, and childhood hunger.

Perhaps MicroBusiness Mentors was born to assist the truly poor by giving them training and microloans as a way forward. It just might be that offering the same kind of microcredit that we BYU friends were doing globally could also assist impoverished Utahns to enjoy a better life. Thus, in my MPA course, I began teaching such terminology as *microcredit, microentrepreneurship, microenterprise,* and *financial inclusion*. Over many years, I had been inspired by the vision and efforts of my longtime friend and colleague Muhammad Yunus, in Bangladesh. His work eventually led to his receiving the Nobel Peace Prize in 2006. Some of the original inspiration for establishing our small NGO, which we named MicroBusiness Mentors, arose from Yunus's book, *Banker to the Poor: Micro-Lending and the Battle Against World Poverty* (1999). The two of us had collaborated for years since my earlier launching of various new microcredit NGOs in the Philippines, Latin America, Africa, and islands of the South Pacific.

The case below is one such venture within the United States that I founded with some of my MPA students, and to which Yunus agreed to be its adviser.

Over the past 50 years, America has gained the reputation of "Big." Super-sized meals, nine-seat SUVs, and gigantic corporations seem to epitomize the culture. Often overlooked, however, is the significant role that "small"—even "micro"—plays in the U.S. economy. In fact, over 80 percent of its businesses today can be classified as microenterprises—businesses with fewer than five employees that require small amounts of start-up capital. Significantly, these businesses employ 41 million people (Association for Enterprise Opportunity, 2013). It has been hypothesized that if so much of America is actually based on the factors of both "big" and "small," then perhaps even the concept of microcredit could take hold in the United States.

Might a land of big cars, big houses, and big appetites also do small things? Could microloans for microenterprises meet a starving niche in the American economy? Studies of microenterprises in the U.S. verify that there is indeed a market for microcredit. This form of lending seeks to serve those underprivileged workers who cannot access traditional financing to build their business (FDIC, 2012). Of the 20 million microenterprise owners in the United States some 15 years ago, nearly 11 million had difficulty accessing financing from traditional banks; 2.3 million were members of minority groups; 5.1 million microenterprises were run by women—the target market for most international microcredit groups and the market in which microcredit in the United States began (Edgcomb and Klein, 2005).

Formally designated, microcredit grew quietly in America beginning as early as the 1980s. Community organizations, primarily those concerned in particular with women's limited financial and enterprise opportunities, saw the benefits of using the microloans and peer-lending strategies that had been so successful in the developing world. The Corporation for Enterprise Development, Community Action Organizations, and even the U.S. Department of Labor began experimenting with microcredit principles to fight unemployment with self-employment. Though growth began slowly, the creation of unified microcredit groups and improvement of practices helped the industry begin to see rapid success using principles developed to help developing countries.

Yet early on, a key difference was noticed, owing to the complex business environment in the U.S. Because starting a small business is much harder in America than internationally, and because the microenterprise sector occupies a smaller percentage of the economy here than in developing countries, U.S. microcredit organizations have placed a strong emphasis on training programs. As a consequence, two fields have emerged from the initial American microcredit movement: microfinance, which deals with the actual providing of finance, and microenterprise development, which deals with assisting microenterprise entrepreneurs with services such as training and technical assistance. Many organizations, such as MicroBusiness Mentors, choose to operate at the intersection of these two by providing training as well as financing for the microentrepreneurs.

Starting Up MicroBusiness Mentors

To create the setting for the emergence of MBM, let us look at an individual beneficiary, Nelly Flores, a Provo resident who immigrated from Mexico. Señora Flores worked for hours each day trying to sell enough jewelry at local stores to keep her small start-up business afloat. But the stores would not pay for the jewelry up front, and they took almost all the profits she hoped to earn, leaving Flores with all the work and no return. "They wouldn't pay me what I deserved," Nelly said, "and I didn't know how to make my business work. MicroBusiness Mentors' classes helped me understand the market for my type of business." After MBM training, she received a $500 microloan to alter her business model and shift in new directions. Commenting on her continued success, she said, "I realized that I needed to sell directly to customers, so I stopped selling my jewelry in local stores, and I opened a booth at the Farmer's Market in Provo.... And my business keeps growing!" (MBM interview, 2006).

Flores's husband complimented her performance, saying, "MicroBusiness Mentors gave my wife a lot more than business skills and a loan. It gave her the confidence she needed to be successful." After attending additional training classes with her fellow alumni, Nelly presented a revised business plan and received a second loan, in the amount of $1,000, to finance her growing business. She reported continual success as she applied the business principles she learned from MBM to keep her business growing.

This example is but one of thousands of such cases from MBM. The nonprofit was launched in a course I developed in the late 1980s in which I challenged students in my Organizational Behavior course at BYU to make a difference. For over a decade, the usual focus was on poverty and social innovations to help people in developing countries help themselves through "sustainable solutions" and family empowerment. The assumption had always been that the poor could wait for solutions from big government, the United Nations, and churches and other charities. Conversely, my own philosophy was that self-help could be even more effective.

Self-empowerment, I had learned, gave people control over their lives. If the poor merely awaited assistance from the "Big Boys," all too often, aid never came, and even when it did, dependency would follow.

So MBM was conceived in a 2002 course as most students in my class were designing other NGO start-ups and projects in Africa, Latin America, and Asia. A small number of MPAs responded to my invitation for at least one group to roll out a local project to benefit those in need within our own community. The basic issue was that if microcredit could have such a revolutionary impact in the developing world, what impact might it have in local neighborhoods near our university? So that semester in 2002, as a social experiment in U.S.-based microcredit, MicroBusiness Mentors (MBM) was founded with the goal of providing business training, financial capital through microloans, and mentoring to microentrepreneurs in Provo. What began as a classroom mini-project has grown into a widespread community movement, reaching thousands of would-be entrepreneurs in the Utah Valley community over the years.

In this chapter I detail its history, illustrate its place in the U.S. microcredit industry, and highlight its effectiveness. To do so, I answer such questions as these: How did MicroBusiness Mentors make such a transformation? Who were the key players, and what were their key steps in putting the organization on its current trajectory? How does MBM fit into the broad U.S.-based microcredit movement? Perhaps most important, as the young microcredit organization evaluates its standing, is Nelly Flores's successful experience the norm? Is the organization still accomplishing its mission to empower students through economic self-reliance? Is the MicroBusiness Mentors format sustainable? In short, how is MBM working?

The Early Process of Building MicroBusiness Mentors

Inventing a small microenterprise nonprofit that would support immigrants, especially from nearby Latin America, seemed questionable to us in some ways, because we realized the migrants were poor, as were the college students wanting to help. But the idea was also seen as logical at another level, because there was often a need among immigrants for ways to have a job and to feed their family. However, such individuals typically fear being caught or arrested by local law enforcement because they may not have the required visas or passports. Nor are they always able to obtain a job because of racism, or, again, the lack of legal paperwork to be hired. So MBM was invented precisely to aid such people.

My MPA students found that many microcredit programs in the United States struggled to maintain self-sustaining operations; they also realized that Provo, Utah, had a growing and largely underserved Hispanic population. Accordingly, for their "Change the World" project that semester they drew up a business proposal for a local business-training and microcredit organization targeted toward Hispanics. Such individuals generally cannot enter a bank to obtain a business loan. They have no credit history, at least in the U.S. They have very little, if any, collateral to secure such a loan. Nor do most even have a credit card. So MBM could perhaps fill the gap with training plus a microloan for poor immigrants, potentially offering a better life for them and their loved ones.

At the beginning, to determine the need for such an organization and in conjunction with their MPA statistics class, the group of BYU students conducted their own survey, using flyers and phone calls, to see if there was interest in microcredit in the community. Of those who responded to the survey, 71 percent had an annual income of $30,000 or less; 48 percent had zero savings; 81 percent were potentially interested in being self-employed; 78 percent were potentially interested in receiving business training; and 55 percent said they were potentially interested in obtaining a loan (MBM 2002). Secondary research showed explosive growth in

Utah County's Hispanic population; data showed surprising geographic discrepancies in income, high school grade averages, and government-subsidized housing between different neighborhoods in the county. Outside research confirmed the findings of the MPA students. For example, a study conducted by the Aspen Institute showed that Utah has one of the lowest concentrations of Microenterprise Development Assistance Organizations in the United States, with a ratio of over 50,000 to 1 (Edgcomb and Klein, 2005). At that time, more than 200,000 businesses in Utah could be classified as microenterprises, employing 17.1 percent of the population. With research to back up their idea, the students moved forward.

Joined by a few others, the group convened regularly during the next year to create a detailed business plan, finally deciding on the organization's official name—MicroBusiness Mentors. They met with several local nonprofit and government groups to gain their feedback and garner support for the new organization. They met with the mayor of Provo and his economic development staff, who expressed their unified support for the idea. Local branches of area charities such as the United Way and Community Action Agency similarly expressed their support, as did the local Chamber of Commerce. In the spring of 2003, the group submitted its business plan to BYU's Business Plan Competition and achieved semifinalist ranking. Along with their prize came $1,000—the first seedling money for the organization!

The original business design called for the organization to reach those Utah County Spanish speakers who wished to improve their financial situation through entrepreneurship. Clients would be chosen to participate in MBM after being interviewed by members of the organization. The curriculum would be offered weekly, initially either on the Brigham Young University campus or at local elementary schools, in eight sessions each lasting three hours. The structure of the loan-giving process was based largely on other NGOs that I, as their professor, had earlier founded in the Philippines, Honduras, and Mali. It was decided that loans would be given based on approval of peers and completed business training, rather than collateral or credit history. Clients' first loans would be based on peer-lending, or what is often referred to as "solidarity groups." After successfully paying back their first loans, clients could qualify for incrementally larger, individual loans. The organization would be administered by a team of students, including a General Director and Directors of Finance, Training, and Marketing.

The students designed an eight-module curriculum based on material from a number of international microlending institutions with which I had collaborated or which I had helped found—Enterprise Mentors International, Ouelessebougou-Utah Alliance, FINCA International, HELP Honduras, and others. Soon after, with curriculum and business plan in hand, the growing group of volunteers put their plans into action and held the first MicroBusiness Mentors class in the summer of 2003. The group advertised at local ESL (English as a Second Language) classes and began MBM's training mentoring sessions on BYU's campus. Five students regularly attended the classes: immigrants from Guatemala, Mexico, and Argentina; four graduated from the program.

The first batches of loans were offered at $500 per client. They were funded out of my own pocket, as I first gave $1,000 to fund the initial two loans, then $2,000, and eventually up to $5,000. Though I began receiving some of my initial investment back as loans were repaid, it was clear to me that the organization needed outside funding to become operational. So MBM leaders connected with several local financial institutions, making them aware of the organization and its potential to spur economic development. Yet not one of the financial institutions responded. Outside funding wouldn't become a reality until 2006.

The values and systems MBM used for its establishment and growth stood in vivid contrast to the ways of many new NGO startups. The lists below suggest the contrasting paradigms:

Typical Old NGO Strategies:	New MBM Strategies:
• Top-down	• Bottom-up
• Large scale	• Small scale
• Bureaucratic	• Self-organizing
• Business–government	• NGOs
• Formal controls	• Participatory
• Big budgets	• Microcredit
• Return on investment	• Ongoing reinvestment

MBM Growing Pains

Gradually, MBM determined on and grew an organizational structure. It began to have key formalized positions to ensure that every student volunteer accepted responsibilities to help move things forward. The organization included a small board of mature students and me as their professor, to oversee everything and make major policy decisions. Organizational roles included managerial positions such as president, vice president, and a director of training who would oversee all the trainers. Another position was the human resource director, who would support everyone in their learning and skill sets. There was also an accountant to track the money carefully, plus a loan committee to dispense microloans and get them repaid for future clients. Additional positions included PR positions to build credibility and marketing, recruiters to find additional volunteers, and more.

One of the advantages of running MBM within Utah Valley was that the two large universities in the area—Brigham Young University and Utah Valley University—as well as several smaller technical colleges in Utah county were educating thousands of students, most of them Americans, who had gained fluency in Spanish, which simplified recruiting for our training efforts. The reason for this was that the area was home to many Mormon returned missionaries who had spent two years of their young lives preaching and providing community service around the globe. They had labored with the people in both large urban cities and small rural villages, and they learned to love and serve the people and to appreciate their cultures. BYU itself offered courses in 76 languages, the greatest number of any university in the world (BYU, 2021); Yale was a distant second, offering only 25 languages. These factors made young adults' willingness to volunteer with MBM for six to eight hours each week very helpful to the organization.

As things developed over the next several years, MicroBusiness had various ups and downs. Part of the difficulty was due to being a new organization suffering all the complexities that most business start-ups experience. But there were unique challenges, too. For instance, MBM had continuous turnover, as student volunteers often needed to leave Provo in summers to fulfill an important internship with a large business or government position. Some graduated from college and moved on to start their careers. Others went on to leading graduate schools, which admitted them, not only as a result of their high grades or international experience, but also because of their entrepreneurial spirit—and particularly their success with MBM. Even if volunteers stayed in the county, many were busy with summer jobs or new long-term career opportunities, marriages, establishing families, and so forth. Trying to maintain the focus and be true to MBM's initial strategy proved daunting for many.

Funding continued to be a challenge. Although microfinance was starting to accelerate globally, few in Utah, even businesspeople and local government officials, knew much about it. So the organization was struggling to gain enough credibility to qualify for substantial outside funding. A solution came when Muhammad Yunus, the 2006 Nobel Peace Prize winner and founder of Grameen Bank in Bangladesh, agreed to make an informal partnership with MicroBusiness Mentors. Yunus expressed his support for the organization, since I had worked with him for over a decade. The *Deseret News*, Utah's largest newspaper, ran a story about our friendship and the early efforts of MBM, which generated growing awareness (Westenskow, 2006). Soon, leaders at several local financial institutions were again contacted, and this time one local community credit union responded, intrigued by the idea of supporting a local microcredit initiative. After long discussions and intricate explanations about the promise of such an organization, the credit union committed to contributing $10,000 to support new MBM loans. That generous move opened up a sense of new energy and commitment on the part of the student team to expand and solidify MicroBusiness Mentors.

Another challenge was that of recruiting Latino immigrants who wanted to start microbusinesses. Many of them felt worried about being arrested by U.S. federal police and other law enforcement employees. Concerns about visas, jobs, racism, taxes, and other issues were big challenges for families from Latin America, especially those lacking the proper government paperwork. From the time of President Ronald Reagan's White House in the 1980s, Republicans and Democrats alike had battled over what to do about immigration, and how to manage the influx of people seeking relief from civil wars, domestic abuse, poverty, drug cartels, and more. The conflicts still raged in the first decade of the twenty-first century, forcing MBM and other groups wishing to support minorities to devise ways of dealing with numerous challenges, beyond simply giving a microloan.

Yet MBM trudged hopefully onward. Little by little its client base grew from 7 to 9 Latinos per course, to 12 to 14. More clients graduated from the courses, and the organization reached a few key milestones, essential for its future growth. Its curriculum was improved and revised, and the organization's community involvement increased—MBM was becoming better known in the community and was being well-received by local organizations and businesses. The organization also had new challenges: leaders of the organization struggled to know if the curriculum was effective, and qualified and confident trainers were hard to come by and even harder to keep around. The organization's next effort was to build on what had been developed thus far to increase its social and economic impacts. Improving the quality of life for Latino families was an important element of MBM's values and ethics.

MBM Expansion of Volunteers and Latino Clients

Clearly, there were positives to the NGO, though the organization had not yet reached the scale its founders had envisioned. So by 2010 a huge effort was launched to recruit more university volunteers to teach and be mentors to our Latino clients. Gradually, not only were business and accounting students joining the effort, but others majoring in engineering, international relations, pre-law studies, and the social sciences were also participating. Also, there was an emphasis on engaging more of Provo's poor immigrant adults to prepare to start their own microenterprises. A variety of media stories at local universities generated a new batch of trainers who turned out to be not only energetic but also increasingly competent. Local Spanish-speaking newspapers began running stories about MBM, or, as they called it on their pages, *Mentores para la Microempresa*.

The results? More and more university students began volunteering as trainers and consulting mentors with MBM clients, helping them with the extensive number of necessary processes for establishing their microenterprises: legal incorporation, business plans, marketing strategies, computer skills, building a website, personnel and HR, finance and accounting, hiring help as growth occurs, obtaining a loan (along with repaying it and getting a larger one), and on and on. Soon MBM had attracted a dozen or more volunteers who, after training in our learning modules for Latino clients, allowed the organization to create two groups of clients when the demand was sufficient. They sought more Latinos who wanted jobs, and the process continued to be more productive. Two sections of college student volunteers provided the mentoring, along with two groups of Spanish-speaking immigrants wanting to become their own entrepreneurs. The results soon produced some 20 volunteers teaching as many as 26 potential microentrepreneurs how to launch their own businesses.

The next BYU semester saw even greater growth. Some of MBM's leadership team embarked on a comprehensive "marketing blitz" that attracted even more student volunteers to become trainers. At the same time, there was a greater push into the Latino community of Utah Valley, which led to recruiting more clients for training than ever. Preparations for new groups intensified. MBM held fundraisers, golfing events, and community festivities to promote the cause and solicit financial contributions from the community. Within a short time, MBM was serviced by some 30 volunteers teaching and mentoring 40 to 45 Latino clients. With increasing interest and growing numbers of participants, the need for new funding soon became critical.

Over time, as the professor and "prime mover," I was able to push, lobby, and cajole additional potential supporters to provide more loan capital. The large American Express office in Salt Lake City, 40 miles to the north, provided a generous check of $10,000 to help. That gift was then advertised to encourage more donations from local banks throughout Utah Valley, several of which chipped in $5,000 to $10,000 each. MBM soon had sufficient funds to grant more microloans to growing numbers of Latinos seeking to launch their tiny enterprises. A community advisory board was developed consisting of donating bankers, along with leaders of United Way, Centro Hispano, and other supportive community groups. Being able to operate MBM with 100 percent volunteer labor and leadership meant the management costs were virtually zero. Thus, all the financial contributions could go directly into funding more microenterprises. We were able to use various training facilities to hold client mentoring sessions, board meetings, and the leadership team's planning and strategizing gatherings, all of which helped keep overhead expenses at zero.

Gradually, MBM received increasing media attention in Utah (Subieta, 2013). Our reputation also grew nationally. I was invited to share our story across the nation. The University of California, Berkeley, invited me to speak about MBM to faculty and students from across the country at a conference of universities (Woodworth, 2014). More recently, I also gave a keynote address on MBM in Tel Aviv, Israel, at a major conference of Nobel Prize Laureates in economics, held at the International Institute of Social and Economic Sciences (IISES), College of Law and Business (Woodworth, 2017).

Ongoing Challenges Today

Slowly but surely, MicroBusiness Mentors has continued to move forward. In recent years, in a series of meetings, trainings, and MBM volunteer discussions, the group assessed its collective progress and explored next steps in perhaps moving above and beyond an emphasis on microenterprise clients from Latin America, to expand services to regular white American citizens who are struggling in the U.S. economy (MBM Team, 2019).

Recent comments from several BYU student volunteers capture the work of MicroBusiness Mentors at this time. Said one, "We just need to keep moving forward as the American economy is in turmoil. Our Latino and other clients need our support as they weather today's storms." Another added: "MBM has provided generous training, microloans, and mentoring for a long time. But perhaps we're more relevant and needed now than at any time in the past." Similar sentiments have been communicated by past volunteers who now have earned law degrees and MBAs from top U.S. universities. While their own careers are successful, their annual incomes well above $100,000 per year, and their family lifestyles quite comfortable, they worry and wonder about MBM families from the past.

Fortunately, over the last several years, from 2017 through 2020, MBM has continued to progress. Its student volunteers typically learn, serve, and then graduate and move on. New Latino clients continue to be trained in business basics for starting new microenterprises. A new dimension of MBM's work has emerged in that the organization works more with white populations and refugees from the Middle East—a significantly different development from its early years. The explanation for this change is sad, but simple. With the Trump administration's violent treatment of caravans seeking to cross the U.S. border with Mexico, the separation of migrant families, the caging of children, and the aggressive searches for undocumented Latinos in major cities, many such people have returned to Latin America and are no longer even attempting to cross into the U.S. Thus, MBM's Latino client base has shrunk, and these days the mentoring and trainings are more often conducted in English than Spanish.

MicroBusiness Mentors continues to expand in 2022. However, its road has not been easy, nor a route of smooth success. Owing to political tensions, outright world conflicts, and failures of leadership in Washington, D.C., its development and maturity have been a process of ups and downs, fits and starts, sunshine and darkness. A major national challenge that affected it was the "Great Recession" that occurred in 2007–2008. It affected millions of American families and wrecked the economy. Huge Wall Street corporations received trillions of dollars to recover. But microenterprises and their struggling entrepreneurs suffered greatly as millions of tiny family firms collapsed. Thankfully, the next administration put together an economic restructuring team of experts, and America's economy finally recovered, and, in fact became stronger than ever by 2016.

Over the next several years, however, the economy began to decline, reaching an 11 percent unemployment and some 32 million people seeking government unemployment aid to survive (U.S. Department of Labor, 2020).

All this has been exacerbated by the new global phenomonen of a coronovirus. The U.S. continued to be economically solid, until hundreds of thousands began to die in the country, millions were infected, and experts feared that the pandemic may become even worse in 2022. So the future for microentrepreneurs and their life-giving tiny businesses is a big question as we consider 2022 and beyond. Still, I remain hopeful that small NGOs and community-based solutions will survive and continue to empower poor families. And I believe that MicroBusiness Mentors will continue to stand and serve with its "forever-commitment" to those who struggle for a better quality of life.

Like the pioneers of old, MBM continues moving forward. It draws on the Latter-day Saint ethic of dedication to God and service to others, male or female, white, black, or brown.

The prophet Brigham Young, the great colonizer of the western United States, sought to build a new economy from the wilderness. He preached and practiced a compassionate community in which people cared for each other. He rejected rugged, cowboy individualism and the land-grabbing culture of the West. Among his many pointed challenges about building a better society was this: "Do we realize that if we enjoy a Zion in time or in eternity we must make it for ourselves? That all, who have a Zion in the eternities of the Gods, organized, framed, consolidated, and perfected it themselves, and consequently are entitled to enjoy it?" (Young, 1941, p. 118). MBM has striven to make its own personal contributions to Brother Brigham's call to action.

References

Articles of Faith. (2020). LDS Church basic tenets. https://www.churchofjesuschrist.org/bc/content/shared/content/english/pdf/language-materials/64370_eng.pdf.

Association for Enterprise Opportunity. (2013.) Microbusinesses in the United States: Characteristics and Sector Participation. September. https://aeoworks.org/wp-content/uploads/2019/03/Microbusinesses-in-the-United-States-Characteristics-and-Sector-Participation.pdf.

BYU. (2021). Brigham Young University. https://www.byu.edu/.

Edgcomb, E. L., and Klein, J. A. (2005). "Opening Opportunities, Building Ownership: Fulfilling the Promise of Microenterprise in the United States." *The Aspen Institute*, 24–25.

FDIC. (2012). National Survey of Unbanked and Underbanked Households. FDIC.gov. Federal Deposit Insurance Corporation. December 26.

MBM. (2002). Team paper by students in the Organizational Behavior course "Becoming a Global Change Agent." Marriott School, BYU.

MBM. (2006). Unpublished interviews by Mentors.

MBM Team. (2019). Unpublished team meetings and interviews. March 9–October 22.

Microenterprise Employment Statistics in the United States. (2009). *Association for Enterprise Opportunity.* January 20. http://www.microenterpriseworks.org/index.asp?bid=159.

Subieta, D. (2013). A new way to give back with MicroBusiness Mentors. BYU NewsNet, May 4. https://universe.byu.edu/2013/05/04/1a-new-way-to-give-back-with-microbusiness-mentors/.

Taylor, J. *Journal of Discourses*, vol. 19, Discourse 43, https://journalofdiscourses.com/19/43.

U.S. Department of Labor. (2020.) Unemployment Claims. https://www.dol.gov/ui/data.pdf. July.

Westenskow, R. (2006). "Nobelist Partners with Provo Group." *Deseret News*, December 16.

Woodworth, W. (2014). Latino Microfinance: Ten Years of Lessons Learned. National Conference of Universities. University of California, Berkeley, November 15–16.

Woodworth, W. P. (2017). Engaged Learning in MBA Programs: Hands-on Microfinance. International Institute of Social and Economic Sciences (IISES), College of Law and Business, Tel Aviv, Israel. March 8–10. Proceedings.

Worldometers. (2021). COVID-19 Coronavirus Pandemic. https://www.worldometers.info/coronavirus/. Accessed November 5.

Young, B. (1941). *Discourses of Brigham Young.* John A. Widtsoe, editor.

Yunus, M. (1999). *Banker to the Poor: Micro-Lending and the Battle Against World Poverty.* Public Affairs.

"Arise, O Glorious Zion"
LDS Hymns, No. 40

1. Arise, O glorious Zion,
   Thou joy of latter days,
   Whom countless Saints rely on
   To gain a resting place.
   Arise and shine in splendor
   Amid the world's deep night,
   For God, thy sure defender,
   Is now thy life and light.

2. From Zion's favored dwelling
   The gospel issues forth,
   The covenant revealing
   To gather all the earth;
   And Saints, the message bringing
   To all the sons of men,
   With the redeemed shall, singing,
   To Zion come again.

   Text: William G. Mills (1822–1895)
   Music: George Careless (1839–1932)

7

Eagle Condor Humanitarian

(Peru, 2002–2022)

A great blessing in my life has always been a feeling of connection with the native peoples of the Americas. Having served various tribes in North America, such as the Oglala Sioux at Pine Ridge and the Navajo Nation, as well as Utes, Paiutes, Hopi, and more, I grew to love those people and have learned much through the years. The same is true for my efforts with indigenous communities in Mexico, as well as my years helping the Amazonian tribes in Brazil. From such friends, I came to understand their cultures and village life, as my associates and I sought to help them build better futures. At times, I'd recall scriptural passages from their ancient, sacred records like this verse recording the plea of Enos in the Book of Mormon to come forth in the last days:

> And after I, Enos, had heard these words, my faith began to be unshaken in the Lord; and I prayed unto him with many long strugglings for my brethren, the Lamanites.... And I had faith, and I did cry unto God that he would preserve the records; and he covenanted with me that he would bring them forth unto the Lamanites in his own due time (Enos 1:11, 16).

▲ Indigenous peoples of the Peruvian Andes with Eagle Condor board and staff

▼ ECH managing director, Jaime Figueroa, and author at the "Moroni Women's Center" high in the village of Patacancha at 12,000 feet

Indeed, as Moroni himself decreed, the truths and promises from the ancient gold plates were written "unto my brethren, the Lamanites" (Moroni 10:1.) These reflections suggest the beginnings of the work my collaborators and I launched to help the indigenous people of the Andes mountain range in 2002.

I want to frame this chapter by drawing on an Inca legend from high in the Andes mountain range of South America that tells of the Eagle and the Condor, two magnificent birds that have flown the skies and held special historical symbolism for the Peruvian people. It's derived from an ancient prophecy made a thousand years ago by Holy Men concerning the reunion between the long-separated people of the Eagle and the people of the Condor:

> In the beginning all the earth's people were one, but long ago they divided into two groups and each followed a different path of development. The people of the Eagle were highly scientific and intellectual, and the people of the Condor were highly attuned to nature and the intuitive realm. At this current juncture in earth's history, the Eagle people will have reached a zenith in their amassing of scientific knowledge, technology and technological tools, expression of high art, and the ability to build and construct. They will even develop tools and technologies that will expand the mind, and they will produce technical miracles of unimagined power and breadth. The enormous accomplishments and technologies will bring tremendous material wealth to the leaders of the Eagle world. In this same era, the people of the Condor, people of the heart, the spirit, the senses, and the deep connection with the natural world, will be highly developed in their intuitive skills. But at the same time they will be hungry and impoverished for knowledge that will enable them to be successful in the material world. Now is the era for the two groups to rejoin and share their knowledge and wisdom. The Eagle and the Condor will fly together in the same sky, wing to wing, and the world will come into balance (Eagle Condor Prophecy, 2016).

Now is the time when the Condor of Peru in South America is beginning to take flight with the Eagle of North America in bridging two worlds of unification and love. This parable inspired the creation of a nongovernmental organization called Eagle Condor Humanitarian, founded in 2002. It grew out of a Brigham Young University course I taught called "NGO Management." The course consisted of readings on microfinance, developing world economics, social entrepreneurship, NGO management, and much more. Underlying all the readings were the teachings of the Gospel of Christ and, in particular, the doctrines of the Restored Church about the necessity of feeding the hungry, empowering the poor, and reaching out to suffering families, parents without jobs, and their children who don't have enough to eat.

Class members not only read research articles, but they also heard my lectures and even held debates. Student teams were also formed to create group projects during the semester. The class consisted of graduate students of the Master's of Public Administration (MPA), Romney Institute of Public Management, in BYU's Marriott School of Business (Marriott School, 2021). One member of the class, a student from Peru, proposed that others join him in planning a new NGO for the impoverished people of his country, Bolivia, and Colombia. Since 2002 that little project has grown through several iterations into what has become an organization named Eagle Condor Humanitarian (ECH), whose primary goal is to help fulfill the ancient Inca prophecy by uniting the people of both regions and building a better future. Thus, I write this chapter as a cofounder and board member, although I eventually left to start new NGOs across the world. But in a sense, the Eagle Condor case is one of participant observation. In some respects, it was an action research project. Our primary focus was on microfinance, but we included additional humanitarian services through the years. ECH has evolved through its various nonprofit strategies in bringing the words of the Holy Men to a vivid reality. Most of the student team and myself, as founders, were North Americans, who collaborated and worked alongside the Peruvian project leader. Since its early days, Eagle Condor has wrought wonderful changes in the lives of thousands of Peruvians as well as those of other nations, and will continue to do more good in the future.

This chapter in *Radiant Mormonism* describes the new radiance of the indigenous people of Peru who are now being blessed with new opportunities to build stronger, healthier families by learning how to increase self-reliance. The effort grew out of my earlier commitments to live and practice the inspired teachings of pioneering LDS prophets as to how we should build a Zion society. As I've studied church history as a seminary and institute teacher over the decades, I've come to know and love deeply Latter-day Saint concepts for carrying out high-impact programs and organizations. They clearly apply to the founding of Eagle Condor Humanitarian, drawn from the social and practical teachings of early LDS Church officials. My article in *Brigham Young Magazine* captures these values for building positive organizations: "Restoring All Things: The Managerial and Economic Views of Early Mormon Leaders" (Woodworth, 1995).

Eagle Condor declared its mission with the following objectives:

1. Create sustainable hope and dignity within people of underdeveloped areas, through purposeful and well-planned humanitarian field programs.
2. Endeavor to provide them with microfinance and employment opportunities through teaching principles of good business practice that enable them to become self-sustaining while raising their standard of living.
3. Through grassroots efforts, provide a rich and predictable real-life experience of LDS humanitarian charity for adults, youth, and families who want to offer a hand of charity, feeling as if they can make a difference in the lives of others.

4. Roll out a perpetuating and respected organization whose members and donors are confident that their contributions are making a difference and aiding God's children of the Andes.

The ECH case below describes and analyzes how the organization originated, along with its program design, systems, structure, funding, and evolution through various phases for two decades. I will also briefly critique some of its weaknesses and failures, and the challenges it will face in the future.

This research may best be described by Professor William Foote Whyte, of Cornell University, who was my mentor for a number of years. In his 1982 address to the American Sociological Association as its new president, he called for social scientists to utilize our concepts and theories in applied ways. He argued that we should not merely study what *is*, but what *ought to be*. His was a clarion call for new "social inventions" to solve human problems (Whyte, 1982). Inspired by Whyte, this paper also draws on research from business, MFI experts, and other sources (Brau and Woodworth (2014); Daley-Harris (2003); Hatch (2002); International Labour Organization, 2006); Jansson (2001); Nogueira, Duarte, and Gama (2020); Otero (1999); and Yunus (2010).

Establishing Eagle Condor Humanitarian

At the outset, I will offer a simple example of an LDS Peruvian ECH client to show, close up, the typical needs of the Peruvian poor, as well as how our organization empowers such people. Jaro Diaz, a 35-year-old in Chiclayo, Peru, worked for a car repair shop, arising early every morning to ride his bicycle to the shop where he would fix car radiators all day. His meager wages were about 40 cents (U.S.) per hour, so a ten-hour day would yield a mere four dollars. With that, he had to feed his family of five people. A neighbor told him about a new organization called Eagle Condor, offering free entrepreneurial training, after which a microloan of the near-miraculous sum of $200 dollars could be had. The training would take one day per week for six weeks. To attend the ECH microenterprise training sessions, Jaro arranged to have a friend take his place at his car repair job on such days. He proved to be an enthusiastic student and became something of a leader to others. As required, he eventually had to create a business plan, so he thoughtfully considered his personal, family, and business goals and wrote them down. Over time, he made changes, then repeated the process several times before he was comfortable, receiving feedback and mentoring from the ECH trainer throughout the process. His goal was to start his own car radiator repair shop.

Eventually, after the entrepreneurship classes, Jaro qualified for a loan, acquired tools of his own, and started finding clients that he could serve after his workday at his regular job. Gradually he paid off his loan and received a second one for $400, then another for $800, and so on. Eventually, he had accumulated sufficient capital to rent a small facility and start repairs for his growing customer base, at which point he resigned from his previous job to be a full-time microentrepreneur. Because of his coherent plan, ongoing mentoring and advice from ECH, and his growing bank account, he was soon able to start hiring additional workers, paying them higher wages than even he had earned at the previous shop (Tello, 2005).

This account is only one of hundreds I learned of during the first several years of ECH's microfinance program. My former MPA student became the first director of the program in Peru, after friends and I raised the start-up capital for our new NGO. We sent him to the Philippines for a month to work and learn from the NGO I had established there in 1990. With advice and direction from the small board of trustees we had formed in Utah, and using the initial start-up plans from the student group in my class, things began to roll out. A small team was hired in Peru, training programs were launched, and the client base grew. Within several years, ECH expanded into the Cusco area and also into the Sacred Valley populated with indigenous villages. Also, efforts were launched in northern Peruvian towns like Piura, Chiclayo, and Trujillo. At that time, unemployment affected more than 60 percent of all people in

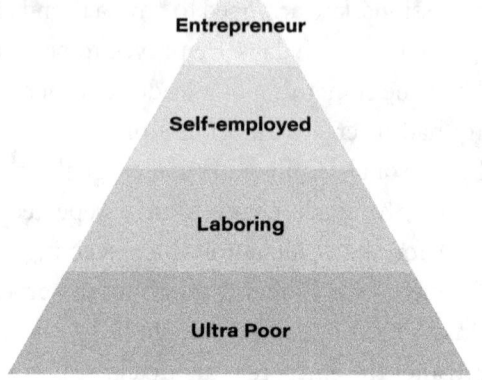

Figure 2: Multiple levels of clients in varying economic situations

northern Peru. Sixty-four percent of the families were categorized as "poor" by government officials. So there was much work to do.

As the NGO was rolled out, the branch of ECH in Trujillo grew from 2 to 60 active loans in its first year. Twelve months later, they had given out about 120 loans since the opening of the area. Some 40 microloans were soon paid off, but another 20 had been lost or forgiven, owing to the borrowers' circumstances. The majority of the loans were between $300 and $1,000 U.S. Some 60 percent of all the loans were to males, and about a fifth of the loans exceeded $1,000, made to those individuals growing larger businesses with multiple employees. As can be seen from Figure 2, there were multiple levels of clients in varying economic situations in Peru. ECH targeted much of its efforts on the ultra-poor, those at the "Bottom of the Pyramid" (Prahalad, 2006).

Analysis of Eagle Condor as an Organization

ECH's structure was led by a volunteer board of directors in the U.S., many of whom had served LDS missions in the Andes. After returning to Utah and getting great educations, they then remembered the impoverished Indians they had met and wanted to return to Peru and help improve life there for those they still loved. Now with successful careers in business, real estate, law, and other careers, they believed the time seemed right to help the "Eagle of the North" fly, in partnership with the Condor of Latin America. ECH then established a Peruvian sister NGO, *Asociación Andes*, with its own indigenous board and organization. At the outset, the organization's paid employees included my former MPA student from BYU, Jaime Figueroa (who coordinated donations, expeditions, and programs) in both Salt Lake City and Lima, Peru, along with Oswaldo Tello (an LDS bishop and the northern Peru field director), three loan officers, an administrative assistant, a nurse, and an engineer—all working and living Peru. ECH also rented a house in which Tello and his family lived and where all activity was based. A retired Peruvian volunteer managed the construction of houses that occurred throughout the year, a parallel program of ECH. Other staffers helped with expedition activities. The engineer even helped in the proper design of sewage systems and construction of houses, schools, and more (ECH, 2006).

I recently thought of the pioneering, valiant efforts of the Utah and Peruvian donors and board as they gave of their money, time, and skills to benefit the jobless and hungry Peruvian saints. Giving of our resources to aid those who suffer was in line with the spirit of consecration and stewardship reflected in the words of an early pioneer prophet, Lorenzo Snow:

> This is the spirit and aim of the United Order . . . that we should endeavor to establish. We should employ our surplus means in a manner that the poor can have employment and see before them a competence and the conveniences of life, so that they may not be dependent on their neighbors. Where is the man who wants to be dependent on his neighbors . . . ? No! He is a man, and is in the image of God, and wants to gather the means around him, by his own individual exertions (Snow, 1878).

Generating Funding for ECH Efforts

To maintain and grow its programs, Eagle Condor raised money through various strategies. They included personal contributions from friends and family of the volunteers. In some cases, supporters secured donations from their LDS wards and stake congregations, neighborhood associations, or business networks. A number of Utah area corporations made significant financial contributions from their business foundations (Eagle Condor, 2003–2017).

Another major instrument for securing ECH resources for microenterprise training and microloans was organizing humanitarian expeditions to Peru of 10 to 14 days in which North Americans would each donate several thousand dollars to ECH, part of which would cover their travel expenses. Usually $1,000 above and beyond travel costs would go to our NGO programs upon arrival in-country. I myself led several groups, including volunteers who were the children and grandchildren of general authorities, even First Presidency members.

Launching ECH Humanitarian Programs and Services

ECH brought real progress to several Peruvian towns, one after another. Gradually, more ECH programs were implemented to supplement microenterprise efforts. They arose from the pleas of the poor as perceived by the staff and interns, who would then provide additional support for individuals, families, and neighborhoods. Over time, Eagle Condor collaborated with or helped to start other NGOs offering various programs to Peru's poorest individuals and families. They include the Andean Children's Fund, Chasqui Humanitarian, HELP International (see chapter 2), Southern Cross Humanitarian, and Crecer, an organization sponsored by one of my other NGOs called Mentors International (see chapter 6). ECH's mission differed from almost all the regulated microfinance institutions in the Peruvian market. Perhaps it was most similar to the mission of Caritas Peru, a Catholic nonprofit that provides economic development programs, along with disaster relief and social services such as housing, food, and other support, to the very poor (Caritas, 2020).

From the outset, Eagle Condor offered expeditions to Peru from the United States. They were established to accomplish several things. One was to increase the levels of public interest in ECH while generating buy-in from donors and supporters in the U.S. that would ensure the flow of future donations. A second purpose was to generate impacts that directly aided Peru's poor. The range of these social services consisted of interventions such as those described below.

ECH launched humanitarian expeditions of North Americans, groups that labored as volunteers in Andean villages most days, but could extend their stay for a tour of Machu Picchu afterward. Volunteers traveled to Peru for 10 to 14 days of volunteering, not only paying for the costs of travel and on-the-ground experiences, but also contributing additional monies that could be used for local needs. Everyone paid their own way, taking extra suitcases full of donated goods such as tools, books, clothing, medicine, or computers, which they could distribute as they labored among the poor. Depending on their skills and backgrounds, they used their time and energy in building houses and schools, offered school teaching, provided microenterprise training, and more. In some cases, U.S. specialists with medical or dental skills provided their expertise in free clinics. Within just a few years, ECH became an impressive example of North Americans reaching out to others and building them up.

These humanitarian expeditioners constructed libraries in towns and villages and stocked them with Spanish-language books brought from the U.S. Over the first 15 years, some 71 small libraries were established and stocked with books, a project led by an LDS librarian dedicated to enhancing access to books and good literature.

Others taught in local schools to supplement already-existing educational services. A number of volunteers assisted in these schools by teaching simple English lessons in area high schools.

At night, others would go to the schools and teach adult literacy, or offer English to the school children's parents who worked days, but wanted to learn more at night.

On one of my visits, neighbors of mine from my Provo ward bought and took a total of 23 computers to set up a lab in a rural school that had just received electric power. That "little" beginning motivated hundreds of subsequent volunteers traveling to Peru to take small laptops, and later brought used but serviceable cell phones and other electronics for use by ECH groups in cities where electricity was available.

Some expeditioners labored high up in indigenous villages such as Patacancha, which sits atop a 13,000-foot-high mountain in the Urubamba region. On one of my trips there, we helped build large greenhouses by constructing walls of adobe bricks and rocks, and erecting frames on top that we covered with clear plastic. Because of the high-altitude cold, the local growing season was a mere two months annually, and these greenhouses effectively doubled that, allowing the residents to grow many more crops, such as potatoes and corn—crops that were critical staples for their diet.

During that trip we also helped finish the building of a women's center high up in Patacancha where female villagers could gather to visit, sew their crafts, and discuss their children. After ECH completed the building, the people asked what they should name it. My student and ECH cofounder, Jaime Figueiroa, said they should name it for "their great ancestor, Moroni." Not knowing anything about that great Book of Mormon general, Jaime explained how Peruvians were descendants of Moroni, a general and a magnificent prophet of God. Over subsequent years, the villagers have been taught about Moroni and the fact that he returned to earth from heaven as a glorious, shining angel bearing the ancient records of Peru's ancient people. The villagers quickly agreed, and a plaque is still affixed above the center's door.

ECH sought to dedicate significant programs and services to oppressed people, and to women in particular, who were often ignored or exploited in the Peruvian male-centered society. The following programs were created and established primarily for Andean women: holistic programs for female clients, health exams, psychological testing, ongoing healthcare services, village construction of schools or additional classrooms, continual business training for women, one-on-one business consulting, monthly women's clinics where females could meet and share ideas with other entrepreneurial female clients without the heavy influence of males—in other words, without the overbearing cultural factors of *machismo* or *chovinismo masculino*.

For nearly two decades, Eagle Condor engaged in multiple efforts to assist and empower the people of the Andes region in South America. In the next several paragraphs I summarize a typical 12-month period of humanitarian efforts (ECH, 2014). Its team established collaborative partnerships with expert organizations including the Innovasis Foundation, Interweave Solutions, Northern Star, AMS Credit Card Processing, and Piura's regional government. It recruited and trained South American students working on higher educational pursuits. It organized holiday parties for over 200 children in Peru, Ecuador, and Colombia. Some 144 U.S. youth expedition participants enjoyed "Away Experiences" for youth in preparation for college and life.

Five family and professional expeditions to volunteer in Peru involved 100 participants who provided dental care to rural communities, built greenhouses, and refurbished schools and community centers. Self-Reliant Training classes were conducted in Piura and at Iquitos Peru Medical. Dental work was offered to hundreds of adults and children who had never been to a dental office. Another medical organization has sponsored 23 medical expeditions to Peru since 2006, completing over 174 surgeries. In Colombia, ECH volunteers worked with over 320 displaced and refugee children, providing food, education, and career-building opportunities. In 2014 ECH completed construction of multiple youth shelters throughout the Andes region. Water projects were carried out for the Uris and Youth Center in Ecuador, as well as in Otavalo and Galapagos, Guayacana and Iltaqui. Staff and volunteers have delivered humanitarian donations to numerous local primary schools and rural communities.

Each year ECH constructs several preschools, along with the occasional middle school. Annually, ECH also renovates schools needing plumbing and electrical systems, such as ones in Cajamarca. On occasion, services were rendered including such activities as 50 to 70 children being fed and mentored. Multiple interns worked one-on-one with poor families and their kids. Interns and partners such as Northern Star Peru in the Sacred Valley near Cusco continued to offer successful rocket-stove initiatives for local communities. Youth facility centers were built that provided nutrition programs in indigenous villages like Ocutuan.

These examples illustrate some of ECH's nonfinancial humanitarian ventures over the decades. Such services were also integrated with microenterprise strategies for economic development and job creation, thus becoming the way forward.

The brief list below suggests the range of support ECH has provided over the years:

- Microfinance
- Microfranchise
- Self-help lending groups
- Literacy
- Square foot/small-scale gardening
- Women's leadership training
- Producer cooperatives
- New technologies
- Healthcare innovations

With this summary of the range of ECH ventures, I turn to more detail about microeconomic strategies in particular.

Peruvian Economics and the Rise of Microfinance

Poverty has always been a critical issue in Andean cities, and is even more of a problem throughout the region's thousands of rural

villages. The paragraphs that follow capture some of the historic and sociopolitical realities that Latter-day Saints who are considering starting their own humanitarian organizations should know, because when we established ECH, we were not fully aware of Peru's complex traditions. Historically speaking, from the 16th through the 18th centuries, Spain's imperialism was in complete control. Exploitation by the Spanish conquistadores, and extraction of the rich deposits of valuable minerals, dominated much of society. Extracting everything of value by enslaving indigenous people offered all necessary labor needed to rob the area. Some researchers argue that the region never recovered from the confiscation of property, terrible oppression, and the degree of abusive slave labor that enabled Europeans to take complete control.

All of that was intertwined with an emerging psychology that made Peruvians and their indigenous neighbors feel like underdogs who were "worthless," were doomed to be passive, and had few opportunities to achieve a better future. Hardships and deprivation were the only constants in life. The dominant Christian religion of the Spaniards reinforced such values by convincing the native people that they must suffer while on earth, but would have a better future when rising into heaven after their deaths. There was to be no well-being, no "peace of mind" during mortality's hardships. These conditions constantly reinforced such a culture, as analyzed by the research and writings of the great sociologist Max Weber (1904), in his classic volume, *The Protestant Ethic and the Spirit of Capitalism.*

Making matters worse in Peru, or perhaps in conjunction with its cultural values, were structural problems that maintained high rates of poverty throughout history, and that exist still today: the oppression of women and the fear that accompanies it, rural regions that lack electric power, inadequate schools and high rates of illiteracy, government corruption and conflicting political parties with frequent coup attempts, lack of essential public services such as roads and a national transportation system, widespread vulnerability of peasants, and insecure rights to land, forests, and water. On this latter point, a convincing argument regarding Peruvian poverty is made in a best-selling book by the Peruvian economist Hernando de Soto (1989) on the informal economy and the critical importance of business and property rights. De Soto's *The Other Path*, as opposed to what was called the "Shining Path" guerrilla movement of the 1980s, decried Peru's impoverishment by phenomena he referred to in a later book as "dead capital" (*The Mystery of Capital: Why Capitalism Triumphs in the West and Fails Everywhere Else*). Until the country's informal economy becomes formalized so that the poor have land titles and other legal property rights, he argued, Peru will remain an impoverished country.

All these realities of Peruvian poverty were primary motivations driving Eagle Condor's founding, owing to its emphasis on microfinance. Over decades, the nation suffered through sky-high inflation of up to 7,600 percent annually! At some points, Peru's GDP dropped by 20 percent, and more than 55 percent of the people were living below the official (and already low) poverty line.

Since the mid-2000s, however, signs of improvement have trended better, including less inflation and higher exports (Parodi, 2000). Through much of the last two decades, however, the abysmal incomes of those under the poverty rate were around $5.50 per day, a meager amount (World Bank, 2021). Certainly, the poor in Peru have continued to struggle over the years (CIA, 2019; Cespedes and Taj, 2018). Latter-day Saints native to and living in Peru are no exception. In fact, anecdotal evidence suggests that our Church members may be worse off than the typical Peruvian family, having less education, poorer housing, greater hunger, and fewer jobs.

Therefore, when we launched Eagle Condor, our goal was to provide "financial inclusion" for the poorest, and back then we concluded that microfinance was the primary tool to do so. Why? Because it provided economic empowerment to Peru's have-nots—the millions of "Unbankables," as they were called. Soon, more-formal approaches to microloans by other groups also began to ramp up. These were not only nonprofit organizations or NGOs like Pro Mujer, Acción, and FINCA International, but major banks, as well. The latter include powerful financial institutions—the "Big Boys" as I call them—like Banco del Trabajo, BBVA Continental, and Banco de Credito del Peru. These huge corporations developed an interest in microfinance in recent times because they saw potential growth and large profits from finally beginning to offer services to extremely poor Peruvians who had long been ignored. Yet the tiny family-firms of poor people made up some 98 percent of the total number of Peruvian businesses, or approximately 3.2 million microenterprises. They generated 77 percent of all employment and accounted for 42 percent of GDP (Moran, 2011). Thus, large banks were eventually attracted to new markets of the disenfranchised.

One of these entities was Mibanco, a Peruvian MFI that deserves a bit of explanation because of its agenda and importance in Peru. Mibanco (began operations in Lima in 1998, based on the experience of an early NGO, named Acción Comunitaria del Peru—a nonprofit civil association with four decades of experience in the microlending and small-business sector. An article in its house organ, *Acción*, highlights Mibanco's origins as it grew from an NGO into a Peruvian MFI powerhouse:

> In 1996, in response to the growing microenterprise sector, President Alberto Fujimori challenged Peru's financial sector to establish a regulated, commercial bank for the poor. A clear leader in microfinance at the time, nonprofit Acción Comunitaria del Perú (ACP) was the logical institution to take on the role. Therefore, in May 1998, with the technical support of Acción International, and both private and nonprofit investors, ACP transformed from a nongovernmental organization to a commercial bank, Mibanco. Today, ACP continues to operate as a nonprofit organization, offering training and rural credit while Mibanco provides its clients with savings and a range of credit products, including working capital, housing, and consumer loans. One of the largest MFIs in Latin America, Mibanco serves 99,121 active borrowers with an active loan portfolio of US$92.3 million. Mibanco is headquartered in Lima, with 28 branch offices in Lima and the nearby port city of Callao, Chincha, Huancayo, and the northern coastal city of Chiclayo. Mibanco is widely considered one of the most successful examples of a commercial MFI in Latin America (Mibanco, 2003, p. 1).

While this summation seems somewhat accurate, numerous critics have attacked Mibanco for its spin-off from ACP in a process that made its board members millionaires overnight. Both Muhammad Yunus and I voiced a number of complaints, as did other scholars, in decrying the fact that these bankers became extremely wealthy while seeming to tackle the ugly reality of poverty among Peru's poorest people.

Eagle Condor's Microenterprise Program

In each of the past 15 years or so, ECH served an average of 150 microenterprise clients who received business training. Upon graduating they qualified for microloans for small-scale enterprise start-ups that provide greater stability for their communities. Ongoing new self-reliance classes were established, as ECH managers continued mentoring and working with participants to create solid, self-reliant business for families. As an illustration, in 2014, among adults who went through microenterprise training earlier, some 73 percent were continuing to operate 18 months afterward. Poor family incomes had averaged the U.S. dollar equivalent of only $146 monthly before starting microenterprises. But they had grown by 32 percent a year later, up to an average of $216 per month. Perhaps more important, these families learned new principles of money management, including the need for personal savings. Thus, families grew their monthly savings from a mere $46 to a new high of $88 per family, a 46 percent jump—results that, while small in terms of the numbers of people served, help promise them a better future.

As such changes occurred, Eagle Condor continued its efforts to foster jobs among the poor by offering workshops and mentoring to clients, along with microloans. Below is a summary of typical EHC microentrepreneurial training, using a range of workshops to foster economic development through small-business creation:

Eagle Condor Peru Training
- Workshop 1a: Business idea generation and evaluation (9 hours)
- Workshop 1b: Strategies to help a microbusiness grow (6 hours)
- Workshop 2: How to design a business plan (9 hours)
- Consulting: Work with participants to elaborate viable business plans (one day per week for 5 weeks)
- Workshop 3: How to obtain funding to implement a business plan (6 hours)

- Workshop 4: Small business ongoing management (32 hours)
- Workshop 5: New and existing small-businesses start-up and launch (15 hours)

Over the years, ECH recruited and trained potential Peruvian staffers to operate its various programs on the ground. As directed by its U.S. board, I myself mobilized some of my BYU university students as research interns who traveled to Peru and worked with the local ECH staff, helping to run their offices, assist in training sessions to offer mentoring skills to clients, and do much more. They also conducted research to track and evaluate program efforts. All were fluent Spanish speakers and had lived for a year or two throughout Latin America.

Below are several Eagle Condor examples of data and analyses from U.S. student evaluators. Table 4 shows the early start-up phases of ECH that demonstrated its humble beginnings in several communities (ECH Report, 2006; Tello, 2005).

ECH Microfinance Features

At its beginning in 2002, Eagle Condor Humanitarian's microcredit program was viewed as unusual. Like many of the regulated MFIs in Peru, but *unlike* other NGO MFIs, group lending and village banking processes were not used by ECH. The original selection of clients back then also did not follow the industry norms of typical MFIs. At the start of ECH programs, a large pool of potential clients was selected based on people's needs and interests. Unlike many microcredit programs that favor female clients, ECH's allocation of funds was not based on gender, and strict emphasis on the poorest of the poor was not followed, as more successful candidates were viewed as agents for job growth as well. By 2004, potential microloan clients were invited to multiple hours of training from ECH personnel regarding business idea formation, business planning, marketing, and basic accounting. These training sessions were free, and represented no obligation to the participants (Rawhouser and Woodworth, 2006).

Those who attended the required training were next eligible to present a business plan, and then they could make a proposal for a loan in order to perhaps receive start-up capital. The ECH Andes board in Chiclayo, which was composed of community members with relevant business experience, reviewed the merits of each application. If rejected, instructions were given for how to improve the proposal. Many times when accepted, the loan amount requested was modified according to the judgment of the board. ECH offered two basic loan types. Participants who did

Table 4: Summary of Early Typical Eagle Condor Reports from a Typical Peruvian City (*continued on next page*)

I. 2004 Goals and Outcomes

Goals	Microenterprise Incubation Program	Microenterprise Development Program
Goal:	Support 10 participants	Support 10 participants
Indicator:	10 new businesses operating by the end of the first year	10 existing businesses experience income and asset growth

Outcomes (from 2004 Annual Report)

Training:	24 participants received basic entrepreneurial training	20 participants received basic entrepreneurial training
Mentoring:	16 participants received assistance to elaborate their businesses plans	14 participants received assistance to elaborate their businesses plans
Indicators:	10 new businesses were operating, having received a total loan amount of US$7,350 for start-up	12 existing businesses started to grow in income and assets, having received a total loan amount of US$7,300 for expansion

Table 4: Summary of Early Typical Eagle Condor Reports from a Typical Peruvian City (*continued*)

II. 2005 Goals and Outcomes

Goals	Microenterprise Incubation Program	Microenterprise Development Program
Goal:	Support at least 25 new participants	Support at least 15 new participants
Indicator:	25 new businesses operating by the end of the second year	15 existing businesses experience income and asset growth

Outcomes (from 2005 First Quarter Report)

Training:	• 190 participants attended Workshop 1: Business ideas generation and evaluation (9 hours) • 130 participants attended Workshop 2: How to elaborate a business plan (9 hours)	• 12 participants attended Workshop 1: Business ideas generation and evaluation (9 hours) • 27 participants attended Workshop 2: How to elaborate a business plan (9 hours)
Mentoring:	17 participants received assistance to elaborate their businesses plans	14 participants received assistance to elaborate their businesses plans
Indicators:	8 new businesses are operating, having received a total loan amount of US$4,570 for start-up Achievement: 32% of the 2005 goal	5 existing businesses started to grow in income and assets, having received a total loan amount of US$4,020 for expansion Achievement: 33% of the 2005 goal

Table 4: Summary of Early Typical Eagle Condor Reports from a Typical Peruvian City (*continued*)

III. Characteristics of Microenterprise Participants and Types of Microenterprises

Gender	Number	%
Male	19	54.3
Female	16	45.7
Total	35	100.0

Type of Microenterprise		
Fast food	8	22.8
Grocery store	5	14.3
Dressmaking	3	8.6
Wood furniture shop	2	5.7
Other commerce business	3	8.6
Other service businesses	6	17.2
Other industry businesses	8	22.8
Total	35	100.0

Locations of Clients		
Piura	12	34.3
Chiclayo	10	28.6
Sullana	4	11.4
Ferreñafe	4	11.4
Monsefu	2	5.6
Catacaos	1	2.9
Reque	1	2.9
Lambayeque	1	2.9
Total	35	100.0

not have their own businesses were eligible for an initial business incubation loan of up to $1,000, while applicants who currently had an operating small business were eligible for a business development loan of up to $2,000. While a participant was repaying that first loan, she or he could potentially become eligible to receive a parallel loan, according to the needs of the business. At the start of my student Hans Rawhouser's study, 37 loans had been made. On all loans, ECH charged a flat rate of 1.5 percent per month, or 18 percent annually, with no other transaction fees.

Services Provided

With an intensive focus on the success of the clients, ECH was committed to what we called a holistic operational approach. Staff worked assiduously to find participants with exogenous factors in their lives that would likely strengthen the success of their participation in the program. The program required health exams and psychological testing in an effort to predict whether potential participants were sufficiently healthy—physically and emotionally—to operate a business successfully over the years to come. Once the potential participant began, each was given basic preventive healthcare from a staff nurse.

ECH also provided extensive business training and coaching. After clients received their loans, they also received continued one-on-one business coaching, as well the opportunity to attend monthly meetings with other clients to discuss their collective business progression. This aspect of ECH's program thus provided a kind of clinic to foster "continuous improvement," a Japanese management hallmark of best practices used by successful corporations worldwide (Deming, 2000).

Metrics Reported

Many microfinance programs measure effectiveness in terms of payback rate and either operational or financial sustainability. ECH put a greater emphasis on gathering data on the strength of the businesses it was financing. ECH records and reports to stakeholders tracked the gross revenues, net income, net profit margin, net assets, return on assets, and net monthly income increase. This monitoring required further monthly client meetings and limited the load capability of loan officers. In fact, while typical MFIs serve an average of 200 clients per loan officer, ECH usually had only three loan officers who were in charge of fewer current and potential participants, and who went the extra mile to develop their project. ECH's emphasis was heavily weighted in terms of quality, not quantity.

Interest Rates

Eagle Condor Humanitarian wanted to be fair in applying one flat interest rate for all loans. This rate, at 18 percent annual interest, was considerably below the market rate in Peru, which was closer to 36 percent. So this essentially was interest-rate subsidization, and represented a benefit to its clients. The subsidization of the interest rate was coherent with the principles of the ECH organization in which interventions were focused on those individuals who appeared to have the characteristics to ensure their success. However, some of these participants represented higher levels of risk than others. Paradoxically, sometimes those who entailed lesser risk were people who were viewed as really the best and most "deserving" clients, as a staffer argued.

Therefore, so that the "best" clients were not required to subsidize the "riskiest" clients, it made greater sense to simply assess the market risk of each client, and then deduct the flat subsidization provided by ECH. This seemed especially appropriate when the business clients had built credit histories with the Peruvian credit bureau and had successfully repaid previous loans.

Intensive Client Targeting

One of the most interesting issues that ECH debated internally was whether intentionally concentrating a high degree of effort on a small client base was preferable to a more operationally efficient program that affected larger numbers of people. For example, more clients could receive microloans if ECH didn't spend capital on salaries for a nurse, loan officers, and an engineer. Another possibility was for ECH to serve an informational role by directing interested parties to the most appropriate lending institution, including competing NGOs and banks, rather than directly servicing clients. In this way, their impact would be distributed to greater numbers of people.

The Peruvian ECH board determined that the key to deciding the proper level of involvement lay in considering the entire mission of the organization. One key differentiating factor between ECH and other larger microfinance institutions was that donors and volunteers from the United States and Peru wanted to be involved in the solution. In addition to donating money, they wanted to feel that they were working *with* the beneficiaries, perhaps using some of their unique skills (whether in construction, crafts, or business organization) to benefit others. This more-personal interaction made the expedition volunteers more of an integral part of the ECH organization, around which other activities could be structured. Thus, the organization's structure needed to be different from a savings and loan institution or a bank that was primarily interested in increasing profits. Therefore, it was decided that the focus had to be different, and so the approach ought to consider multiple parts of the complex problem of poverty.

Because such interventions needed to be more focused in order to have this type of personal interaction, proper client selection was crucial to the success of the program. In most of the advertisements in the press or on TV or radio for microfinance institutions, a few clients had actually experienced tremendous results as advertised. However, not all clients experienced the same level of impact.

The success of ECH's program grew, in part, from an accurate determination of which clients would likely benefit the most. ECH also required character references from each client's neighbors, or from a church or other nonprofit organization in their community. This helped to decrease substantially the level of information asymmetry between clients and the organization. Potential participants were also required to attend significant amounts of training before receiving loans, which helped to reveal the level of seriousness of the client. Based on ECH's early, nonperforming clients, the staff found that physical and emotional health significantly affected the clients' ability to manage a business. So ECH gradually introduced screening processes in order to determine whether business failure due to a client's health problems might become an issue. This was important, and coherent with the focus on a limited pool of participants. However, ECH could see early on that some microentrepreneurs appeared to be prime candidates, but then performed poorly. It was finally determined that certain client characteristics were difficult to measure prior to providing microenterprise loan capital. So the staff ultimately determined that it was not appropriate to devote so much effort to those who had not proven their ability as microcredit clients.

As the "Big Boys"—traditional banks and their ilk—increasingly were entering the Peruvian microfinance market, they brought various services that ECH was not equipped to make, such as larger amounts of capital, more loans for the masses, and a host of additional products. These services ranged from allowing the poor to have bank accounts, letting them obtain credit cards, permitting them to enjoy the benefits of insurance, receive loan guarantees, and more. While I myself was critical of charging high interest rates for microloans, I admitted that these additional benefits from the "Big Boys" were proving helpful in bringing Peruvians, particularly rural people and peasants, into the nation's economy. As large institutions grew, ECH began to seem less relevant. It had neither the financing, scale of operations, person-power, nor clout with the national Peruvian government to excel on a significantly large scale. Today ECH is more of a humanitarian NGO than a true microfinance provider. Overall, the above issues reflect the many questions and challenges of building a microfinance institution that can be successful over the long haul.

Criticisms of Eagle Condor

In summarizing the extensive efforts and successes of Eagle Condor Humanitarian, I must mention that it has experienced various ups and downs through the years. While the successes predominate, as described above, there have been some notable failures. They include a number of board and staff conflicts, as well as intercultural clashes between the leading directors and staffers of the two countries, Peru and the U.S. Some were a result of the "American Way" of doing business being quite distinct from the traditional management cultures of Latin American nations. Nonprofit management often faces the same challenges.

Another difficulty was—and still is—that ECH has had to struggle through not only the typical challenges of a start-up or the ongoing management of a nonprofit in a foreign land, but also doing so during natural disasters, in light of the fact that Peru suffers earthquakes, volcanoes, massive mudslides due to rain and snow storms, and more. Added to these were national political upheavals, terrorism, economic crises, civil conflicts, and tight economic conditions. To varying degrees, these all affected the success of ECH.

An additional major source of economic stress in Eagle Condor's first decade was the so-called Great Global Recession of 2008, in which millions of people around the world lost jobs and salaries. It hammered nations everywhere, including millions of LDS families globally. With declining donations, ECH suffered a great deal. In fact, though it is not unusual for nonprofits to have financial ups and downs, ECH found it especially difficult to maintain an even keel in hard economic times. ECH has also struggled with the devastation of the coronavirus pandemic. It has affected many Peruvians, who got ill or watched loved ones die. From February 2020 until summer 2021 when things picked up again as the pandemic receded in some countries and expanded in others, it wasn't possible for ECH to enjoy the typical levels of financial contributions from previous years because so many people were unemployed, and in some cases had even lost their homes. Even worse was the fate of those falling victim to the devastating illness pandemic (2.2 million Peruvians) or succumbing to it (200,000 as of November 2021) (Worldometers, 2021). Peru takes an astonishing sixth-place ranking in the world for deaths per mllion residents.

There have certainly been other problems at Eagle Condor Humanitarian over its nearly two decades, but in spite of various difficulties, it continues to help the Peruvian people.

Conclusion: Help Them Help Themselves

From its inception in 2003, Eagle Condor became a small but important player in the rolling out of grassroots rural microfinance efforts in Peru, especially among those working independently from the government and outside the nation's large financial sector. Over time, along with a growing number of other institutions, including NGOs initially and larger banks in recent years, Peru has become one of the hottest countries engaged in financial inclusion for the "poorest of the poor." Perhaps the words of Enrique Iglesias (2005, p. 2), president of the Inter-American Development Bank, are a fitting conclusion to this case. In his firm's newsletter, he reflected on the struggles of Latin America's poor and the need for financing them in order to aid "the people with the untapped capacity to create the millions of businesses and millions of jobs we need to overcome poverty. Let's help them help themselves. This type of help isn't charity; it is an investment in dignity."

Thus was the inception and rollout of this "radical" little Peruvian NGO, intended to help the descendants of Father Lehi, his sons Laman and Lemuel, and their descendants now seeking to return to the Savior's fold today and enjoy a better quality of life with more-fulfilled blessings. I've always loved the counsel of George Q. Cannon, an early Church apostle and a First Presidency counselor:

> The leading Elders of this Church, as their talent is used for the benefit of Zion, so must the talent of men who are gifted with business capacity be used in like manner—not for individual benefit alone, not for individual aggrandizement alone, but for the benefit of the whole

people, to uplift the masses, to rescue them from their poverty. That is one of the objects in establishing Zion, and anything short of that, as I have said, is not Zion, it is not the Zion that the Prophets have foreseen, it is not that which God has promised (Cannon, 1882).

References

Brau, J., and Woodworth, W. (2014). Financing for Social Enterprise: Third World Impact Strategies for 'Necessity Entrepreneurs.' *Academy of Management Annual Proceedings* 2014 (1):16605–16605, 10.5465/AMBPP.2014. Accessed October 2, 2020.

Cannon, G. Q. (1882). *Journal of Discourses*. Vol. 23, 281–82.

Caritas. (2020). https://www.caritas.org/where-caritas-work/latin-america/peru/. Accessed November 4, 2020.

Cespedes, T., and Taj, M. (2018). Peru Poverty Rate Rises for First Time in 16 Years: Government. *Reuters*, April 24.

CIA. (2019). *WorldFactbook*:Peru. https://www.cia.gov/library/publications/the-world-factbook/geos/ml.html. Accessed April 3, 2020.

Daley-Harris, S. (2003). *State of the Microcredit Summit Campaign Report 2003*. http://www.microcreditsummit.org/pubs/reports/socr/2003/SOCR03-E[txt].pdf. Accessed November 28, 2019.

de Soto, H. (1989). *The Other Path: The Invisible Revolution in the Third World*. Harper and Row.

Deming, W. E. (2000). *The New Economics: For Industry, Government, Education*. MIT Press.

Eagle Condor Humanitarian. (2003–2017). Internal documents including board minutes, staff notes, emails, and more (unpublished materials).

Eagle Condor Prophecy. (2016). https://www.eaglecondor.org/what-we-do. Accessed September 9, 2020.

ECH. (2014). *Annual Report*. https://irp-cdn.multiscreensite.com/62d1fe59/files/uploaded/ECH-2014-Annual-Report-PROOF.pdf. Accessed March 2, 2021.

ECH Report. (2006). Unpublished microfinance evaluation.

Hatch, J. K. (2002). *Innovations from the Field* (ed., Sam Daley-Harris). Kumarian Press.

Iglesias, E. V. (2005). Intel was once a start-up: Why Latin America's microentrepreneurs deserve more attention—and assistance. *IDB America*, p. 2, September 2005.

International Labour Organization. (2006). "Peru: Economia." http://www.oitandina.org.pe/pagina.php?secCodigo=55. Accessed February 27, 2021.

Jansson, T. (2001). Chapter 8 of the Economic and Social Progress in Latin America—2001 Report. Digital version retrieved March 29, 2021, from http://www.iadb.org/publications/index.

Marriott School, BYU. (2021). https://marriottschool.byu.edu/. Accessed February 12.

Mibanco. (2003). Poverty Outreach Findings. In *Insight*, a U.S. publication of Acción, no. 5, 1, May.

Moran, M. R. (2011). Microfinance in Peru: Key Findings and Perspectives. *Profinanzas*. http://mddb.apec.org/Documents/2011/GFPN/WKSP1/11_gfpn_wksp1_010.pdf. Accessed December 19, 2020.

Nogueira, S., Duarte, F., and Gama, A. P. (2020): Microfinance: Where are we and where are we going? *Development in Practice*. doi: 10.1080/09614524.2020.1782844. Accessed June 25, 2020.

Otero, M. (1999). Bringing development back into microfinance. *Journal of Microfinance*. Vol. 1, no. 1, Fall, 1999.

Parodi, C. (2000). *Peru: 1960–2000*. CIUP.

Prahalad, C. K. (2006). *The Fortune at the Bottom of the Pyramid: Eradicating Poverty Through Profits*. Pearson Education.

Rawhouser, H., and Woodworth, W. (2006). Microfinance Innovation and Standardization in Peru. Western Social Science Association Conference paper, Phoenix, Arizona, April 19–22.

Snow, L. (1878). *Journal of Discourses*. Vol. 19.

Tello, O. (2005). Mini case of Peruvian client, Jaro (unpublished).

Weber, M. (1904). *The Protestant Ethic and the Spirit of Capitalism*. Dover Publications.

Whyte, W. F. (1982). Social inventions for solving human problems. *American Sociological Review*, vol. 47, no. 1, 1–13.

Woodworth, W. (1995). Restoring All Things: The Managerial and Economic Views of Early Mormon Leaders. *Brigham Young Magazine*, November, 35–41.

World Bank. (2021). Peru. https://www.worldbank.org/en/country/peru/overview. Accessed February 26, 2021.

Worldometers. (2021). Coronavirus Statistics Today. https://www.worldometers.info/coronavirus/. Accessed November 5.

Yunus, M. (2010). *Building Social Business: The New Kind of Capitalism That Serves Humanity's Most Pressing Needs.* Public Affairs.

"Lord, I Would Follow Thee"
LDS Hymns, No. 220

1. Savior, may I learn to love thee,
   Walk the path that thou hast shown,
   Pause to help and lift another,
   Finding strength beyond my own.
   Savior, may I learn to love thee—
   Lord, I would follow thee.

2. Who am I to judge another
   When I walk imperfectly?
   In the quiet heart is hidden
   Sorrow that the eye can't see.
   Who am I to judge another?
   Lord, I would follow thee.

3. I would be my brother's keeper;
   I would learn the healer's art.
   To the wounded and the weary
   I would show a gentle heart.
   I would be my brother's keeper—
   Lord, I would follow thee..

4. Savior, may I love my brother
   As I know thou lovest me,
   Find in thee my strength, my beacon,
   For thy servant I would be.
   Savior, may I love my brother—
   Lord, I would follow thee..

Text: Susan Evans McCloud (1945–)
Music: K. Newell Dayley (1939–)

8

Unitus

(1999–2022)

Ever thought of raising a billion dollars for the global poor? Two decades ago I met up with a few wealthy LDS friends and we decided to raise an "insane" amount of money to foster the growth of the microcredit movement. As the idea, originally referred to in the 1980s as *microcredit*, one barrier blocked much of its progress: there simply wasn't sufficient capital for generating the necessary growth to fund poor people's struggles. The first few dozen initiatives were mostly small, underfunded, and limited in terms of managerial competence. Thus, Unitus came into being as a social business to remedy these deficiencies. In 2000, we as a group of LDS friends and colleagues became founders who sought to design a radically visionary approach that would offer a new model for doing microfinance with its investment partners. We ultimately raised a grand total of $1.2 billion, partnering and providing loan capital to various nongovernmental organizations in 23 countries, and benefiting many millions of people. However, in 2010 Unitus shifted strategically and morphed into several other organizations throughout the next decade, up until the present. This chapter analyzes the origins, systems, and strategies we employed in achieving such results, as well as delineates some of the challenges, difficulties, and problems we faced as of 2020.

▲ Impoverished peasant women in Kenya where Unitus began

▼ Microentrepreneurs with their family dairy enterprise in India where Unitus has channeled over $300 million to empower poor families

When we first began talking about doing this, we had many discussions based on a volume I had recently coauthored, titled *Working Toward Zion: Principles of the United Order for the Modern World* (Lucas and Woodworth, 1996). According to some experts, I had offered the most comprehensive history of early Mormonism's communalism, its amazing success in building equality in Zion, the various factors that made it work, and its potential applications for our own lives today. It was read and praised by leading Brethren of the Church, including several apostles, and it featured a forward by the scholar Hugh Nibley as well as recommendations by eminent historians like Richard Bushman of Columbia University. The volume led to considerable media coverage, presentations at LDS and academic conferences, and more.

The book's core concepts were practical gospel values, such as the integration of the spiritual and the temporal, the dignity of work, consecration, self-reliance, having decent jobs, stewardship, and more. Among the hundreds of quotations we included from prophets of the past and present was this from President Spencer W. Kimball: "We are stewards over our bodies, minds, families, and properties.... A faithful steward is one who exercises righteous dominion, cares for his own, and looks to the poor and needy" (Kimball, 1977). Another favorite of mine is the declaration by the Lord that we are stewards for those in need—words that prophets have uttered that contain some of the strongest language in scripture: "if any man shall take of the abundance which I have made, and impart not his portion ... unto the poor and the needy, he shall, with the wicked, lift up his eyes in hell, being in torment" *(Doctrine and Covenants:* 104:118). These, along with numerous other admonitions, motivated my friends and colleagues to consider ways that we might reduce poverty and build up Zion. This chapter, then, tells the powerful story of what we did, how we accomplished it, and what the worldwide impacts of our efforts were that helped provide microloans and jobs for literally more than 20 million struggling people in dozens of nations.

Introduction: The Need for Financing the Poor

I will begin with an exploration of why the "poverty problem" throughout human history has been so immense. The world's working poor suffer greatly from a lack of income, and many millions, even in 2021, will never find jobs in the formal economies of business and government. Instead, they must try to make do in the informal, or underground, economy where they eke out an existence as rural farmers or street vendors producing goods to sell so as to feed themselves and their families. To state the obvious, such individuals will never go to an office job in a business building, get a paycheck, have a pension for retirement, enjoy benefits like healthcare and vacations, or receive a promotion. Instead, they have to create their own jobs while facing considerable opposition, never having things like paid leave, retirement benefits, or job security. This is the reality for hundreds of millions of people who work 10 to 15 hours to feed their children only one or twice a day.

So, one wonders: what prevents them from succeeding? A primary factor is the lack of capital with which to create or expand business opportunities. Furthermore, there has been growing global momentum to strengthen and scale-up economic inclusion for the poorest people, as advocated by the United Nations' Sustainable Development Goals (SDGs), which seek to "end poverty in all its forms everywhere by 2030." Its Eighth Goal spells out the importance of "inclusive and sustainable growth" (United Nations, 2015). Such a proposition is a far cry from human history in which the have-nots were largely ignored, constantly faced survival challenges, and typically died fairly young.

Despite greater efforts that a few countries made to help the poor in recent years, the challenges of striving to reduce human suffering and poverty were brutally confronted with staggering difficulties beginning in March 2020, as COVID-19 began to infect people worldwide (some 250 million having falling ill by November 2021) and depressed more than a hundred countries' economies. By 2030, if "business-as-usual" thinking continues to dominate economic strategies, an estimated 479 million people will be trapped in the ugly realities of extreme poverty. The coronavirus devastation may thrust more than 80 million into worse poverty than they have ever faced (CGAP, 2021). That possibility may make microfinance and other services for the poor more critical than ever.

For decades, we have debated the best ways to reduce extreme poverty. There are no shortages of strategies proposed by large-scale organizations such as the World Bank; the International Monetary Fund (IMF); the United Nations (UN) and its many agencies; the United Kingdom's Foreign, Commonwealth, and Development Office; the United States Agency for International Development (USAID); the Overseas Development Institute (ODI); and hundreds of smaller organizations. Yet numerous critics of such institutions and their programs, often backed by extensive research, have opined and decried such efforts over decades (Easterly, 2006; IMF and World Bank, 2010; OECD, 2005; UNDP, 2019).

This chapter draws on my action research efforts to identify and mobilize a few wealthy Mormons to create a new NGO called Unitus, which we termed a social business because it recruited professional associates to launch a remarkable strategy for fighting extreme poverty and hunger, beginning in 2000. In defining the Unitus organization, we chose to associate it with Muhammad Yunus's (2009) views, although he had not yet published a definition. Basically, to the fledgling Unitus this meant creating an organization that would be entrepreneurial in solving social problems but would not simply be a charity. Rather, it would adopt a business management approach that would be financially viable yet would result in a nonprofit entity that reinvests surpluses into its operations. In the vernacular of business, it would be a nondividend, non-loss firm whose economic resources would be dedicated to building social impacts rather than generating profits. Capital for operations would be important so that the entity could become operational and remain sustainable. But becoming rich was not the goal. Instead, our goal would be to provide pro-poor services and seek to do good in the world.

As it evolved, Unitus's energy and funding shifted away from helping our own church members and was channeled to non-LDS individuals, including Catholics, Muslims, Hindus, Protestants, Buddhists, and those of other spiritual traditions. The reasons for this are beyond the scope of this book. But suffice it to say that our original group of founders included dedicated LDS Church leaders; current, past, and future bishops; mission presidents; area and General Authority Seventy; as well as ward and stake leaders from across the U.S. Early on we established various programs to grow the amount of good we could muster.

In October 2000, we organized what I perhaps bravely called the first and only LDS Economics Conference in history. It mobilized "movers and shakers" from across the nation to a huge event at the Joseph Smith Memorial Building in Salt Lake City. It was a day when 562 such people seeking to help LDS members globally learned about modern United Order innovations. We invited a series of top-rated speakers to provide gospel insights about self-reliance and empowering the poor. In numerous breakout sessions, attendees talked about microfinance, worker-owned cooperatives, and nongovernmental organizations. Other topics and themes taught how virtually every LDS family could serve and empower the poor through microcredit and organize their own local Unitus Action Groups with friends and relatives to learn about and apply microfinance and other innovations that would bless fellow saints everywhere, especially in terrible economies where there were few jobs and opportunities. In these groups, friends and relatives would meet in people's homes, learn about microcredit, and explore how it can be applied to reduce human suffering. We hoped that group members would pool whatever financial contributions their little organization could make and donate it to microfinance institutions (MFIs) of their choosing. It was an informal idea, but we hoped it would succeed. Unfortunately, it had meager results. Several of these groups were established throughout the state of Utah. Perhaps the most successful was established by folks in California, in the city of Elk Grove, south of Sacramento (which was named for the Holy Sacrament), where friends and neighbors pooled resources and joined my expedition to expand microfinance in Guatemala for a week. But unfortunately, most of the Unitus board of trustees didn't venture forward on this agenda item with their own associates.

I arranged for President Gordon B. Hinckley to attend and speak at the fall 2000 economic conference. As my wife and I sat with him at the banquet table for the luncheon before he spoke, he was extremely encouraging, expressing happiness that we sought to assist the Church in building Zion—taking initiatives that the big bureaucracy itself would have difficulty taking. That was because, among other things, we were entrepreneurial, able to take risks, and learned quickly what worked best, and we were generating our own funding, never seeking a dollar from Church headquarters.

I presented our dear prophet with a new award we established: the "Humanitarian of the Millennium Award," as well as an early 1841 copy of the Book of Mormon. The prophet spoke powerfully in support of efforts to aid those who suffer: "My heart has ached in a way that I don't know how to express it," he said, "as I've seen those people in Brazil and all throughout South America in those little paper shacks." With poverty "goes ignorance and a lack of education. Without [education] those people cannot be lifted. I'm so grateful for the microcredit loans you [Unitus] have been making and encouraging to be made. It seems almost impossible that a few paltry dollars can span the difference between walking in the mud throughout one's days or getting started in some little business that will grow and lead to a decent living and the means with which to do what the Lord would have us do." President Hinckley went on to say, "I can't believe our Father in Heaven enjoys seeing his sons and daughters walking in poverty. I think he would be pleased if they all prospered and lived well enough to live properly and decently." He declared that God is truly pleased when people accumulate wealth "when those means are used to bless the needy of the Earth" (Moore, 2000 in the *Deseret News*).

Afterward, he and Sister Hinckley signed a large calfskin we had designed for hundreds of the attendees to autograph as a commitment. Instead of the old "Title of Liberty" raised by Moroni, in the Book of Mormon, ours announced a new banner, the "Title of Unity," in the hopes that we could help church members become more united, more committed, and more faithful in combating extreme poverty and improving the number of jobs and incomes of the saints worldwide. Our Unitus vision was to uplift God's saints who struggled everywhere and to help them enjoy lives of great faithfulness and well-being.

Another of our early innovations at Unitus was to establish a United Order type program, called the PRINCE Cooperative of LDS members in Kenya, after the mission president asked us to help the few struggling church members there who had converted. Our research efforts took me and other Unitus board members to Nairobi to survey families in the main branches of the church there. It revealed that the unemployment or underemployment rate was above 70 percent (Unitus Survey, 1999). The church had only been organized in Kenya for 10 years or so, but there had been no improvement in that statistic. Most East African LDS individuals subsisted on less than a dollar per day. So we organized a series of member informational meetings to explore ways we could be of assistance in helping them create a Latter-day Saint Zion, with jobs and better living conditions for the members, supported by the district presidency at the time.

With those depressing numbers, the Unitus board began discussing with the Nairobi saints ways that we might establish a workers cooperative to employ some members who lacked educations and jobs. We shared with them examples from our LDS heritage of cooperative economic strategies. We told them of Lorenzo Snow and Brigham Young. Little by little, the idea took hold. Hope increased. A spirit of cooperation and trust grew.

We sent a Kenyan MBA student at BYU to be our intern and conduct training sessions with over 200 Nairobi saints. Members of the new little cooperative studied business practices and learned how to develop an effective business plan. They practiced assessing various business opportunities and began thinking like investors. They gradually developed rough business plans, and more than a hundred met with me and another board member to hammer out bylaws and select the first business they would start. They elected a Managing Committee and formed a cooperative. Eventually, they collected capital contributions from about a hundred members, who each invested small funds to demonstrate their commitment. Unitus in the U.S. provided background information and additional financing for the project. On July 24, 1999, which happened to be Utah's Pioneer Day, the PRINCE Multipurpose Cooperative Society of Kenya, Ltd., was inaugurated as the first-known United Order-like cooperative by African Latter-day Saint pioneers. It was named PRINCE, a reflection of the values the cooperators adopted: *P*urity, *R*esponsibility, *IN*itiative, *C*ooperation/*C*harity, and *E*quality. The co-op name PRINCE also symbolized Christ, the *Prince* of Peace.

The Kenyan cooperators agreed to start a bakery business first. It would pay well enough to get workers out of the slum and yet was not so complex that they could not operate it with their existing skills and experience. However, the large group of members had to raise some starting capital to join, with the expectation of gaining membership with their righteous LDS friends. The cooperative successfully launched, with Unitus providing a large loan to supplement the financial resources available at the start. The group remembered our training and the Mormon pioneer history of building United Order systems throughout the American West. Brigham Young saw the early saints' development as having more spiritual than economic purposes. In 1869 he preached that "This cooperative movement is only a stepping stone to what is called the Order of Enoch, but which is in reality the order of Heaven" (Young, 1997, p. 326).

After a year or more of success in creating a hundred new and decent jobs for the Kenyan saints and pointing to a promising future, the project unfortunately came to an end. The reasons for the demise included co-op conflicts, some members not being productive, a decline in bakery orders by several Nairobi markets, complaints to the Church's Area Presidency in South Africa, unauthorized use of the PRINCE delivery van, and more. The decision to dismantle the program was painful for many members

However, we would continue to use the hundreds of thousands of dollars we had raised for Honduras, the Philippines, and elsewhere in promising ways. We simply turned our energy to serving the larger world, not just Latter-day Saints. Those of us involved in Unitus in Kenya jokingly made a vow to raise more money for development and humanitarian efforts than the entire church was doing. To our astonishment, within a decade, we did exactly that, ultimately generating over $1.2 billion, mostly for microfinance, benefiting more than 20 million impoverished people in 27 nations! That was truly awesome.

What Unitus Accomplished After Kenya

Regardless of Unitus's challenges in Africa, the board trekked forward. So this chapter draws from my personal experience, having spent some 40 years engaged in microfinance strategies that I often called "barefoot banking" in the informal economy, social business, or social entrepreneurship (Woodworth, 1997). With respect to Unitus, I have assembled this chapter from information such as journal notes, field trips, Unitus internal documents, speeches, slide presentations, board minutes, news coverage, and interviews with staff, board, and clients, among other resources spanning more than a decade. Admittedly, this chapter outlines only a few key efforts, but it suggests a rather complete narrative woven with one's eyes wide open. It concludes with some honest criticisms and an update from 2017–2020, after Unitus split into several different pursuits that continued to provide poverty-alleviation strategies and programs.

Unitus embraced microfinance as the new movement emerged globally as a promising strategy to remedy the problems of unemployment, hunger, lack of savings or access to healthcare, and, worst of all, extreme poverty. At the time Unitus was launched in 1999–2000, most of the world's population was trying to live on less than $2 per day. Only several million people around the world had access to any of these new microfinance services. Hence, Unitus was born to address this scarcity.

How Unitus began
The organization emerged from discussions I was having with several associates who had read my book and began wondering how they could perhaps get involved in my "crazy new idea" of microcredit, as one colleague put it. I was becoming known as a social entrepreneur and also a management professor in the Marriott School of Business at Brigham Young University in Utah. Along with a New York attorney, James Lucas, I had published a major LDS book on wealth, poverty, consecration, and stewardship, which we titled *Working Toward Zion: Principles of the United Order for the Modern World* (Lucas and Woodworth, 1996). Those seeking to know more about our book and my various ventures were typically wealthy associates—executives in large technology firms and investment companies living on the East or West Coasts. Others were corporate consultants or Utah entrepreneurs. After months of private, one-on-one dialogue, I proposed that instead of having separate, individual discussions, we start meeting as a group to explore how we might collectively merge our business and professional skills in beginning to practice some kind of microentrepreneurial outreach efforts as successful Latter-day Saints. From that start-up, we chose the name "Unitus," drawing on our desire to unite the world in empowering the poor—that is, to *"Unite Us."*

We met regularly. Some in the group flew to Utah and held monthly debates with local participants now and then. Eventually, we determined that it was time to take action, so Unitus was born. It started by pooling some money (several hundred thousand dollars), which we donated to a few nongovernmental organizations affiliated with me, including Humanitarian Link and HELP International. The latter was an organization I had founded to provide microloans in Honduras in 1999 after Hurricane Mitch destroyed much of that country (see chapter 2 herein). As a small NGO, HELP

International was established in my Microfinance course at BYU, and consisted of 70-plus MBAs and undergraduate students. Teams were established, plans were laid, and 46 individuals spent their summer on the scene helping to provide training and microcredit for self-employment among hundreds of impoverished Hondurans whose lives were upended by the destruction. HELP also rebuilt communities wrecked by the flooding. That humble small beginning, aided for a year by Unitus, has since grown to mobilize, train, and send college-age social entrepreneurs to labor in more than 28 nations to date, involving some 3,200 students from Brigham Young University, Stanford, Virginia Tech, Colorado State, University of Utah, Harvard, and many more (Woodworth, 2020).

Finally, in 2000, during its early deliberations, the board of trustees legally established Unitus as an NGO in Utah. The cofounders debated about how to establish a unique social business that would be "audacious," make a great impact, and provide antipoverty capital globally. These debates concluded with a consensus that the group did not want to work with governments or corporations but rather wished to enter the war against poverty from the nonprofit or "third sector." Three of us took materials from sections of my earlier book, *Working Toward Zion*, to draft a new little volume especially for building an LDS powerhouse to serve impoverished church members. It was titled *United for Zion: Principles for Uniting the Saints and Eliminating Poverty* (Woodworth, Grenny, and Manwaring, 2000). But after being rebuffed by the aforementioned church bureaucrats, we didn't pursue its programs, as we felt we must turn to the needs of other populations.

As the first board of trustees' chair, I suggested we travel as a team to Bangladesh when I could perhaps arrange for an opportunity to spend a week there meeting with Dr. Muhammad Yunus to seek his insights about our efforts. This event became critical to all of Unitus's future success, so I will describe it further here. Because I had collaborated with Professor Yunus for several years—both of us speaking at conferences, him addressing some of my courses and university NGO conferences, and our serving on each other's NGO boards—I thought this would be doable. I had long admired his Muslim spiritual traditions, and he often expressed his admiration for my LDS faith and works to serve humanity. Fortunately, he agreed to meet with some of my wealthy American colleagues seeking his wisdom. After we flew to Dhaka in January 2001, he generously agreed to meet with us in the boardroom of his company, Grameen Bank, every morning for a week so we could exchange ideas, pick his brain, and explore what kind of innovation Unitus might carry out. After our morning seminars, we spent the remainder of each day in the offices of that institution's managers, who oversaw departments such as marketing, operations, accounting, human resources, finance, and the like, interviewing them and inspecting their financial records to learn precisely how the bank had become such a powerhouse for poor women. We also visited several of Grameen's field operations to interview women, attended a local women's bank meeting to learn how things operate, and so forth.

By our last day in Dhaka, we had determined to carry out one of Yunus's suggestions that we had hotly debated—that we should not simply become yet another ordinary MFI. Rather, Unitus would seek to be the world's first *Microfinance Accelerator*, focused on helping other NGOs grow their own programs to serve more clients. In other words, rather than having Unitus hire staff, recruit borrowers, give and track loans, train clients, and collect repayments, we would help *others* do these grassroots things. We would raise the money to give or lend them capital so that they could grow and ultimately carry out their own microlending NGO programs. This turned out to be a radical concept that, over the years, has proved highly successful. The objective was to assist small, yet competent MFIs so that they could expand dramatically instead of being limited by a lack of resources when the need was so great. This was an innovative strategy, as our initial research revealed that most MFIs were simply unable to provide the demand for capital required by microentrepreneurs in many nations. In fact, we found that most NGOs that provided microcredit reached their client maximum growth numbers and then plateaued within the first five years. Few

Each 👤 represents 10 million clients

Only 30 million clients (10%) had access to microcredit (👤) out of 300 million potential clients (👤)

Figure 3: Demand for microfinance

were able to grow further, due to lack of capital. The section below offers another way of seeing the problem.

Demand for Microfinance

Our Unitus research estimated the global demand for microcredit to be about 300 million clients, yet only some 30 million clients at the time had access to existing microcredit—a mere 10 percent of the total demand, as shown in Figure 3. So we decided that, since we weren't going to assist Latter-day Saints and the few small NGOs at the time in Utah, we would "go big" in enabling the best small MFIs in the world to grow bigger and better. Perhaps, we thought, we should first generate large amounts of needed capital for the most promising—not the most needy, but those with great potential.

We believed that the unmet demand was approximately 270 million clients, or 90 percent of the total number of people in need. The chief question was: could Unitus become an accelerator to ramp up this new movement in providing capital so that small MFIs could rapidly expand to serve more clients?

Over several months, Unitus thus identified key elements for approaching poverty alleviation needs and opportunities with a

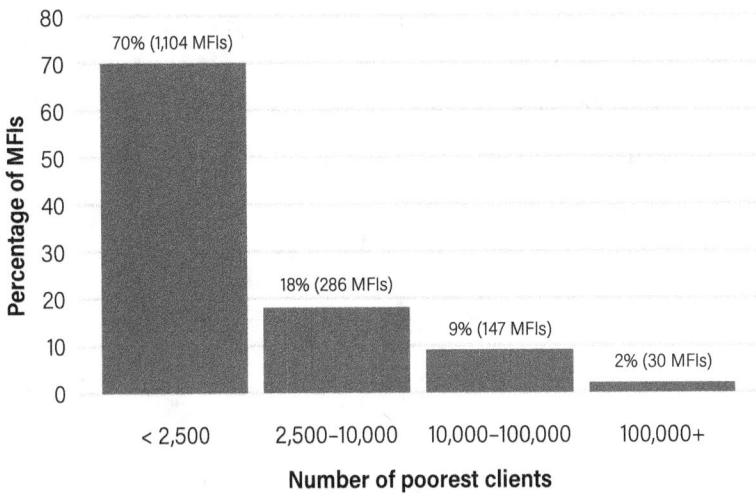

Figure 4: Capital limits to poverty reduction through microcredit

strategic framework of the following elements, making it different from any other organization:

- **Innovate** Seek out an innovative contribution.
- **Invest** Function as an investor and supporter, not an operator.
- **Scale** Pursue opportunities with the potential for impacting millions of working poor families.
- **Take Risk** Take risks to prove the efficacy of our methods and linkages so that others will follow in our tracks.
- **Catalyze** Attract capital markets to areas where the market doesn't exist or is broken.
- **Exit** Stop donor-funded activities when we perceive we've reached (or won't reach) a tipping point.

Figure 4 suggests further details about future possibilities we considered.

Early on, the Unitus board continually asked this question: "Why, if there is such a huge global demand, is there currently so little money available to provide microloans?" The answer came down to two issues.

First was the lack of capital, explained by the following:

- Nonprofits depend on being funded by individuals and grants.
- MFIs are viewed as risky prospects for commercial loans.
- To become profitable, a critical mass must be reached.

Second, MFIs needed better systemic capacities to be successful, including:

- Well-established organizational structures
- Effective management procedures
- Internal controls
- State-of-the-art IT infrastructure
- Innovative product development methodologies

Thus, Unitus began to address these challenges through numerous, intense board meetings and debates. This process took several months but a plan gradually began to take shape. The initial goal was to start out by forming two or three new partnerships each year and then to take the following steps with each one:

- **Phase 1** Identifying potential regions and partners
- **Phase 2** Evaluating and selecting an ideal partner with good systems
- **Phase 3** Structuring the investment
- **Phase 4** Growing the MFI
- **Phase 5** Exiting the investment

The two graphs in Figure 5 depict how Unitus planned to dramatically ramp up the microfinance movement worldwide. They show how its efforts over seven years could change from only

MFI growth with Unitus investment

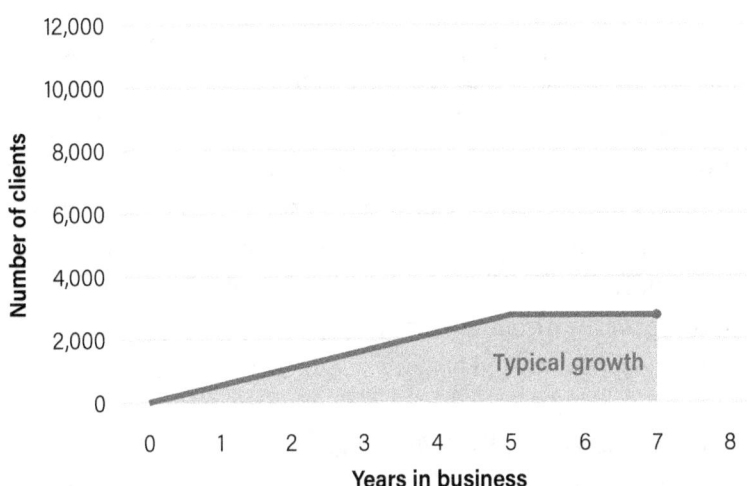

MFI growth with Unitus investment

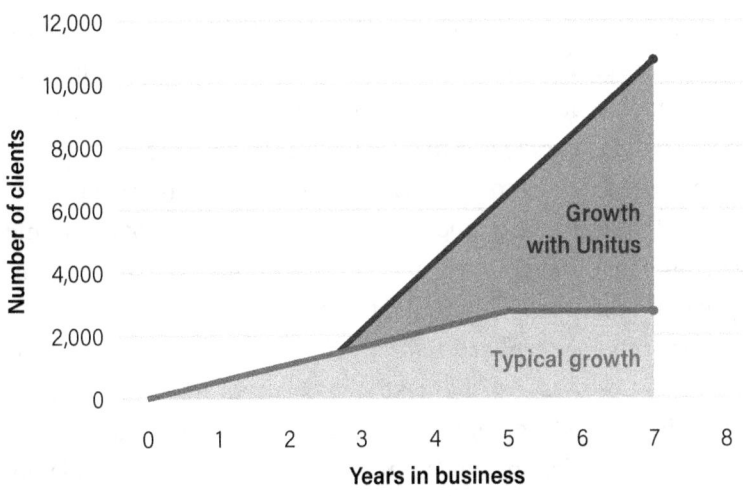

Figure 5: From status quo to Unitus expansion

modest trends (having plateaued at the left) to a significant expansion (at right).

We had been operating Unitus with a few of my BYU graduate students in the Department of Organizational Behavior. But as we began ramping up, it was clear we needed to hire a professional Unitus staff. So experienced professionals were engaged and, under the direction of its board of academics, entrepreneurs, and finance managers, the roll-out ramped up our innovative strategy to build a more rapidly growing, long-term, and sustainable industry to fight extreme poverty. Although our future partners were not Latter-day Saints, the objectives and benefits of each new MFI partner's acceleration were clear.

For *borrowers*, Unitus would foster such things as improved standards of living, increasingly successful microenterprises, enhanced business skills, and strengthened social networks. For *small MFIs* that would begin receiving funding from Unitus so they could begin to grow, the organizational outcomes were to consist of achieving greater scale, operational and financial self-sufficiencies, increased capacities, and access to sustainable funding for the long haul. Benefits could also be foreseen for the *MFI industry* as a whole. Unitus would validate this new systematic growth model; it would lower the risk profile for the formal financial sector (enticing other entities to jump in to support this radical new sector of economic development), and it would also encourage broader participation by major philanthropists around the globe.

Over time, we realized that larger and more dramatic visions would be necessary, so the next step occurred in Mexico. To get the Unitus model implemented, in 2002, we established our own little MFI in Tula, an indigenous region in the state of Hidalgo, Mexico, to experiment with assisting tiny business start-ups. That practical fieldwork gave the team the ability to learn quickly what was successful and how to design and launch a new organization in Latin America. The board reached out to partner with a Peruvian NGO called *Pro Mujer* ("Pro Woman") that was beginning to expand throughout the region. Efforts began to lease facilities, hire and train a small Mexican staff, and then begin to offer training in microlending, savings, and budgeting one's income. Starting from scratch in January 2002, the first loans were issued that April. By December, the Tula MFI had grown to serve some 2,500 clients. Astoundingly, the new MFI enjoyed 100 percent of expected repayments, along with a 99 percent client retention rate! The average loan size for clients was $95. Pro Mujer grew to a total of 10,401 clients within several more years. Altogether, Unitus had invested some $1.87 million U.S. in our first Mexico project. By the end of 2020, the humble beginnings of the Unitus outreach in Tula alone had grown to serve more than 26,000 women.

The Unitus Acceleration Game Plan

In Unitus's first several years of operation, 2000 through 2002, as the new approach began leveraging its Acceleration Model, the highest-potential early-stage MFIs in developing countries were identified by our consulting team. These were then given access to financial support (in the form of loans, capacity-building grants, and catalytic debt guarantees), consulting advice, time-tested business strategies, mission-critical business solutions, technology tools, strategic planning, capital advisory services, social networks, information systems, and human resource capacity building. These multiple resources were intended to increase each MFI's capacity and thus empower it to reach the poor in its own region with microfinance products and services. By utilizing this model, the first of Unitus's MFIs partners began to experience *instant* exponential growth rates greater than 100 percent each year—thus potentially serving millions of the world's poorest people with microcredit loans, savings products, insurance, and other financial products and services.

Many of these relatively small MFIs began doubling their client base each year, soon reaching *eight times* the traditional microfinance industry average. Because of their newfound success, some even started winning industry recognition in their countries for efficient operations, transparency, and lower interest rates for their clients. Thus, Unitus began to demonstrate that MFIs could be profitable, large-scale, one-mission-focused businesses with links to local capital markets, rather than charities. Once linked to capital markets, such MFIs had the resources they needed to offer loans of as little as $100 to the working poor, who then started tiny microenterprises to lift themselves out of poverty. Overall, this was the process by which Unitus established itself as a leading social venture capital investor for the microfinance industry.

Unitus's Rapid Growth Began Reaching Millions of the Poor

In a few short years, Unitus started securing larger donations from individuals as well as from big family foundations, often drawing on relationships between board members and their professional colleagues. A few of these were members of some of Mormonism's wealthiest families. And thanks to some Unitus board members' personal wealth, several million more dollars was obtained. Then, with that success, even-larger contributions came from our friends, including $3 million from the Bill Gates Foundation early on; several million dollars more from Pierre Omidyar, the founder of eBay; additional funding from one of Facebook's founders, Mark Zuckerberg; and donations from Apple cofounder Steve Jobs's family foundation. The Omidyar Network, for example, gave Unitus several one-to-two-million-dollar grants early on. In 2008, it contributed $9 million to be used over the next three years. It was clear that, if Unitus developed a businesslike model for expanding microcredit, considerable potential lay in securing the necessary capital for reaching huge success as a "partner to the poor."

As Unitus revenues grew, the need for more staff became apparent. Previously it had employed several of my graduate business students at Brigham Young University, but it was clear that we needed greater expertise and deeper managerial heft. So we began recruiting executives beyond the LDS Church and Utah. Hiring strategies were developed to find some of the best and brightest candidates with strong track records of corporate management success. These included people who knew how to scale-up organizations, and who also shared the board's values about love and serving the poor, as well as some who were interested in designing innovative strategies to acquire and leverage donations both quickly and coherently.

Beyond the Mexico operation, in early 2002, a new potential partner was identified in India, called SKS Microfinance (Swayam Krishi Sangam), a small MFI located in the state of Andhra Pradesh. Its founder and the Unitus board found common interests: Unitus sought an outstanding partner with high potential for growth and, in turn, SKS required an infusion of capital so that it could enjoy explosive growth while serving poor rural Indians. It appeared to be a good model with a creative approach that was perceived to have high growth potential. Yet it only achieved some 5,000 clients, despite seeming to have much promise. It was well run, was efficient, had good technical systems, and possessed other qualities. Without more funding, however, it could only serve several thousand microentrepreneurs in a nation of more than a billion souls, because it lacked sufficient capital. Instead of a promising future, its limitations were clear.

Thus, beginning with small grants of $50,000 or $100,000, Unitus took some risks and began to spur major new growth at both SKS and other MFIs internationally. One of the Unitus board members also joined the SKS board to provide ongoing technical assistance in mapping future growth plans. Soon, Unitus also evaluated other partners in India for potential success. Large loans were extended to some institutions after they were evaluated and adjudged good candidates, and the number of such loans grew dramatically. In a very short time frame, many thousands of new clients were benefiting from the services of Indian NGOs, assisted by American capital. This had become a genuine win-win arrangement for the poor of India, their local MFIs, and Unitus itself. The initial Unitus support to scale-up SKS also led to significant internal growth. By 2010, it had engaged with 6.8 million impoverished Indian borrowers and held $624 million worth of microloans (Strom and Bajaj,

2010). Eventually, after tripling its capital and client base, as well as for multiple growth reasons, SKS rebranded itself with a new name—Bharat Financial Inclusion Ltd.—and added new services. Since then, it has merged with IndusInd Bank and expanded those numbers even further. By 2020, it had some 19,000 employees, 3,600 offices, and 16 million customers. Not bad growth from humble beginnings in 2002 with a Unitus partnership!

Adding More Unitus Partners

Beyond SKS, Unitus established partnerships with other small MFIs that were well run yet lacked capital for significant client growth. Below are brief highlights of four of the early MFI partners that Unitus began funding as acceleration plans were implemented.

Fondo de Inversion Social (FIS) | Argentina   I had been working on Latin American social entrepreneurship projects in 2008 when I met up with the Argentine founders of FIS. They saw the challenges of over three million people struggling under the national poverty line in the capital of Buenos Aires alone. A mere 2 percent had access to financial services, in part because the economic crisis of the late 1990s had left the nation suffering from a massive currency devaluation and the world's largest debt default. FIS was established in 1999 to provide financial services to the working middle-class and urban poor. Unlike people enduring extreme poverty in Bolivia and Nicaragua, Argentinians lacked microentrepreneurial traditions and had widespread distrust of the financial system. I shared with our board that FIS believed that microfinance, business, and the pursuit of social benefit could be combined to improve things. Eventually, our Unitus team agreed that our resources could assist FIS with funding to leverage its client base beyond Buenos Aires to rural areas, growing from some 4,500 clients to many more. It soon became the largest MFI in Argentina.

Swadhaar | India   In India, three of four poor people live in the country's rural regions where more than 21 percent of the population suffers chronic poverty. Swadhaar became a new MFI in the urban slums of Mumbai, an enormous struggling metropolis that the 2001 Indian Census reported had 54 percent eking out an existence in city slums without even running water or indoor plumbing. Swadhaar was launched in 2006, providing a mere $85 per microloan. It was serving over 2,000 borrowers when Unitus analyzed its programs and began offering MFI funding as a complement. Swadhaar's initial objective was to reach 200,000 clients within five years, which it did. Today it remains heavily focused on women's financial literacy, as well as the use of new technology to access capital and operate microenterprises. Several of the Unitus board and staff began flying to India frequently to find and develop new partners there. As a Marriott School professor, I recruited several graduate students to do field research with Indian MFIs in assessing those with high potential that we could assist.

LifeBank Foundation | The Philippines One-third of all Filipinos struggle in poverty, with some 80 percent suffering from severe conditions in rural areas where people live on less than $2 per day. I launched one of the first MFIs in Manila in 1989–1990, now known as Mentors International (Woodworth, 2020) (see chapter 5 herein). Since then, it has raised some $147 million and provided over one million loans that have improved the lives of some five million people. Despite these achievements, the Philippines continues to suffer much from destructive cyclones, an Islamic insurgency in its southern islands, and extensive government corruption. Thus, LifeBank was founded in 2003 on the island of Visayas where poverty was extreme. It began providing not only $80 microloans to impoverished individuals, but other financial services as well. Over time, its programs, ethics, and strong management capabilities impressed Unitus; thus, a partnership was born. Gradually, LifeBank has grown through the years of collaboration, from extending a few hundred loans in 2003, to 61,000 only four years later, and on to more than 126,000 clients. With a vision for nationwide growth and assisted by early financing from Unitus,

LifeBank scaled up to serve 270,000 clients by 2009, and as of 2020 it supports over 350,000 microentrepreneurs.

Bandhan | India Another of the many other partners Unitus worked with as an MFI was Bandhan. Individuals in and around Kolkata (formerly Calcutta) merely earned $46 per month while confronted with poverty that was epidemic in Unitus's early rise. Founded in West Bengal in 2000, this organization was impressive because it provided services mostly to poor women through programs like healthcare, education, and disaster management, supplemented by microfinance and microentrepreneurship training. Its name, Bandhan, means "togetherness." It grew quickly when Unitus entered the picture to accelerate its outreach further. In 2008 alone it grew more than 300 percent, and reached two million borrowers the following year (Team VCC, 2009). That successful accomplishment resulted in *Forbes Magazine* ranking it third among the world's leading MFIs that year. Unitus aided Bandhan further by advising how it could achieve greater cost controls, efficiencies, and impacts. By standardizing its operating systems it was able to lower its rates for clients, thus propelling it to further success. In 2015, it evolved into Bandhan Bank so it could offer additional customer services while continuing to keep its primary effort on serving India's poor. A *Fortune* article in early 2021 reported that Bandhan today has over $7 billion in market capitalization, yet primarily continues aiding India's poor though its 3,500 MFI offices that are aiding a total of 21 million clients (Ghosh, 2021).

In addition to the four MFIs detailed above, Unitus also evaluated a number of other prospective partners and began channeling funding for their growth.

Beyond Nonprofit Microlending Partners to For-Profit Venture Capital Tools

Eventually, the Unitus managers and a board team determined that to substantially accelerate the process of financial inclusion, it would need to include for-profit efforts that would add the appropriate resources and services of capital markets to enable significant further growth. As the original founder and first chair of the Unitus board, I felt conflicted about microcredit ventures turning to capitalism for their money. I preferred upholding my ideals of following the "pure" motives of doing good while making personal sacrifices to help the oppressed. Yet I have always felt that *anyone* can make a difference. I often spoke out vehemently against several global MFIs that were beginning to privatize or were conducting IPOs (Initial Public Offerings) on the stock market. I'd seen several ramp up interest rates on their microloans to the poor, which angered me. Then I'd see the early investors and certain board members from such ventures become millionaires.

Our Unitus discussions suggested, however, that small, private contributions from ordinary people were never going to achieve the scale of global self-reliance to which we were committed. Perhaps what we called "humanistic capitalism" could be a good fit with charitable values, we thought. Otherwise, our continually asking people for financial contributions would lead to "donor fatigue," as we were already seeing. Having an equity fund would give an MFI independence and enable it to become master of its own destiny. Furthermore, its managers could begin to plan for the future without outside factors such as grants being cut or reduced. Being able to plan, understand, and manage its resources could likely be the key to the success of any growing MFI. Equally critical would be the fact that the organization would need to have better finance and accounting systems, as proficient businesses do. Simply offering donors a "feel good" story of an MFI client who, say, received a loan in Nicaragua would not suffice.

In most capitalist societies, it's clear that regulators, investors, and other constituents affect and constrain the market system. So Unitus decided that by starting an equity fund, "guardrails" could be added to microfinance efforts to ensure that they keep their focus on the unbanked sector and the very poor, especially their women clients. Having social guidelines and priorities in place could prioritize against pure profit decisions of an equity fund that pursues money interests alone. In sum, at Unitus's partner MFIs, we felt that the social benefits of making loans to the poorest women should be prioritized *before* maximizing profits. Ultimately, such social safeguards were outlined and documented to ensure that MFI managers kept their focus on the targeted, unbanked poor.

Below were three of the primary instruments for adding new capital-based strategies:

Unitus Equity Fund   UEF was our first fund and was rolled out in 2006. It would seek money from people's investments, not donations. They would not get IRS charitable contribution receipts. Rather, they would be considered not as "donors" but instead as "investors" expecting to get their investment monies back with earnings, not maximizing profits, yet doing good and getting a decent return. UEF launched in 2006 with a first close of $9 million U.S. on an expected $20 million fund. This made UEF the very first equity fund in the history of microfinance. Its characteristics included focusing on high-growth MFIs that would offer microfinance monies to the poor not currently being served; generating purely private monies; and emphasizing equity, not debt investments in microfinance institutions. The UEF fund was structured like a venture capital fund so that one's money was locked up in order to provide immense poverty impacts for up to 10 years. The target was a return of 8 to 12 percent per annum. Unitus hoped that UEF would succeed as a demonstration effect for social investing, thus inspiring additional private capital from others to flow to social enterprises. The group had come to the conclusion that equity investments like UEF's would be critical for future MFIs. UEF ultimately raised $23 million from wealthy Unitus founders on its board. Along with funds from investors, it secured contributions from Kensington Investments LP, Abacus Wealth Partners, and several smaller sources. One of its most impressive programs was linking UEF with Elevar, an Indian MFI fund led by a former Unitus manager. This partnership fueled impressive MFI growth.

Elevar's first fund grew to serve more than 10 million borrowers or clients with MFI loans worth more than $1 billion. Its second fund helped a broader set of businesses that collectively served a million more clients/borrowers. Jointly these funds brought $3.7 billion in debt and $500 million in equity in subsequent rounds to its investments such that by 2013 it had averaged 155 percent revenue growth. The funds together had invested in 16 early- to growth-stage companies serving close to 11 million total households in Asia and Latin America through services such as microcredit, savings accounts, rural healthcare, home improvement loans, small business credit, and migrant and information services, and more (Clark and Thornley, 2013).

The Dignity Fund   Dignity was the second fund launched to secure new capital sources for the MFI industry with the goal of "fueling the social empowerment of the poor." Its goal was to increase the number of poor households with access to credit, savings, and other financial services by providing debt financing to promising microfinance institutions. The Unitus managers and board envisioned that Dignity would generate additional new funding to help MFIs needing and deserving of more capital for growth to reach a greater number of impoverished clients throughout the Third World, enabling ever more entrepreneurs to lift themselves out of poverty with dignity.

Unitus Capital   This new fund was established in 2008 and located in Bangalore. Its focus was on generating more money from investors who sought to empower extremely poor families through the rapidly growing demands for microlending in the subcontinent of India. Our analysis suggested that Unitus would have a greater impact by "spinning out" its capital markets team into a new social enterprise that provided corporate finance services. Money was raised from seed investors, and thus Unitus Capital became a reality. It soon began expanding to serve social enterprises in China and Southeast Asia and brought in clients from nonfinancial services sectors.

New Awards and Marketing Successes

Our Unitus team began exploring new ways that could promote the agenda so that it could grow in both impact and repute, thus attaining greater public awareness along with new funding. We moved from seeking LDS Church news and Utah media public relations to a more-global outreach. We hatched various innovative schemes to enhance our MFI strategies and resources. For example, we approached The Police, a globally known rock group, to provide public relations to new audiences. They agreed to partner with Unitus by featuring us at their concerts and soliciting monies from ticket sales across the U.S.A. They also agreed to film a promotional video that was sold worldwide. A few superfans even won the opportunity to sing on stage with the lead singer, Sting, and the band's other top performers as they traveled to stadium venues throughout North America. This marketing effort netted Unitus over $200,000. It was successful enough that, when The Police launched their European tour, similar fundraising occurred there as well. It provided fans with front-row concert tickets and pre- and post-concert private venues to interact with the band. For the music group itself, the effort showed its commitment to helping reduce poverty through microfinance.

Through the years, Unitus had enjoyed success in raising enormously significant sums of money for combating poverty and numerous awards and public recognitions. A summary of some includes the following: For three years in a row (2005–2008), *Fast Company* magazine and the U.S. consulting firm Monitor Group announced that Unitus had won a Social Capitalist Award; it was then honored in New York for "using the tools of business to solve the world's most pressing social problems" and "demonstrating a consistent and unusually large impact on society." It was also awarded the prestigious four-star rating for sound fiscal management from Charity Navigator in both 2007 and 2008.

Other recognitions occurred. Unitus Capital was ranked the No. 1 Investment Bank by Deal Volume for several years in a row, up through 2019, by Venture Intelligence and other institutions. From

2014 to 2018, it was named the "Best for Investment Banking – India" for 2015 by Wealth & Finance International. In earlier years, it was recognized for its work advising Morgan Stanley, Opportunity International Australia, Microventures India, and others institutions. It was "highly rated" as a "best company to work for" by Glassdoor and other global HR companies. It has been featured nationally in *The New York Times* and *The Wall Street Journal;* on *PBS* and *National Public Radio;* in many smaller media outlets like the *Seattle Times, Salt Lake Tribune,* and dozens more; as well as in major magazines and journals like *Newsweek, Time,* and *Harvard Business Review.* As well, key news sources in India, Kenya, Cambodia, Mexico, and dozens of other international cities have featured stories on Unitus's impact over the years.

As Unitus expanded its accelerated MFI impacts, it became a "darling" of the movement. Earlier organizations such as the Grameen Bank, Acción, FINCA, and others were still operating, but Unitus itself was generating a great deal of new enthusiasm. Its fame continued to grow as board and staff were invited to present their work at dozens of global conferences and at top universities. In academia, MBA and other graduate students along with professors wanted to learn more, hoped for internships, and in some cases received Unitus job offers. By the mid-2000s Unitus was growing its staff from a handful to a dozen individuals, then to 23, on up to 37 and eventually some 45 managers. Most had extensive experience with major tech, banking, and other industries. Many had been entrepreneurs or top executives at Apple, Citibank, and Microsoft; others had been head of Advisory Services for the International Finance Corporation (IFC) or managed British or South African investments. Programs were being operated from Unitus offices in Seattle, Washington; Bangalore, India; and Nairobi, Kenya.

Mid-2000s Partners and Microentrepreneur Client Growth (2006–2010)

By utilizing its Microfinance Accelerator—a tool for large-scale rapid poverty alleviation, developing new marketing strategies, creating new investment funds, reinventing the microcredit movement, and partnering with other major MFI organizations throughout the planet—Unitus itself was becoming a powerhouse. It had entered into a rapid growth phase. By early 2006, it had expanded to seven MFI partners serving more than 540,000 poor clients in India, Mexico, and Kenya in East Africa. It installed a new board chair and expanded its management team, then shifted its headquarters away from Utah to Redmond, Washington, where new staffers were being hired from tech firms like nearby Microsoft. Next, with a heavy Indian presence, a field office was established in Bangalore. That same year, Unitus also hosted its first-ever Unitus Leadership Summit in Malaysia. The conference brought together representatives from Unitus's many MFI partners, as well as leaders from several non-Unitus MFIs in India, Mexico, and the Philippines. It offered attendees the opportunity to share ideas on leadership, innovation, and sustainable growth for microentrepreneurs.

As of November 2006, Unitus was serving more than 1 million clients in India, Kenya, Mexico, Argentina, and the Philippines. By reaching such numbers in less than five years, Unitus had built the fastest-growing microfinance portfolio in the microfinance industry. A year later, in 2007, Unitus held another three-day annual leadership summit, this time in the Philippines. Leaders in microfinance, business, and philanthropy, including those from Unitus's MFI partners, met to chart the next chapter of poverty alleviation through social business. That summit provided a platform for social entrepreneurs and private sector experts to confront barriers and explore new solutions to scaling poverty-fighting enterprises. The summit's highly interactive sessions focused on strategy, technology, financing, and business efficiency. Together, participants engaged in dynamic, forward-looking discussions centered on identifying trends and evaluating new opportunities emerging in the field of microenterprise. Conversations focused on the need to lower operating costs, boost innovation, develop new products and services to meet the growing needs of the poor, devise strategies to leverage inflows of private capital into the microfinance sector, and enhance the potential for MFIs to serve as distribution channels for other products and services, such as healthcare and clean water.

By 2007, Unitus had hired an increasing number of managers and staffers and was operating from three offices—in Redmond, Washington; San Francisco; and Bangalore, India. It had grown to serve 16 partners worldwide, and collectively they were providing financial services to over 2.4 million microentrepreneurs in India, Kenya, Mexico, Argentina, the Philippines, and Indonesia. In addition to offering ever-larger amounts of capital, it was also promoting and supporting knowledge-sharing among its 21 MFI partners. By 2008, Unitus and its partners had reached more than 3.5 million poor families worldwide since its incorporation back in 2001, making it one of the fastest-growing MFI networks in the world. Within another year, the Unitus portfolio had surpassed the six million client mark, nearly double the number of clients served in the previous year. The organization by that time had 23 MFI partners in Argentina, Brazil, Cambodia, India, Indonesia, Kenya, Mexico, Tanzania, and the Philippines. No more a little Utah-based MFI serving the relatively small LDS population around the world, Unitus was having huge impacts with many NGOs needing our assistance, helping lift millions of the world's poorest families. Although I bemoaned the fact that our efforts had been blocked by a few jealous Mormon bureaucrats, we certainly had become a far greater blessing to people of other spiritual traditions. The LDS Church's humanitarian programs have increasingly served families in many nations. They've given temporary aid, distributed wheelchairs, and provided food and clothing in times of crisis. I trust that the church's small programs will keep growing. But in retrospect, I'm glad our Unitus strategy has focused on helping the poor climb out of poverty and become self-reliant in moving forward. Helping struggling families become truly independent has always been my objective around the globe. Unitus has succeeded in doing exactly that.

In 2008, Unitus held its annual Leadership Summit in Bali, Indonesia, attracting more than 20 microfinance innovators. It was the third such gathering of Unitus partners. In its sessions, industry experts and executive coaches addressed microfinance challenges such as how MFIs were dealing with the ongoing 2008 global credit crunch of a major international recession; how to grow an MFI rapidly while maintaining its core mission; which products and services were working, beyond simply providing microcredit loans, and then how best to design and implement them; and ways in which MFIs could measure both their own success and that of their clients. During this summit, Unitus presented the Unitus Acceleration Award to Equitas, a recent MFI partner in Chennai, India, that had reached 100,000 clients after a mere nine months of operation. The award began to be presented each year to a Unitus partner that best exemplified the goal of accelerating microfinance by achieving outstanding growth in a challenging market, through innovation, growth, and commitment to client needs.

Also in 2008, Unitus also launched a new program called "Empowering the 'Ultra Poor,'" funded by the Sorenson Legacy Foundation, based in Utah, to provide a two-year initiative to increase impacts on the poorest internationally.

In 2009, Unitus Labs launched the "Social Performance Management" (SPM) project as an effort to improve metrics on the impact of microfinance in borrowers' lives. At its core, it was doing research on what actually happens to microcredit recipients after receiving a loan. How does it impact one's quality of life and income levels? In addition to providing an avenue for qualifying such impacts, SPM served as a tool for MFIs to evaluate and improve financial products, services, and operational procedures to learn how a tiny loan increased client satisfaction and retention. This project was later transferred to MicroSave, another MFI organization, for completion. During that same year, Unitus Labs also opened an Africa Microfinance Growth Centre in Nairobi, Kenya, to help identify and catalyze stronger microfinance outreach for poor populations in rural East Africa. It later was funded by the Omidyar Network,

Boeing, FDSK, and SV2's Silicon Valley Social Venture Fund. This project was completed in 2010.

Also in 2009, Unitus announced a new partnership with Yehu Microfinance Trust, an MFI recognized for its strong leadership and strategic operations in underserved areas of coastal Kenya near Mombasa. It had been founded by an early board member and Utah entrepreneur one decade earlier, becoming Unitus's third partner in East Africa, Yehu had reached more than 8,000 clients while serving marginalized populations whose members earned less than $2 per day, and had committed itself to commercially scaling its operations to expand its reach. Yehu thus became the 24th MFI partner. By September 2009, a mere seven years since its launch, Unitus had helped its partners serve more than 9 million families worldwide.

Upon securing new funding from major sources of capital such as the Michael and Susan Dell Foundation, the Boeing Corporation, and Deutsche Bank, further impacts were achieved. Unitus held its 2009 Unitus Leadership Summit in Mussoorie, India. Unitus MFI partners, microfinance industry experts, and other attendees shared experiences and best practices in microfinance during the event. This fourth and largest summit brought together 27 representatives from 16 MFI partners in six countries on three continents. At the end of the summit, seven Unitus partners were recognized for reaching significant client outreach milestones that year. Samhita Community Development Services, a Unitus MFI partner since 2008, won the Third Annual Unitus Acceleration Award. Operating in Madhya Pradesh, India, one of the poorest regions with more than 37 percent of the population living below the poverty line, it had faced many start-up challenges. The region is characterized by low population density and poor infrastructure and is primarily peopled by landless, agricultural wage laborers with limited general education and no previous access to financial services.

In mid-2010, Unitus Labs decided to alter its own business model. Its strategy was shifting to explore other sectors of economic development, not microfinancing per se. Its management team had been debating other issues for some time, seeking advice from a mix of partners and experts and also conducting research on other global needs and opportunities that would continue to be in sync with Unitus's purpose and mission. In a 2010 press release it announced to the public that it would halt the funding of the poorest in deploying solely microfinance services through its NGO.

In other words, a new Unitus 2.0, in effect, would be created. Its objective was to become an organization focusing on improved livelihood opportunities for the working poor. The group formed a team that was willing to set up a new venture and launch a fresh vision that could catalyze a brand-new market for livelihood ventures. It was designated to become a venture named *Unitus Impact Fund*, and began to be rolled out in 2011. The plan was to become an investment management firm focused on creating livelihood opportunities at global scale and significant impact.

Also, by 2011 Unitus itself had officially changed its name to *Unitus Labs* to better reflect its historical approach and to emphasize both its current and going-forward focuses on engaging in early-stage research on and support for market-based solutions that reduce global poverty. The "Unitus Family," so to speak, had evolved into four independent entities, each with its own managers and boards: Unitus Labs, a nonprofit focused on research and early-stage development; Unitus Equity Fund, a strictly microfinance venture fund; Unitus Capital, an investment bank focused on Bottom-of-the-Pyramid interventions (Prahalad, 2005); and the Unitus Impact Fund for investing in innovative livelihood ventures.

In October of 2011, Unitus Labs renamed a pilot initiative in India as Unitus Ventures, having earlier been known as the Unitus Seed Fund. Its objective emphasized developing new businesses in emerging markets with innovative strategies that possessed high potential for millions of people to better their lives. Unitus Labs managers had begun to feel that enormous numbers of ideas for reducing poverty on a large scale would emerge from start-up entrepreneurs who generated disruptive ideas and models to eventually become for-profit firms. Thus, by mid-2012, Unitus Ventures was off-loaded from Unitus Labs to become a separate capital management firm to scale-up investing operations and impacts. It has become the leading venture fund in India supporting early-stage tech start-ups with "India scale" and global potential. It helps capitalize early-stage fintech, education, healthcare, and job tech start-ups get ready to grow via funding, strategic and operating support, and securing growth capital to validate market potential. Recently, Unitus Ventures continued to provide capital to various projects, including an ed-tech start-up named Habitat, in Bengaluru in 2020, with an investment of more than $500,000, another with $800,000, plus more. The portfolios of its companies then exceeded $144 million in revenue generated while impacting over 12 million "bottom-of-the-pyramid" people.

It should be mentioned that by 2011, *Unitus Capital* had successfully raised over $550 million of debt and equity capital for social enterprises, primarily in the Asian financial services space. It has continued to grow ever since. Here are a few milestones from its long-term focus in India: by 2013 it had become the No. 1 investment bank by volume of deals accomplished; by 2014 it had raised more than $1 billion for pro-poor investments throughout Asia; by 2017 it had closed the largest private equity transaction in microfinance, more than $100 million, for Spandana, another Indian MFI; and then, finally, after years of confronting hurdles such as Indian demonetization, government restrictions, and more had cropped up, in 2019 an entirely new entity was established: the *UC Inclusive Credit Pvt. Ltd.* (UCIC). It operated in Bangalore, a leading region of Indian social innovation and entrepreneurship. It was incubated by *Unitus Capital* as an impact-focused *Non-Banking Finance Company* (NBFC) registered with the Reserve Bank of India.

The cluster of current Unitus entities appears as shown in Figure 6.

Certain critics of Unitus and other large players in the MFI industry, however, complained that the microcredit movement was drifting away from zeroing in on empowering the "poorest of the poor"—those living in absolute squalor, trying to survive hand-to-mouth on only one meager meal per day—toward giving most

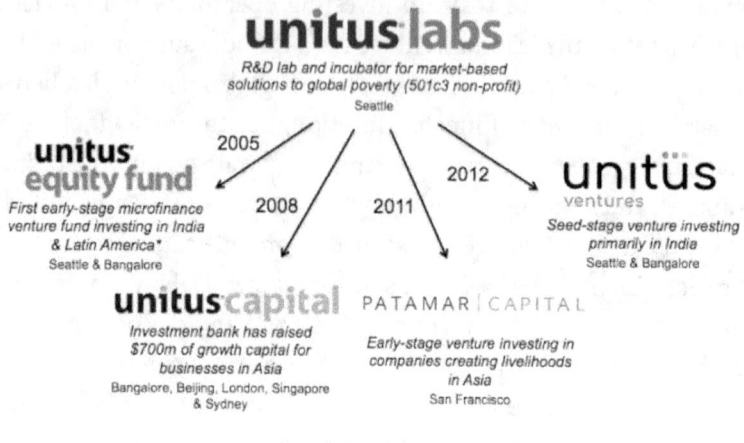

Figure 6: Unitus Labs entities worldwide

loans to those a little more well off. The rationale for doing so was that such clients had more possibilities to expand their microenterprise, knew how to succeed, had gained additional experience, and maybe had even received a bit more education. All these things held promises of recipients of microcredit doing better with their loan capital, and then paying off their debts, promptly and with interest. The justification for this included the argument that those living under the poverty line, as well as the near-poor, also require and deserve access to capital.

Conclusion

Regardless of positive or negative assessments regarding the ultimate success of the microfinance movement and further attempts to explain and justify all its facets, the fact is that this trend is here to stay. The promise continues that financial inclusion will change lives so that poor families have access to loans and other financial services, thus earning more wealth, having a better quality of life, building assets, and cushioning themselves against future external shocks. Increased income provides the means for poor families to acquire land, construct or improve their homes, and purchase livestock and consumer goods—as well as to expand their businesses. Joining others in their small rural or large urban community helps them to accrue and access savings, since engaging with an MFI increases families' trust that they can safely store, grow, and utilize their funds. This, in turn, reduces the vulnerability of the poor. They are more able to achieve everyday survival as well as plan for the future. Parents can pay for their children's tuition, enjoy better living conditions, gain access to healthcare services, and enjoy multiple other desired benefits. For these and other reasons, microfinance and financial inclusion are critical strategies to help alleviate poverty and to build a world of greater equity and opportunity.

I must acknowledge that the huge capital generation of MFI funds made its global success truly amazing—far more than we folks at Unitus, Muhammad Yunus himself at his Grameen Bank in Bangladesh, or up and down Wall Street could have imagined. From only a few institutions giving a microcredit loan in the 1990s before the rise of Unitus, Acción, FINCA, and BRAC, by early 2010 more than *100 million microentrepreneurs around the globe* were receiving credit to expand their tiny businesses and create jobs not only for themselves but for family and friends, as well. Some 20 million people were beneficiaries of the $1.2 billion generated by Unitus Microfinance in its various forms. Today the numbers are even larger, and money in the global market for microfinance is projected to reach $313 billion by 2025 (Globe News Wire, 2020). Meanwhile, increasing inequality in wealth distribution and the rise in the number of unbanked people continues. The divide between extravagantly wealthy billionaires and humanity's bottom 50 percent keeps expanding. In fact, during the COVID-19 pandemic in 2020 alone, billionaires dramatically increased their financial holdings by a trillion dollars of massive additional wealth (Stebbins and Suneson, 2020).

As an early advocate for the global microfinance movement, I will continue to advocate using it to reduce extreme poverty and press for greater empowerment among women. I hold that despite capitalist ventures' attempts to seize control of social innovations that serve the poor while maximizing their own agendas, microcredit should be a fundamental human right. But it needs to be centered on uplifting the masses, not enhancing the major instruments of capitalism such as large, for-profit banks. Effective MFIs must protect the "poorest of the poor" from becoming victims of capitalism's ravages, to counter the grinding weaknesses and vulnerabilities of having too little capital, work, or food.

Unitus was clearly a critical player in the early mechanisms for financial inclusion, thus benefiting those who suffered globally. It generated enormous new sources of capital for uplifting the poor from the depths of despair. Unitus successfully found donors and convinced them to help join the MFI movement such that between its small individual contributors and large institutional investors, some 20 million-plus of Unitus's struggling clients secured individual or solidarity-group loans to launch or expand their microenterprises. Unitus's tools for accelerating the movement were extended by other microlenders, both large and small, to the extent that approximately 195 million people had obtained microloans by 2012–2013, according to the Microcredit Summit (Reed, 2013).

Since then, even after Unitus moved on to other strategies through Unitus Labs and its additional innovative vehicles, the microfinance movement has expanded to literally thousands of new MFIs, giving impoverished clients access to thousands of new MFI institutions and reaching as many as 400 million borrowers worldwide today. As global inequality grows, while the COVID-19 pandemic continues to wreak worldwide havoc on small businesses and poor families' lives, the need for tiny amounts of microenterprise capital will surely continue unabated for the coming decades.

I end this chapter with an LDS commentary that suggests support for all righteous efforts to bless the poor and needy. Whether one commends Unitus fully, partially, or not at all, its work benefited millions of the global poor. I sincerely believe that all those who labored to conceive, plan, implement, or institutionalize its work should know the good they did over the years.

In conclusion, as I reflect on our work through Unitus, the words of my great old spiritual mentor, Brigham Young, come to mind. He declared we need not await the Second Coming or sit idly by until the LDS First Presidency commands us to act. No. He avowed that for us to reduce poverty, we must unite God's people in the principles of consecration, stewardship, and United Order values globally—*that it's up to us, here and now.* "We are not going to wait for angels ... we are going to build [Zion ourselves]" (Young, 1954 edition, p. 443).

References

CGAP. (2021). *The State of Economic Inclusion Report 2021: The Potential to Scale.* World Bank.

Clark, C., and Thornley, B. (2013). Elevar Equity: Unitus Equity Fund and Elevar Equity Fund II. *Impact Investing 2.0.* Duke University's Fuqua School of Business, 1–18, November.

Doctrine and Covenants: 104:118.

Easterly, W. (2006). *The White Man's Burden: Why the West's Efforts to Aid the Rest Have Done so Much Ill and so Little Good.* Penguin Press.

Ghosh, D. (2021). Bandhan Bank: An Ear to the Ground. *Fortune India*, January 18.

GlobeNewsWire.(2020).https://www.globenewswire.com/news-release/2020/09/04/2089263/0/en/The-global-market-for-Microfinance-is-projected-to-reach-US-313-7-billion-by-2025.html

IMF and World Bank. (2010). *Global Monitoring Report 2010: The MDGs After the Crisis.* World Bank.

Kimball, S. W. (1977). "Welfare Services: The Gospel in Action," *Ensign*, Nov. p. 78.

Lukas, J. W., and Woodworth, W. P. (1996). *Working Toward Zion: Principles of the United Order for the Modern World.* Aspen Books.

Moore, C. A. (2000) Humanitarian Group Hails Pres. Hinckley. *Deseret News.* October 11.

OECD. (2005). *Paris Declaration on Aid Effectiveness*. Organization for Economic Co-operation and Development.

Prahalad, C. K. (2005). *The Fortune at the Bottom of the Pyramid*. Pearson.

Reed, L. R. (2013). Vulnerability: The State of the Microcredit Summit Campaign Report. *Microcredit Summit Campaign*.

Stebbins, S., and Suneson, G. (2020). Jeff Bezos, Elon Musk among US Billionaires Getting Richer During Coronavirus Pandemic. *USA Today*, December 1.

Strom, S., and Bajaj, V. (2010). Rich I.P.O. brings controversy to SKS microfinance. *New York Times*, July 29.

Team VCC. (2009). Bandhan Raises Rs 50 cr Equity Capital from Sidbi. *Reuters India*, December 25.

UNDP: United Nations Development Programme. (2019). *Human Development Report 2019*. United Nations Development Programme. Oxford University Press.

United Nations. (2015). *Transforming Our World: The 2030 Agenda for Sustainable Development*. United Nations.

Unitus Survey. (1999). Unpublished survey of LDS members in Nairobi, Kenya, conducted by several board members, February.

Woodworth, W. (ed.) (1997). *Small Really Is Beautiful: Micro Approaches to Third World Development—Microentrepreneurship, Microenterprise, and Microfinance*. Third World Think Tank.

Woodworth, W. (2020). Incubator for Social Innovation: HELP International as an NGO Start-up for Deep Impact. *Journal of Research in Business and Management* (JRBM), vol. 8 (5) 1–8.

Woodworth, W., Grenny, J., and Manwaring, T. (2000). *United for Zion: Principles for Uniting the Saints and Eliminating Poverty*. Unitus Publications.

Young, B. (1954). *Discourses of Brigham Young*. Selected by John A. Widtsoe. Deseret Book.

Young, B. (1997). *Teachings of the Presidents of the Church, Brigham Young*. Intellectual Reserve, Inc.

Yunus, M. (2009). Creating a World without Poverty: Social Business and the Future of Capitalism. Public Affairs.

"Teach Me to Walk in the Light"
LDS Hymns, No. 304

1. Teach me to walk in the light of his love;
   Teach me to pray to my Father above;
   Teach me to know of the things that are right;
   Teach me, teach me to walk in the light.

2. Come, little child, and together we'll learn
   Of his commandments, that we may return
   Home to his presence, to live in his sight—
   Always, always to walk in the light.

3. Father in Heaven, we thank thee this day
   For loving guidance to show us the way.
   Grateful, we praise thee with songs of delight!
   Gladly, gladly we'll walk in the light.

Text and music: Clara W. McMaster (1904–1997)

9

How to Design Your Own NGO

Tools and Methods for Launching New NGOs

(January 2022)

This chapter in *Radiant Mormonism* goes beyond the cases and experiences of my friends, students, and myself in laboring to combat the travails of the poor in this life. Instead, it offers a few suggestions and strategies for readers seeking to design and launch their own humble nongovernmental organizations. In a sense, the next pages will help a person who wants to become a social entrepreneur. I will describe examples and suggested tools that may assist you in your goal to personally practice consecration and stewardship. Perhaps you will mobilize others—family and relatives, neighbors, colleagues at work, folks in your LDS ward, and others.

As readers consider ways to address the challenges of the worldwide poor, whether in your local community or in Africa and beyond, consider the counsel from a nephew of the Prophet Joseph (the son of his brother, Hyrum), President of the church in 1918, Joseph F. Smith, who taught that the Church "has always sought to

▲ Working in the Middle Eastern refugee camps of Greece with Syrians, Afghans, Yazidis, Iraqis, and more

Laboring with the global poor through effective NGOs is a powerful solution to societal problems

▼ Scene of photo the author took of a female microentrepreneur pushing her products through the streets of Hanoi, Vietnam

place its members in a way to help themselves, rather than adopting the method of so many charitable institutions of providing only for present needs.... Our idea of charity, therefore, is to relieve present wants and then to put the poor in a way to help themselves so that in turn they may help others." The basic purpose is that "we depend on mutual helpfulness" (Smith, 1998).

This advice could guide you in establishing a microfinance institution in East Africa, perhaps. It would also be useful for launching an education program to build schools in Central America. I will explore how you might create a nonprofit organization to serve many village women in Asia. How may it best be done? Which elements are critical? Where do you even start? What are the potential pitfalls? How can you get a new nonprofit established? What legal requirements exist? How and where are donations possible? In seeking to build a board of trustees, which steps should occur first (should one start with an all-volunteer staff, of will they need salaries?). Any advice on whether or not to grow quickly? Or evolve slowly? What is the most effective process for taking action, reducing human suffering, and lifting the poor?

Reflecting on these chapters describing my experiences of tackling hunger, impoverishment, and suffering, I deeply feel both the pain of others and the joy of serving and empowering struggling families. The cases are global: the Philippines, Mali, Honduras, Peru, Thailand, Haiti, India, and even Utah. Have you ever dreamed about wanting to change the world? Have you sometimes felt powerless as you witness massive human suffering around the world? At times, have tears filled your eyes as your television screen shows children's bodies on the nightly news? Then these stories have been exactly for you.

Having led management consulting efforts for five decades in providing expertise to large corporations in nine countries and from coast to coast in the United States, I know a bit about management and the skills necessary to build effective organizations, lead change, and produce high-quality results. In addition, I've advised LDS Church leaders during the same decades, ranging from headquarters in Utah to area presidencies, mission presidents, stakes, and wards globally. Further, I've worked with governors, mayors, and legislatures nationally and, in a few instances, internationally. All these professional successes have strengthened my abilities in helping NGOs, whether creating start-ups or being asked to consult and train managers and boards. Using "best practices" from the field of Organizational Behavior, in which I earned my Ph.D. at the University of Michigan in Ann Arbor, I came to be pretty effective at helping design, launch, and grow nonprofits that succeed over the long haul. Such practices I have inculcated include training in Third World problems and needs, cross-cultural understanding, organizational diagnosis, NGO design, socio-technical systems, decision-making, team building, total quality management, strategy implementation, crisis interventions, financial systems, managerial leadership, and additional competencies, and many others. All are critical to building NGO systems to achieve ongoing success.

Steps to Starting an NGO

I will begin by stating that a core principle is to *not try doing this alone*. I know very few nongovernmental organizations that were started by a single individual and have continued operations for 10, 20, or 30 years with amazing success. Perhaps it can be done, but it's vanishingly rare. Virtually all the best NGOs were formed by a small group of like-minded friends or professional colleagues who shared a dream. Cases like Ouelessebougou, in Mali (chapter 3), began with 8 to 10 of my associates seeking to aid West Africa. The "big money" instance of Unitus (chapter 8) was launched by 7 or 8 quite wealthy friends. Mentors International (chapter 6), which I conceived of originally, but then partnered with, included just two acquaintances and myself. And of course, many of the NGOs I established were launched by a couple of dozen amazing students in my BYU courses. The goal was seldom "Me, Me, Me!" but rather "We, We, We!" With others collaborating, there's great power in leveraging our best skills and abilities, leading to amazing social and economic impacts globally.

This chapter guides readers through a series of stages for establishing a project, including making it a viable NGO. They include such things as Identifying Your Motives, Setting Up a Nonprofit, Doing Your Homework, Building Systems and Infrastructure, Deciding Your Target Population, Training and Education, If Doing Microfinance . . . Identifying a Savings Program and Establishing Social Collateral, Setting Up Contracts, Preparing for Setbacks, Documenting the System, and finally Being Ready to Change the World. I will describe a bit about each of these processes.

This chapter is a step-by-step guide for anyone interesting in starting a new NGO, including references where appropriate, to the specifics of rolling out a MicroFinance Institution (MFI). It assumes that you have clear and ethical motivations, have your own money to begin with, or at least some access to capital, and have the desire to improve society.

Step 1: Identifying Your Motives

Understanding why you seek to design and roll out a new NGO is a critical action before beginning to build your new program. Key questions should include queries about your inner motivations along a spectrum of introspections such as (1) Why do I want to do this? Is it primarily a matter of altruism? Or perhaps a more mundane approach, perhaps to egoism?; (2) What's in it for others?; (3) What's in it for me?; (4) Am I seeking to reduce humanity's struggles, and if so, for how long? In other words, are my goals driven by empathy?; (5) Do I possess decent values that will uplift others?; (6) Am I hoping for fame or glory out of all this? In other words, will my efforts bring me desired credibility or other psychological results?; (7) To what extent is launching my NGO organization tied to Christ's gospel and LDS teachings? Will those commitments strengthen me in moving forward?; (8) Do I have the spiritual strength to follow through?; (9) Do I enjoy sufficient health to move forward?; (10) Are my circumstances sufficient to devote a good deal of my time (and perhaps money) to making this work? Have I considered the effects of doing this on my spouse, children, and others who are most important to me?; and (11) Will my family and friends be supportive, or at least tolerate my new venture?

Perhaps other questions will arise from such introspection, and if so, take the time to reflect and evaluate on as many issues as you can.

Step 2: Setting Up a Nonprofit

It can be daunting to set up a nonprofit to serve as a nonprofit business or an NGO, whether in the U.S. or in another country. Below you will find some items you will need to consider to initially setup your organization.

Board of Directors

In order to apply as a 501(c)(3) charitable organization in the U.S. under the regulations of the Internal Revenue Service, you must set up the organization with at least three board members. The board of directors is ultimately responsible for the success of the organization. The only legal requirement to be a board member is that you must be at least 18 years of age. Even though this is the sole required qualification, selection of the board members is important. You will preferably want members who have connections to funds or at least have a diverse and well-established contact list. Also, look for board members who come from diverse backgrounds and who are committed to the mission of the organization.

Also, board members must meet ethical standards of conduct to fully carry out their responsibilities to the organization:

- **Duty of Care** This standard has to do with the competence that is expected of board members. It requires them to exercise "reasonable" care when making a decision on behalf of the organization.
- **Duty of Loyalty** This standard has to do with honesty and disclosure. The board member must be able to put the organization's interests ahead of personal

interests. It specifically prohibits personal gain from any transactions entered into on behalf of the organization.
- **Duty of Obedience** This standard has to do with faithfulness to an organization's mission and goals. The board member's actions must be consistent with the central goals of the organization. This duty ensures that those who lead the organization will manage funds to fulfill the stated organization mission.

Legal
Articles of incorporation that formally document the organization name, address, purpose statement, and so on, must be filed with the state. Bylaws that indicate internal rules for the organization (such as board operations and anything that you wish to be legally binding regarding organizational processes) should also be formed at this time. In addition, IRS form 1023 must be filled out in order to be granted nonprofit status. Also, IRS form 990 must be filled out and submitted to the IRS each year in order to maintain tax-exempt status; this form provides the IRS with annual financial information.

Step 3: Doing Your Homework
As with any other business operation, preparation and planning can be the difference between a good NGO and a great one. Before you can change the world, you need a solid foundation upon which your organization can be built and supported. This section will give you a general outline of what needs to be determined before you do anything, and also suggests some factors that need to be considered after setting it up.

Choose a Location and a Country
Just about every place in the world could benefit from a well-run NGO! You can go wherever you want, but always make sure that

you know exactly where you want to end up. Below are a few tips that will assist you, no matter where you decide to start your nonprofit.

Culture

If you can understand your target population's culture, you will be able to better understand what motivates and drives the people you are eventually going to work with. Either you or your associates will need to be fluent in speaking, reading, and writing in the local language. You will need to understand how the people approach business transactions, what motivates them, and what drives and inspires them. Most important, you must believe that you will eventually be accepted by them. Trust must play a crucial role in the success of your organization (especially in the beginning stages), and if individuals feel as if you understand them and their culture, they are more likely to trust and work with you.

Rural vs. Urban

You need to decide whether you want to work primarily in rural areas or within an urban population. Working in an urban setting is generally easier and may see higher rates of success. This is because communication and transportation are faster and cheaper. Also, more imminent entrepreneurial opportunities could exist there. Similarly, NGOs working in more urban settings typically grow at a faster pace and work with a wider variety of individuals than organizations in rural settings. Having said this, I assure you that achieving success with rural populations is also very doable and rewarding, even though these populations often have greater needs than their urban counterparts. Just note that additional time and funding will be needed to overcome the obstacles facing your efforts in rural communities.

Serving Men vs. Women

Gender may be important in your efforts. For instance, since the beginning of the microfinance movement, women have become the primary target population for microloans and microfinancing. Why? Because long experience has proven that women generally pay back their loans and are more likely than men to create a successful business with the funds that they receive. But if you do want to work with men and women, or just men, this is possible, too. Just know that working with men is more risky than with women. You may be able to adjust for this risk through other practices, such as changing the loan rates (explained below). It is important to note that in some patriarchal cultures where men have no access to microloans, the men may force the women to take out loans on their behalf, and then will use the money as if it were theirs for other pursuits and not necessarily to start a microenterprise. This often leads to a variety of negative unintended consequences.

Previous Exposure

Do some research to see if your target population has had any exposure to microfinance or other services you want to provide, and if so, how much. Similarly, find out if there are any other NGOs currently working with your intended population, and figure out how or what they are doing. Will your organization enhance theirs? Duplicate theirs? Compete with theirs? Understanding what your target population already knows, or doesn't know, regarding such issues will play an important role in some of your decisions in the future.

Socioeconomic Target

This question is asking: "Who do you *really* want to work with?" Do you want to work with the "poorest of the poor," or with a disabled population, or with individuals who are poor but have some degree of education? After you have chosen which socioeconomic population you want to work with, do some research on the additional liabilities that could potentially accompany this population. Try to narrow down your target population as much as possible.

Software

You must decide how the financial information is going to be recorded and preserved. There are numerous options for using software within the NGO community. Of course, the more sophisticated software costs more. If this is a concern, you can use Microsoft Excel for basic functions, or you can use an open-source program such as Octopus Microfinance Software. Other pricier but more sophisticated options include Beacon software, MiFI (which acts as a mobile WiFi hotspot), and MFin software products.

Accountability

As an organization, you must decide how you will keep track of financial data, ensure the safety and security of the funds, and agree on an institution where the actual money will be kept, both in the U.S. as well as wherever your international program will be established.

You have to seriously consider the safety and security of the funds that will be transacted on a daily basis. You must decide how physical money will be kept, transferred, and stored. You must also decide how to protect personal information from lenders and loan recipients. You must have a security policy in place to address these concerns and reduce fraud.

Establish Base Interest Rates if Doing Microfinance

Check to see the competition in the area. What are other MFIs charging as their base interest rates? What is reasonable to charge in similar geographic or socioeconomic regions? You must answer these and other questions when determining your ideal program's microlending strategy.

Budgeting

The next step in the process is devising a budget that will meet your organizational needs. It is important to think about all possible sources of revenue. To do this, you need to be able to make accurate projections regarding the number of people who will be participating in the NGO. Also, make sure you think about fixed costs such as full-time employee salaries, rent, and any other recurring expenses. Estimate variable costs, such as utility fees that you will have at the physical office in the country in which you will be operating. Perhaps the same information will be necessary if you establish an office in the U.S. where you will be based.

Make sure to explore the possibility of having a "rainy day fund" or separate budgeted expense for unforeseen items that will inevitably come up. Most unforeseen expenses are legal fees that unexpectedly arise when filing for a permit or locality applications. This is especially true in Third World countries where it will be harder to research all possible legal fees.

Exit Strategy

Before you begin to set up shop, it will be critical to create an exit strategy. If sustainability is a goal of your organization, you should plan a time frame of when you expect your organization to be self-sufficient and then create goals to meet this expectation. Eventually, your original client population should be able to function without your assistance.

Do some research and try to determine how long it has taken a similar organization to become self-sustaining. Be clear with your expectations, and create more-manageable goals in smaller increments to ensure that your organization is on pace to exit at the preestablished time.

Measure Success

Know how you will measure success. If doing an MFI, will success be determined by quantitative results such as payback rates and individuals' earned income, or will success be measured through qualitative results that are harder to measure such as "overall well-being" or increased standard of living? If doing some kind of social or educational program, how will success be determined? Knowing what you are going to measure, as well as exactly how, will have a large impact on how your organization will serve its intended population.

Step 4: Building Systems and Infrastructure

Now that you know where you want to labor, an important objective should be to find individuals to work with who are well-versed in your location's culture and customs. I always prefer to identify and work with natives of the country or area within the country. The right employee(s) will save you a lot of time, energy, and embarrassment. They will help you with all the necessities that you didn't account for (since it's impossible to know everything beforehand). Likewise, you will need some basic infrastructure from which your organization can function, such as office space, security, desks, phones and computers, and furniture. Make sure that you have all the necessary infrastructure that will enable your employees to work efficiently and effectively. Similarly, make sure that your employees have all the necessary tools to carry out their functions properly.

Establish Accountability Expectations

It is essential that your new employees know what is expected of them, and how their performance will be measured. Create and maintain an accurate job description, and be clear and open about compensation. Likewise, make sure your employees know and understand the consequences of not meeting expectations. Have frequent employee training on organizational policies such as safety, security, communication procedures, and more. Do not assume they already know what is expected of them.

Establish Effective Communication Processes

Communication has the potential to make or break your NGO. Work so that all your employees have the necessary technology and infrastructure to efficiently communicate with clients and headquarters as necessary.

Before you start working to establish good communication networks, ensure that all interpersonal communication will be direct and nonoffensive. Give—and receive—training on how to communicate in difficult situations without insulting others. Also establish the cultural and social norms that will be appropriate and clear, thus preventing inadvertent or accidental communication problems that may cause major problems.

- **Communication with Clients** Your ability to communicate effectively with clients will largely depend on your NGO's situation. One method of communication is to have employees physically go to villagers or microfinance clients, and talk with them in person. If possible, employees can communicate with people via phone calls, text messages, and emails. No matter the method of communication, there should be some established criteria that all employees should follow when communicating with their clients, and what they should avoid in all circumstances. Finally, set standards of professionalism for your employees, and decide how you plan to enforce said standards.
- **Communication with Headquarters** Set up networks so that in-country employees can easily communicate with headquarters and vice versa. Establish how often in-country employees should communicate with and report to headquarters, how this process will work, how they can make special requests, and more.

Step 5: Deciding Your Target Population

Now that you know where and with whom your organization will be established, it is time to go out and find the population that will benefit from your new NGO. Because you have already established your target population, work with your new staff to find where this population resides and how to best approach them. This may appear difficult at first, but once you have a solid connection with the locals, you will find that they can lead you in the right direction.

Participation

Once you have established contact with your target population, and you know that you have found the people with whom you want to work, you should gather them together to see who is interested in what you have offer. Make sure to explain in detail the benefits and costs of what you have to offer so that they can make an informed decision. You will find that after you have explained your purpose for being there, your target population will organize itself until there is a group or groups of individuals who want to learn more about receiving services or microloans, or both, from your NGO. If they fail to self-organize, you may need to help build a new network of local leaders with whom your organization can collaborate. It may also be helpful to return after a week or so and verify that the previously interested individuals are still interested.

Step 6: Training and Education

Having found your target population, your next step should be to educate them about basic NGO principles, and much more. Many people in the Third World have never had bank accounts, for example, or learned financial principles in school. Before they receive a microloan, they have to understand what a "loan" is, what "interest" is, and what other basic financial principles are.

Training

Ongoing training sessions will need to occur, and should be done consistently at the same time and location each week. This allows potential participants to see that your organization and its leaders are dependable. Having regular meetings also gives them stability and establishes good practices for the future, perhaps including when their payments come due at a specific time each week or month. It is often recommended that these courses take four to five weeks, depending on your clients' backgrounds and skill level.

Lessons may include the following subjects: importance of education, literacy, hygiene factors, training children effectively, environmental sustainability, and more. If your focus is on microfinance, training should include loan principle, interest, savings, loan repayment schedules, good business practices, financial concepts, and any other subjects you feel your participants would need to know about so they can succeed with their new enterprises.

You should also consider setting up attendance policies such as minimum attendance requirements before receiving NGO benefits, whether the people will help build a village school or work at digging a well for accessing clean water. Good attendance shows their level of commitment, and is also an indication of their trustworthiness in the future.

Choose Leaders

After a given number of weeks, have the regular attendees at your training program select their *own leaders* within their population. The leaders will receive additional training in management areas and could be a pool to select from when considering hiring locals for your organization. Leaders would be in charge of overseeing small groups of their fellow compatriots and would learn additional responsibilities that leadership entails.

Have the leaders set up meeting times with the people they directly oversee. In these meetings have them gather information regarding their home lives and things that may affect their timely repayment of any loans distributed. Have the leaders take ownership over their groups so that participants feel more connected to the NGO.

Step 7: If Doing Microfinance, Identifying a Savings Program and Establishing Social Collateral

Before having potential clients sign contracts or giving them loans, it is important that they put into practice the basic skills they learned in the training. This can be achieved through savings accounts. As they deposit money into a savings account, they can see financial principles, such as interest accumulation, unfold before them. Again, remember that some of the most poverty-stricken people in the Third World have never had access to a bank or a savings account.

Set Clear Standards

Establishing standards, such as minimum savings deposits each week, puts your potential clients into a habitual routine where they are depositing a certain amount of money at the same time at the same place each week. You will need to instill these habits before you can expect them to make routine payments after being granted a loan. Minimum savings amounts should be enough that they would have to sacrifice a little to be able to make the payments. The payment each week should in some small way make the person question whether they should deposit the money or not. By setting it up this way, they must exert a little bit of loyalty and trust when depositing the money each week. It should simulate other experiences that they will face when they have to repay a loan instead of depositing a savings amount.

Make sure potential clients understand that before they can receive a loan, a certain amount of savings has to be deposited. This gives them a goal to work toward and helps them understand that you are granting a privilege in loaning them the money and that it will not simply be handed to them without their first working for a loan.

Set Interest Rates for Savings

Be sure to look up competitive savings rates in the area that you will be working in. Consult with banks and see if you can match the savings interest rates. Also be sure to check with other MFIs in the area to make sure you are offering competitive rates.

In establishing social collateral, it's perhaps best to follow the principles of Grameen Bank of Bangladesh, developed by Dr. Muhammad Yunus. Thus, the next step for doing microfinance is to establish social collateral. This means that the participants have to understand that while the loan is given individually, as a "solidarity group" they are responsible for each other's payments in the event of anyone's default.

Solidarity Groups

Now that your customers have spent several weeks with each other, have them form into groups of four or five people who all trust each other. This becomes their solidarity group. They will be given individual loans, but they will be responsible for each other's debts. This means if one member defaults, the other members of the solidarity group must make the next payment to cover for the person who wasn't able to pay for a portion of their loan that week. Make sure that they understand this protects them as borrowers as well as the MFI itself.

Establish Rules

In each solidarity group, borrowers should come up with rules to govern themselves. This method works better than having the MFI set rules for them, because the borrowers will feel more autonomy and ownership of the process. There will be more compliance with the rules they set for themselves than with the rules the MFI imposes on them.

Step 8: Setting Up Contracts

As with any type of lending organization, creating a contract is an essential part of lending capital. Make sure that borrowers clearly understand all terms and procedures, and that they know exactly what they are getting themselves into. As mentioned above, it is best not only that the contract be between the borrower and your MFI, but also that the borrowers feel responsible to someone or something else, not just you.

Loan Amount

You will need to do a lot of research to determine what a suitable loan amount is for a potential entrepreneur in the nation where you are working. The objective here is to give the borrower enough capital, but not too much. Also determine if the loan amounts should be the same for everybody, or if they should vary, depending on the nature of the proposal from the borrower.

In traditional MFI methods, an initial small amount is loaned out to the borrowers. As they pay back these small loan amounts in a timely manner, they are then able to borrow larger sums of money. This teaches them a form of credit rating whereby the more timely their payments are, they will be rewarded with greater trust in their ability to repay larger debts in the future.

Interest Rates

This may be the most difficult aspect of starting your own MFI. To create a sustainable organization, your MFI must be sustainable, which usually means slightly profitable. At the same time, you don't want to have such high rates that your customers are put in excess debt. As the MFI movement continues to grow, websites exist that can help you decide what the best rate for your location and target population should be. Interest rates must also be adjusted to take into consideration any and all types of risk associated with your loans, target population, and organization.

Repayment Schedule

The timing of repayments will vary, depending on the location, size, and infrastructure of your organization. Having a frequent repayment schedule may be costly and time consuming, while a prolonged repayment schedule can hurt the borrower by leaving money in their hands for too long, thereby possibly resulting in a loan default. You can also experiment with repayment schedules, and from there, determine the best schedule for your area and circumstances.

Default Terms and Rules

It is generally the practice that if borrowers default on their loans, they will lose their ability to receive another one. As mentioned above, the borrower should clearly understand this procedure. It may be necessary to have other rules or regulations—such as not allowing anyone in the defaulter's group to borrower larger loan amounts. Always make sure that said policies are enforced. Likewise, do your best to ensure that your policies are fair to both the organization and the borrowers.

Step 9: Preparing for Setbacks

Always keep in mind that wherever you work, you will face various challenges and setbacks, especially in the first few years of any organization start-up, whether it's for-profit or nonprofit. In some cases, you may be able to prepare for such eventualities, but in others you will not be able to prevent failures. However, having a good understanding of the region can sometimes help you predict difficult times, and will help you prepare for such future scenarios.

Establish Procedures for Unforeseen Events

Make sure that you have—and that all your employees are familiar with—well-defined and established procedures for a variety of potential unforeseeable events. These can range from natural disasters and political unrest to uncontrollable economic instability or epidemics, to name only a few. So train and *retrain* your employees, and your clients also, in said procedures. In a worst-case scenario, create an "emergency exit" plan to minimize loss to both clients and the organization in extreme circumstances. Below are a few policies that will mitigate damage or help revamp your organization after an unforeseen event.

Insurance

A simple way to mitigate loss from an unforeseen event is to have insurance. One way to approach this situation is for the NGO as an organization to buy insurance that will protect it in difficult times. Another way to approach this situation, if you're operating an MFI, is to have the borrowers pay for the insurance. Either you can automatically add a fraction of the insurance costs into their regular repayment schedule, or you can give the borrower the option to pay an additional fee that would cover her or him in a difficult future situation.

Loan Modification

This is a practical method of helping those whose livelihood has been severely damaged or wiped out in a natural disaster or other similar unforeseen event. In short, by either lowering the borrower's loan rate or changing their repayment schedule, you split the loss between the organization and the borrower. This will give needed assistance to the borrower, and will ensure that the borrower maintains a relationship with your organization.

Step 10: Documenting the System

As with any well-run business, accurate documentation is key to an efficient and sustainable organization. So spend the time and resources necessary to ensure that your employees have the means and knowledge of how to document their work accurately and effectively. In the long run, this will create a more efficient organization and prevent many of the problems organizations face. Document, document, *document!*

Celebrate and Openly Discuss Victories

Share success stories freely and frequently. If borrowers see the success of others, they will often work harder to achieve success for themselves. Sharing success stories by either word of mouth or local newspaper or radio coverage encourages and instills a sense of hope among those receiving benefits such as schools, wells, medicines, better houses, or the microloans themselves.

Evaluate the Program

Make sure to evaluate the operations of your NGO, at least yearly. The more frequent the evaluation, the better you will adapt to changing conditions among those you are lending. Make sure to get input from the participants, managers, and anyone else who is important in the organization. Finding any way to improve processes will help the NGO better in the long run.

Learn from Mistakes and Adjust Accordingly
Too often, nonprofit organizations seek to hide or push away their failures, fearing that such information if shared may hurt or weaken the organization. Yet if problems and failures are swept away, then they will never be addressed, thus preventing needed corrections and solutions from surfacing. Always keep in mind that a successful organization is forever practicing what the management literature has emphasized for decades. Adhere to the motto that the astoundingly successful Japanese auto industry developed long ago: *"Continuous Improvement."* Publicly acknowledging problems may hurt you in the short term, but if addressed, that will definitely be beneficial in the long run. Similarly, if you have gathered good documentation, it can help other organizations that are likely to run into similar problems that your organization has already faced.

Step 11: Being Ready to Change the World
Whether you achieve the success you want initially or not, keep on going. There are a plethora of opportunities and thousands of individuals who desperately need your help. In the wise words of Robert F. Kennedy, "Each time a man stands up for an ideal, or acts to improve the lot of others, or strikes out against injustice, he sends forth a tiny ripple of hope . . . and crossing each other from a million different centers of energy and daring, those ripples build a current that can sweep down the mightiest walls of oppression and resistance" (Kennedy, 1966).

Creating a New NGO: Suggestions from Unitus
In addition to the preceding model for establishing a new NGO, the final paragraphs below capture significant nonprofit start-up advice from Unitus, the influential NGO we established in Provo,

Utah, in 1999. My edits and reframing of suggestions were done in 2021 exclusively for this new book, *Radiant Mormonism*.

Before we get complicated, let's simplify something.

An important way you can take action is to create your own nonprofit organization. Compared with simply volunteering to serve with another NGO, in this chapter I have detailed effective steps to establish a new organization. You will learn that such an option increases in complexity and commitment as time goes on! So, even if you have any hesitation at all about getting involved, I suggest that you start simply. But the most important thing is to *start!*

I also urge you to be prayerful about your decision to begin. Don't overcommit. "It is not requisite," as King Benjamin said, "that a man should run faster than he has strength" (Mosiah 4:27). One reason some people resist getting involved in LDS economic development is that they feel that their lives are already too complicated and busy. I firmly believe that by following the Spirit and taking some easy first steps, you will find that while joining in this great effort will add some complexity to your life, it will be far more than matched by the joy it will add. You will literally be able to point to a part of Zion—wherever it may be on the globe—that has become more beautiful because of your sacrifice.

In his journal, Wilford Woodruff describes a meeting he attended in Kirtland, Ohio, in 1834. At this point the membership of the church numbered only a few hundred. The future of the kingdom didn't look particularly bright. Persecution and financial difficulties were increasing in proportion to the growth of the church. It was in this context that the Prophet Joseph Smith asked each of the Brethren assembled in a log cabin that day to bear a five-minute testimony about the future of the church. When they finished, Joseph sustained what had been said, but added that they did not have "any idea of the magnitude of the work in which they are engaged. It will go to the Rocky Mountains, and will eventually fill all of North and South America" (Woodruff, 1969, pp. 38–39).

When this prediction was made, all members of the LDS priesthood in Kirtland were listening in a 14-foot-square log cabin.

It says a great deal about Joseph that in a dingy little Ohio cabin, in the midst of overwhelming opposition, his vision could extend so far beyond his current reality. He saw not only the saints in our day, but beyond. Today, the growth of the church is breathtaking. In places like the Philippines, where there was little more than a branch only three decades ago, we now have thousands of strong wards and branches. Both Brazil and Mexico exceed a million LDS members each, and continue to grow rapidly. In Joseph's day, in the 1840s, the biggest barrier to growth of the church was finding the honest in heart. Today there are many around the world willing to listen and join, but too few who are able to lead. According to President Gordon B. Hinckley, "As the church moves out across the world and into the future we face two very serious problems. The first [problem] is the training of local leadership" (Hinckley, 1999).

And so it is with nonprofits doing economic development. Today we could probably fit the leaders of LDS-focused economic development efforts in a cabin only 14 feet square. The handful of examples of strategies I describe in this book are not merely a representative list, they are almost an exhaustive one! While I'm confident that there are dozens of small-scale efforts under way that I'm not yet aware of, I'm equally certain there are nowhere *near* the thousands of NGOs that are needed. If Zion is to put on her "beautiful garments" (Isaiah, 52:1), if we are to abolish her slums to history, millions of people will need to be involved in ways I have outlined in this book. And before millions can be involved, we will truly need thousands of leaders.

I hope this volume points to some strategies you can take to get started for those so inclined. I pray that *Radiant Mormonism* can be a resource, as well, to linking you with others who are joining the search for solutions. I trust that the case histories and principles described in these pages will be like a Liahona pointing to possible directions in a couple of ways. First, they are not a roadmap—they don't lay out the whole terrain and show the specific steps. Those who want a roadmap will not make it as leaders in the work before us, because no such map exists. What we have instead are multiple cases of NGO interventions that can inspire and guide us, as well as principles that we can use to judge whether the direction we're taking is valid. Second, as we head in a basically "right direction," we'll need the confidence in continued revelation that Nephi had who went "not knowing beforehand" the things he'd do (1 Nephi 4:6). Experience in the workings of the Spirit and comfort with ambiguity are twin qualifications for those who would lead in this exciting and fulfilling work.

May you continuously add your own nongovernmental organization "ripple effects" to the pool of hope in the communities and villages in which you will operate. In so doing, the counsel of a church prophet early in the 20th century may inspire you in designing your own NGO to serve God's suffering children, the masses of the Third World. Declared Joseph F. Smith: "The great commandment, as taught by our Lord and Master, is to love God with all our heart, with all our mind, and with all our strength; and the next is like unto it: love thy neighbor as thyself. 'On these hang all the law and the prophets.' Therefore, let us exercise charity and forgiveness, love and mercy, one towards another; and *go out of your way to help those that are in distress*, so that the widow's voice shall not ascend to God in complaint against the people for lack of food, or raiment or shelter. See to it that charity pervades all your actions and dwells in your hearts, *inspiring you to look after the poor and afflicted*, comforting those that are in prison, if they need comforting, and ministering unto those that are sick; for he that giveth a cup of cold water to a prophet in the name of a prophet will receive a prophet's reward" (Smith, 1998, p. 193).

In concluding this chapter, let us recall the admonition of the Prophet Joseph, who declared that the too-narrow assumptions and practices of many Latter-day Saints are far too meagerly on our own little nuclear families. His plea was for us to seek and fulfill his clarion call to action: "A man filled with the love of God is not content with blessing his family alone, but ranges through the whole world, anxious to bless the whole human race" (Roberts, 1961, p. 227).

References

Hinckley, G. B. (1999). National Press Club Speech in Washington D.C., March 9.

Isaiah 52:1. Old Testament.

Kennedy, R. F. (1966). University of Cape Town So. Africa, June 6. https://images.history.com/images/media/pdf/RFKRippleofHope_Study_Guide.pdf.

Mosiah 4:27. Book of Mormon.

1 Nephi 4:6. Book of Mormon.

Roberts, B. H. (1961). *History of the Church of Jesus Christ of Latter-day Saints*, 3rd ed., vol. 4.

Smith, J. F. (1998). *Teachings of Presidents of the Church: Joseph F. Smith*. Intellectual Reserve.

Woodruff, W. (1969). *Discourses of Wilford Woodruff*. (Edited by G. H. Durham.) Bookcraft.

Note I express appreciation for the last few paragraphs above, about establishing an NGO start-up. I acknowledge my collaboration on those paragraphs with my friend Joseph Grenny and my student Todd Manwaring, coauthors with me of a small book about Unitus, issued in 2000 by Zion Cooperative Publications, titled *United for Zion: Principles for Uniting the Saints and Eliminating Poverty*.

"A Poor Wayfaring Man of Grief"
LDS Hymns, No. 29

1. A poor, wayfaring Man of grief
   Hath often crossed me on my way,
   Who sued so humbly for relief
   That I could never answer nay.
   I had not pow'r to ask his name,
   Whereto he went, or whence he came;
   Yet there was something in his eye
   That won my love; I knew not why.

2. Once, when my scanty meal was spread,
   He entered; not a word he spake,
   Just perishing for want of bread.
   I gave him all; he blessed it, brake,
   And ate, but gave me part again.
   Mine was an angel's portion then,
   For while I fed with eager haste,
   The crust was manna to my taste.

3. I spied him where a fountain burst
   Clear from the rock; his strength was gone.
   The heedless water mocked his thirst;
   He heard it, saw it hurrying on.
   I ran and raised the suff'rer up;
   Thrice from the stream he drained my cup,
   Dipped and returned it running o'er;
   I drank and never thirsted more.

4. 'Twas night; the floods were out; it blew
   A winter hurricane aloof.
   I heard his voice abroad and flew
   To bid him welcome to my roof.
   I warmed and clothed and cheered my guest
   And laid him on my couch to rest,
   Then made the earth my bed and seemed
   In Eden's garden while I dreamed.

5. Stript, wounded, beaten nigh to death,
   I found him by the highway side.
   I roused his pulse, brought back his breath,
   Revived his spirit, and supplied
   Wine, oil, refreshment—he was healed.
   I had myself a wound concealed,
   But from that hour forgot the smart,
   And peace bound up my broken heart.

6. In pris'n I saw him next, condemned
   To meet a traitor's doom at morn.
   The tide of lying tongues I stemmed,
   And honored him 'mid shame and scorn.
   My friendship's utmost zeal to try,
   He asked if I for him would die.
   The flesh was weak; my blood ran chill,
   But my free spirit cried, "I will!"

7. Then in a moment to my view
   The stranger started from disguise.
   The tokens in his hands I knew;
   The Savior stood before mine eyes.
   He spake, and my poor name he named,
   "Of me thou hast not been ashamed.
   These deeds shall thy memorial be;
   Fear not, thou didst them unto me."

Text: James Montgomery (1771–1854)
Music: George Coles (1792–1858)

10

Conclusion— Practicing Personal Consecration Globally Through Private, Personal, and Social Innovations

(December 2021)

To the left is the final LDS hymn in this book for the reader to reflect on, printed in its entirety. It always reminds me, not only of the suffering of the Prophet Joseph Smith, who languished in Missouri's Liberty Jail, imprisoned by a ruthless mob who killed him soon after. A fellow prisoner, John Taylor, humbly sang these words. I think of the many people I've seen struggle and languish in prisons of poverty, simply hoping for a slice of bread, a clean drink of water, or a bed for their child.

This final chapter of *Radiant Mormonism* briefly seeks to integrate the various gospel principles that should guide us as Latter-day Saints in living the "abundant life." It does so by summarizing prophetic teachings about how to live lives of dignity by serving the living globally, beginning with close friends and neighbors, but

▲ This book's author with caregivers at a Nepal orphanage where children were abandoned after their parents committed suicide over their inability to feed, educate, and otherwise care for their families

▼ Meaning in the author's life has included trying to live like Jesus, including washing and applying oils to the legs and feet of India's lepers. Empowering those who struggle is always a source of joy. We should never, ever ignore or forget the struggling children of a Heavenly Father.

then spreading far beyond our nice little comfort zone with an expansive view. We can either hunker down and play it safe, focusing on our nuclear family and local neighborhood. *Or* we can feel the spirit of Zion that changes our perspective, reaching out to bless dozens of others, followed by hundreds, and perhaps thousands. It's totally up to us.

These paragraphs will include a few quotes from earlier chapters in a sort of review and synthesis, along with new sources that integrate and summarize our callings to change the world. I begin with the stirring words of President Gordon B. Hinckley, who said, "If we are to build that Zion of which the prophets have spoken and of which the Lord has given mighty promise, we must set aside our consuming selfishness. We must rise above our love for comfort and ease, and in the very process of effort and struggle, even in our extremity, we shall become better acquainted with our God" (Hinckley, 1991, p. 59).

A century earlier, the church's radical and fiery leader John Taylor cried out against the greed and selfishness of the Utah pioneers, calling on them, even demanding that they provide economic support to create jobs for the many saints who were unemployed and hungry. "Talk about financiering! Financier for the poor, for the working man, who requires labor and is willing to do it, and act in the interest of the community for the welfare of Zion, and the building up of the kingdom of God upon the earth. This is your calling; it is not to build up yourselves, but to build up the Church and kingdom of God.... Do not let us have anybody crying for bread, or suffering, for want of employment. Let us furnish employment for all" (Taylor, 1878, p. 308).

Twentieth century LDS apostles and prophets have consistently admonished church members to move above and beyond their conspicuous consumption and materialism by actually seeking to practice principles of stewardship, consecration, and United Order values today. As President Lorenzo Snow articulated the matter, we are to dwell essentially as equals, "for the purpose of uniting the Latter-Day Saints, the people of God, and preparing them for exaltation in the celestial kingdom, and also for the purpose of preparing them here on this earth to live together as brethren ... so that there shall be no poor found in the midst of the Latter-Day Saints, and no monied aristocracy in the midst of the people of God" (Snow, 1878, p. 342).

For instance, the apostle John A. Widtsoe, a respected scientist and one of the church's most brilliant leaders, told church members to closely adhere to such ideals, not in some distant future or hoped-for millennium, but here and now. He saw that the criteria for judging any economic strategy should be to compare it with the system of the United Order. Why? Because it has "a practical value as an ideal by which any proposed economic system may be tested for the degree of its worthiness. The nearer any scheme for economic betterment conforms to the principles of the United Order, the more likely it will be to assist humankind in their efforts to attain material happiness ... for human welfare, for developing human lives, and for providing the prosperity needed on the path of human progress" (Widtsoe, 1943, pp. 633–34).

Based on the principles and strategies of various nongovernmental organizations that I have described in the chapters of *Radiant Mormonism*, many of these programs seem to closely match many aspects of the gospel methods for achieving both temporal well-being and economic development. As President Ezra Taft Benson put it, United Order values are critical to worthy LDS living: "We must not lose sight of the fact that all we are doing now is but a prelude to the establishment of the United Order, and living the law of consecration. The individual saints must understand this" (Benson, 1988, p. 123). Are we following his admonition?

Joseph Smith taught that we have the opportunity and responsibility "to feed the hungry, to clothe the naked, to provide for the widow, to dry up the tear of the orphan, to comfort the afflicted, whether in this church or any other, or in no church at all, wherever he finds them" (1842, p. 732). One of Joseph's earliest apostles, John Taylor (1879), preached the doctrine of full employment for God's children, declaring "that you require among yourselves; and also find employment for every man and woman and child within this Stake that wants to labor. That is what you should do" (p. 165).

Today in 2021, our challenges are every bit as great as in earlier years of church history, because we must unite God's children, not merely spiritually or psychologically, but economically as well. Let us remember the counsel cited in chapter 1 from President Joseph F. Smith (1905). He pointed out that the Prophet Joseph believed that "a religion which has not the power to save people temporally and make them prosperous and happy here, cannot be depended upon to save them spiritually, to exalt them in the life to come" (p. 242).

In raising and teaching our large family the full meaning of the gospel, my wife, Kaye, and I have sought to educate and—more importantly—practice the fullness of a "Zion lifestyle," giving as much money as possible to the church and to the many good organizations seeking to assist those who suffer. We've been blessed with sufficient resources to manage on roughly half of our income so that we could donate the other half to those needing temporal support.

In doing this, we've drawn on several magnificent scriptural sources to guide our lifestyles. One is from Nephi's record in the Book of Mormon after Jesus's atoning sacrifice and resurrection when he appeared to the surviving, yet vanquished, Nephites. Readers will recall reading that he admonished the people to unite as a genuine Christian community. They did so, and it led to the transformational fact that they soon "had all things common among them; therefore there were not rich and poor, bond and free, but they were all free, and partakers of the heavenly gift" (4 Nephi 1:3). Over the next roughly 200 years there was equality and the prevalence of love, such that "surely there could not be a happier people among all the people who had been created by the hand of God" (4 Nephi 1:16).

Many excerpts from the Book of Mormon warn us about the problems of pride related to our obsession with material things. Today, in 2021, I worry not only about many Americans' obsessions with fancy cars, their ever-ending acquisition of electronic toys, and their insatiable "need" to dine at the most expensive restaurants and travel to exotic resorts. I also worry about their fixation on designer brands of jewelry and clothing. "And it came to pass ... that the people of the church began to wax proud, because of their exceeding riches, and their fine silks, and their fine-twined linen ... and in all these things were they lifted up in the pride of their eyes, for they began to wear very costly apparel" (Alma 4:6).

A valuable religious story about living simply and observing the values of a more-righteous economics that has always guided decisions of righteous people comes from the scriptures detailing the works and words of the ancient prophet Enoch in the *Pearl of Great Price*. I've especially appreciated the insights about the City of Enoch from one of our most literate and scholarly apostles, Elder Neal Maxwell. He wrote a small, 64-page volume entitled *Of One Heart: The Glory of the City of Enoch*. In it, Apostle Maxwell writes of how that particular utopian society grew out of the righteous, Zion practices of God's people over hundreds of years. But how were they able to practice consecration and stewardship during those turbulent times? Elder Maxwell (1979, pp. 37–39) points out that they had "learned not to withhold affection and esteem from each other" and this practice eventually led to their "no longer holding back" their goods. "Enoch tells us that it is not given that one man should possess that which is above another, wherefore the world lieth in sin." Maxwell also articulates important gospel principles and cultural values of the followers of Enoch, including the fact that they achieved greater efficiency by laboring in love; they highly valued the work ethic; and they used cooperation rather than competition as their motivation. The ultimate result? "The Lord called his people ZION" (Moses 7:18).

How to achieve this is, of course, a major question. Apostle George Q. Cannon, counselor in the First Presidency of Brigham Young, is one of many leaders besides Jesus Himself to call on us to reduce human suffering. But even he admitted this is a complex issue. As he once pointed out, we must be up to the task because the Lord of Heaven Himself had "chosen his people, the Latter-day Saints, to solve these knotty problems that have troubled the brains and afflicted the children of men for so many centuries" (Cannon, 1869, p. 99). I sincerely hope that this book offers some useful guidance.

As one of the perhaps-radical early pioneers, Elder Cannon (1878) also voiced his concern that the LDS people would become too proud and greedy—which apparently has come true, when we observe Utah's many wealthy mansions and expensive automobiles while the masses have no access to low cost-housing and must use public transportation for their often-menial jobs. We witness far too many poor families, children without medical care, and rejection of migrants fleeing crime and poverty south of the U.S. border. As Lorenzo Snow preached, "Now let things go on in our midst in our Gentile fashion, and you would see an aristocracy growing amongst us, whose language to the poor would be, 'We do not require your company; we are going to have things very fine; we are quite busy now, please call some other time.' You would have classes established here, some very poor and some very rich. Now, the Lord is not going to have anything of that kind. There has to be an equality; and we have to observe these principles that are designed to give everyone the privilege of gathering around him the comforts and conveniences of life" (Snow, 1878, p. 349).

Joseph Smith (1977) himself declared: "The greatest temporal and spiritual blessings which always come from faithfulness and concentrated effort, never attended individual exertion or enterprise"—a sharp contrast to the so-called rugged individualism of the early West, as well as the extreme greed and selfishness of the present era (p. 183). In addition, he taught that it is our responsibility "to feed the hungry, to clothe the naked, to provide for the widow, to dry up the tear of the orphan, to comfort the afflicted, whether in this church or in any other, or in no church at all, wherever he finds them" (1842, p. 732).

Elder Cannon (1878) also decreed that a "man who has got the blessings of God around him, should be willing to sacrifice a portion of his surplus means to establish some industry, that this poor man can work and obtain a good remuneration for his labor, that he can see comfort and convenience before him, by persevering as he has done who has been thus blessed. This is the spirit and aim of the United Order, and that we should endeavor to establish. We should employ our surplus means in a manner that the poor can have employment and see before them a competence and the conveniences of life, so that they may not be dependent upon their neighbors" (p. 349).

We learn by carefully focusing on this principle stated in the revelations received in the church's early days. For example: "If any man shall take of the abundance which I have made, and impart not his portion, according to the law of my gospel, unto the poor and the needy, he shall, with the wicked, lift up his eyes in hell, being in torment" (*Doctrine and Covenants* 104:18). I've often inquired of some of my LDS friends and close neighbors about this verse. The occasional replies include such responses as these: "Well, I don't read it exactly that way." Or, "This is referring to the future when the millennium is on earth." Or even "When the president of the church orders me to share what I have with the poor, I'll do so. But not now."

If our responsibility in becoming a "beloved community," as the Rev. Martin Luther King, Jr., called for, or in building a Zion community, as LDS scriptures mandate, the question of our willingness to live simply so as to give our extra money and things to help the poor is quite problematic. At least this seems to be true, according to Brigham Young. Said he, when stressing the principle of consecration during a great 1855 sermon in the Salt Lake Tabernacle:

> The brethren wished me to go among the churches, and find out what surplus property the people had.... Before I started, I asked Brother Joseph, 'Who shall be the judge of what is surplus property?' Said he, 'Let them be the judges themselves.... I never [found] a man yet who had a dollar of surplus property. No matter how much one might have, he wanted all he had for himself, for his children, his grandchildren, and so forth.... Occasionally,

some were disposed to do right with their surplus property; and once in a while you would find a man who had a cow which he considered surplus, but generally she was of a class that would kick a person's hat off, or eyes out, or the wolves had eaten off her teats. You would once in a while find a man who had a horse that he considered surplus, but at the same time he had the ringbone, was broken-winded, spavined in both legs, and had the pole evil at one end of the neck and a fistula at the other, and both knees sprung (Young, 1855, p. 307).

Apparently, after the pioneers began emigrating to territorial Utah, in what was then called the early Great Basin Kingdom, they had the same love of material things and reluctance to hold onto every single possession as do many Latter-day Saints living comfortably today.

    A dear friend of mine, Joe Christensen, raised this point in one General Conference. He had been the director of the Institute of Religion at the University of Utah when I was an undergraduate student there, and I had taken his inspiring class. Later he was named head of the Church Education System and was my supervisor when I founded the institute program in Ann Arbor at the University of Michigan. After serving as president of BYU Idaho, he was appointed a General Authority Seventy. In General Conference he once offered good insights about the extent of our giving to disenfranchised, struggling families, including citing C. S. Lewis's 1952 little volume *Mere Christianity*. Joe's suggestion? "In addition to paying an honest tithing, we should be generous in assisting the poor. How much should we give? I appreciate the thought of C. S. Lewis on this subject. He said: 'I am afraid the only safe rule is to give more than we can spare.... If our charities do not at all pinch or hamper us . . . they are too small. There ought to be things we should like to do and cannot do because our charitable expenditures excludes them'" (Christensen, 1999, p.4).

    President Spencer W. Kimball (1977) saw the folly of our latter-day possessiveness and greed that apparently block the powers of heaven from radiating down on us. He reminded us that "Pres.

Joseph F. Smith said: 'You must continue to bear in mind that the temporal and the spiritual are blended. They are not separate. One cannot be carried on without the other, so long as we are here in mortality.' The highest achievement of spirituality comes as we conquer the flesh. We build character as we encourage people to care for their own needs. As givers gain control of their desires and properly see others' needs in light of their own wants, then the powers of the gospel are released in their lives. They learn that by living the great law of consecration, they ensure temporal salvation and spiritual sanctification. Isn't the plan beautiful? Don't you thrill to this part of the gospel that causes Zion to put on her beautiful garments? When viewed in this light, [this is] the essence of the gospel. It is the gospel in action. It is the crowning principle of a Christian life" (1977, pp. 76—79).

President Kimball's counsel is akin to the prophetic words of the Book of Mormon prophet Jacob, who clearly informs us regarding how riches can be acquired and the things for which they should be used: "But before ye seek for riches, seek ye for the kingdom of God. And after ye have obtained a hope in Christ ye shall obtain riches, if ye seek them ... for the intent to do good—to clothe the naked, and to feed the hungry, and to liberate the captive, and administer relief to the sick and the afflicted" (Jacob 2:18–19). I don't read into these words anything about building my personal empire, or acquiring an expensive new car every year—not even a Tesla for a discounted cost of "only" $92,000. I have many friends who spend much of their time seeking new jobs, better compensation, and new career adventures in large corporations. They acquire multi-million-dollar homes every 12 to 18 months, owning one, two, or three simultaneously. An acquaintance of mine in Salt Lake City finally decided to sell his $47 million home because his two daughters were going off to college and he said he didn't need such a "large" house anymore.

As one of my mentors, the great LDS humanitarian Lowell Bennion, told me about such things: "I'm not judging. But I do question some people's point of view" (Bennion, 1982). I learned much from him since I was a young University of Utah college student, enjoying our wonderful conversations. Over the years, Lowell wrote a slew of official church manuals, integrating the LDS faith with writings of the world's great philosophers and some of their theories. He advised top LDS Church leaders through the decades. He helped develop the Church Education System (CES), including being greatly honored by President Gordon B. Hinckley, the main speaker at Lowell's funeral. I have tried to follow his motto since we were both Institute of Religion directors who collaborated with LDS students in teaching the gospel for many years. In fact, the Brethren called him to establish the very first University of Utah Institute program. After he finally left that position on campus, he became a professor, as I did also. But on doing so, and forever after, he would say: "I used to teach religion; now I practice it."

As I remember "Brother B," as he was affectionately called by many students at the University of Utah, including some who became General Authorities, even apostles, one of his published insights comes to mind. In a small, simple 1996 volume, he raised the specter of what ancient prophets from Old Testament times might decree today in challenging our modern LDS comfortableness with practicing our religion on special days with designated ordinances, yet overlooking the very essence of true religion. "Much of the Old Testament ritual rejected by the prophets, such as burnt offerings, has little meaning for us today. To sense the full impact of these prophetic teachings, we need to use present rituals. Wouldn't we be shocked if a prophet today speaking for God should say to the Saints: 'I hate your baptisms and sacrament service. I will not hear your prayers and songs any more. Amen to your priesthood. Be honest in your dealings, be merciful to the poor and afflicted, be understanding to the needs of others. Then my spirit will be with you and you will be with me'" (Bennion, 1996, p. 32). "Brother B's" philosophy centered on charity and compassion—not status, authority, and ritual. To me this suggests that we are to find our deepest religious experiences in feeding the hungry and aiding impoverished widows. Such a view parallels my own. He worried about our materialism as LDS members, including our emphasis on luxury, which he explains "by its very definition means going beyond need. I also see a strong motivation of self-indulgence and vanity" (Bennion, 1988, p. 44).

I truly hope that my friends and co-laborers who seek to build a better world have enjoyed and will profit from a few ideas and experiences detailed in *Radiant Mormonism* by those of us who have launched new social ventures to reduce human suffering and empower the poor. Some years ago, I was asked to write a brief testimony about my faith on an LDS website, "Mormon Scholars Testify," a project that several members of the LDS religion faculty at Brigham Young University established for FAIR Mormon, a research organization. I add it today in bearing witness to the church and the entire world:

> The highest level of Mormonism is that of Stewardship and Consecration, meaning we are called to practice what we preach. While some Mormons feel that such practices are reserved for some future date when the Church announces we should begin building consecrated lives, many of us understand on deeper levels that the time to do so is here and now. The bulk of my adult and family life has centered on offering all I have to God and His children. Related principles are equality, simplicity, sacrifice, pure motives, cooperation, and other United Order values which inspire us to serve the poor and needy. As saints of the latter days we are told to give of our time, money, and skills to building Zion, a condition in which there is no poverty, no tears, no sorrow.... My testimony is a matter of practice, a way of living. *My life is my witness. Service to others is Warner Woodworth's testimony.* In conclusion, let me affirm my commitment to the practices of the LDS Church. It is an article of my faith that I believe in being honest, true, chaste, benevolent, virtuous, and in doing good to all. I believe all things, I hope all things, I have endured many things, and hope to be able to endure all things. If there is anything

virtuous, lovely, or of good report or praiseworthy, I seek after these things (Woodworth, 2010).

As I conclude this book, I recall a great sermon by Brigham Young (*Journal of Discourses*, 1868, p. 153) delivered in the Old Salt Lake Tabernacle as he sought to inspire the early Latter-day Saints—not only about how heaven would be in the future, but how we are able, here and now, in this life, to eliminate poverty, serve God deeply, practice our own beautiful United Orders, and build our own personal Zions. He called for love and unity, in which efforts to achieve success, fame, and power become nonexistent. We can build our utopia here on earth, not needing to await the Savior's Second Coming. Nor do we need to passively depend on our church leaders to issue the command to move to a New Jerusalem. No, that is not necessary. Below is the great pioneer prophet's vision for us, here and now, today:

> I have looked upon the community of the Latter-day Saints in vision and beheld them organized as one great family of heaven, each person performing his several duties in his line of industry, working for the good of the whole more than for individual aggrandizement; and in this I have beheld the most beautiful order that the mind of man can contemplate, and the grandest results for the building up of the kingdom of God and the spread of righteousness upon the earth. Will this people ever come to this order of things? Are they now prepared to live according to that patriarchal order that will be organized among the true and faithful before God receives His own? We all concede the point that when this mortality falls off; and with it its cares, anxieties, love of self, love of wealth, and love of power, and all the conflicting interests which pertain to this flesh, that then, when our spirits have returned to God who gave them, we will be subject to every requirement that he may make of us, that we shall then live together as one great family; our interest will be a general, a common interest. Why can we not so live in this world?

References

Alma 4:6.

Bennion, L. L. (1982). Personal conversation with the author.

Bennion, L. L. (1988). *Do Justly and Love Mercy: Moral Issues for Mormons.* Cannon Press.

Bennion, L. L. (1996). *How Can I Help: Final Selections by the Legendary Writer, Teacher, and Humanitarian.* Aspen Books.

Benson, E. T. (1988). *Teachings of Ezra Taft Benson.* Bookcraft.

Cannon, G. Q. (1869). *Journal of Discourses*, vol. 13.

Cannon, G. Q. (1878). *Journal of Discourses*, vol. 19.

Christensen, J. J. (1999). "Greed, Selfishness, and Overindulgence." General Conference, April. https://www.churchofjesuschrist.org/study/general-conference/1999/04/greed-selfishness-and-overindulgence.

Doctrine and Covenants 104:18.

Hinckley, G. B. (1991). "Our Mission of Saving." *Ensign*, November.

Jacob 2:18–19.

Kimball, S. W. (1977). *Ensign*, November.

Maxwell, N. A. (1979). *Of One Heart: The Glory of the City of Enoch.* Deseret Book. (See pp. 20, 37–39, 49.)

Moses 7:18. *The Pearl of Great Price.*

4 Nephi 1:3, 16.

Smith, J. (1842). *Times and Seasons*, March 15.

Smith, J. (1977). *Teachings of the Prophet Joseph Smith.* Joseph Fielding Smith (ed.). Deseret Book.

Smith, J. F. (1905). "The Truth About Mormonism," *Out West*, vol. 23.

Snow, L. (1878). *Journal of Discourses*, vol. 19. https://jod.mrm.org/19/341.

Taylor, J. (1875). *Journal of Discourses*, vol. 20.

Taylor, J. (1878). *Journal of Discourses.* vol. 19, Discourse 43. Also published in the *Latter-day Saint Millennial Star*. April 8.

Widtsoe, J. A. (1943). *Evidences and Reconciliations.* Bookcraft. Also in *Improvement Era*, vol. 43.

Woodworth, W. (2010). Mormon Scholars Testify. FAIR Mormon website. https://www.fairlatterdaysaints.org/testimonies/scholars/warner-p-woodworth. September.

Young, B. (1855). *Journal of Discourses*, vol. 2.

Young, B. (1868). *Journal of Discourses*, vol. 12.

Appendix I

Private NGOs with and without a Latter-day Saint Connection

This appendix provides a listing of humanitarian organizations that have either an economic development or a Latter-day Saint focus—or sometimes both. Additional sources indicate nongovernmental organizations and organizations that are not LDS-connected, but are still relevant. Those contained in this appendix have been divided into four categories. At the time of printing, some of the connections may have relocated or disbanded completely. Yet they derive from the author's previous lists and may still be pursued from their previous origins until now in 2021. The assignment of organizations to these categories is based on a fairly rough scale but may not be entirely accurate; if some are not fully up-to-date, perhaps more information can be accessed on the internet, as well as on social media such as Facebook, LinkedIn, and other sources.

The authors have included myself and several volunteer students during the various iterations of this NGO appendix, which I have used as a handout at conferences, at presentations at the University of Utah and Harvard, and also internationally.

Economic Development with a Latter-day Saint Connection

The organizations listed below have both an economic development and a Latter-day Saint involvement, or at least, being based in Utah, they have had many church members volunteer or donate to their causes. To qualify for the economic development component, organizations should be working, at least in part, with microfinance, cooperatives, or business training. Likewise, in order to qualify for the Latter-day Saint component, organizations should have an LDS connection with either the provision of aid or the receiving of aid.

Academy for Creating Enterprise

P.O. Box 299
Lehi, UT 84043
https://www.the-academy.org/

(801) 609-7448
info@the-academy.org

The Academy for Creating Enterprise is a nonprofit educational training center designed to teach Filipino returned missionaries skills that will enable them to become self-reliant by starting and growing small businesses in the Philippines. It is organized by members of the LDS Church, and has more closely connected with the Church recently. The Academy's purpose is to help build up the income-earning capabilities of Filipino returned missionaries so they can financially strengthen their families in the provinces and become self-reliant. In that way it provides an opportunity to contribute to the grass-roots development of the Philippine economy.

Acción Contra la Pobreza

615 South State St. (801) 932-2404
Orem, UT 84058

Acción Contra la Pobreza, translating as "Action Against Poverty," is also called the ACP program. It is a microcredit model that has grown out of the experience of BYU students working with HELP International. The ACP methodology of microlending specifically caters to the needs of the poorest of the poor. This program provides loans to groups of five to nine women year round in Tegucigalpa, the capital city of Honduras.

Alma Success Academy

1431 North 1200 West (877) 472-4705
Orem, UT 84057 (801) 426-9500
www.almasuccessacademy.org milt@almasuccessacademy.org

Organized in the fall of 1999, the Alma Success Academy provides scholarships and volunteer teachers to help returned missionaries and other Latter-day Saint young adults in Latin America qualify for family-supporting jobs in the professions or trades. The first Alma Success Academy at Quetzaltenango, Guatemala, is enjoying success in its mission to provide, as President Gordon B. Hinckley said when he announced the creation of the Perpetual Education Fund, these "young men and women of capacity...a ladder by which they can climb out of the impoverishment that surrounds them to make something better of their lives, to occupy places of honor and respect in society and to make a contribution of significance to the nation of which they are a part." In addition to their scholarship-funded university or trade programs, ASA students are taught English, Computer Applications, Spanish Business Writing, Christian Ethics, and Personal Money Management. Elective courses include Entrepreneurship, Accounting, and Economics. ASA plans to open other centers throughout Mexico and both Central and South America.

CHOICE

(Center for Humanitarian Outreach and Intercultural Exchange)

    1937 South 300 West, Suite 110   (801) 474-1937
    Salt Lake City, UT 84115
    www.choice.humanitarian.org   info@choice.humanitarian.org

Organized out of the Andean Children's Foundation in 1988, CHOICE is a nonprofit, nonsectarian (though principally LDS in membership) organization that sponsors "volunteer expeditions" in which families, organizations, groups of associates, or single persons (either trained or previously untrained) "work side by side with the rural poor to develop projects which the villagers request and will be able to sustain after the expedition departs." CHOICE volunteers have worked with water supply systems, greenhouses, and schools and literacy, and have provided health and medical assistance.

Eagle Condor Humanitarian (Formerly Chasqui del Sol)

    7135 S Highland Dr.   (801) 263-2000
    Salt Lake City, UT 84121   https://www.eaglecondor.org/

Eagle Condor (Chasqui Humanitarian) is a 501(c)(3) nonprofit corporation based in Salt Lake City, Utah. Working in Peru and Bolivia, the Foundation works with local civic and LDS Church leaders through projects that will empower them to acquire for themselves what they need, and even want, so that they will raise their own standard of living and have a more fulfilling life. With a variety of projects, volunteers work in several areas including education, health, hygiene, housing, water, family gardens, agro-industry, small enterprises, microcredit, job and vocational training, and English and computer classes.

Fundacion Dignidad

Oriente 176 No. 220 011-525-571-68-04
Col. Moctezuma 2a Seccion dignidad@laneta.apc.org
Deleg. V. Carranza, Mexico, D.F.C.P. 15530

This is the partner NGO of Enterprise Mentors in Mexico, providing training, consulting, and microloans to the poor.

Grameen Support Group

270 HRCB (801) 422-3548
Brigham Young University
Provo, UT 84602 grameensupport@byu.edu

This is the first campus-affiliated Grameen support organization in the world. Its purposes include educating BYU and its larger community about microcredit, raising funds to support microlending, informing students and faculty about Third World needs, and translating Grameen materials into various languages, especially for use in Latin America.

HELP International

455 N University Ave #212 (801) 374-0556
Provo, UT 84601
www.help-international.org

In 1999, in the aftermath of Hurricane Mitch, students and faculty of Brigham Young University developed HELP International. The mission of HELP is to assist the poor of the Third World to improve their quality of life while developing competent student and community leaders for tomorrow's continued fight against poverty. By working in conjunction with other microfinance institutions, HELP provides students a hands-on experience working with microcredit. Volunteers are also given the opportunity to create, implement, and sustain their own humanitarian service projects, microcredit programs, and other development projects in the Third World.

International Development Enterprises (iDE)

IDE Worldwide (720) 924-1227
1031 33rd St., #270
Denver, CO 80205
https://www.ideglobal.org/ community@ideglobal.org

This innovation hub, called iDE, was founded in Denver by Paul Polak in 1982 to use business strategies in empowering the poor. He saw value in using "human-centered design" to create innovative solutions that improve Third World lives. For four decades the organization has mobilized farmers, technologists, teachers, and entrepreneurs to listen to the poor and to coinvent new solutions to better the world. With a staff of over a thousand experts and three main offices in the U.S., Canada, and Europe, iDE has accomplished nearly 300 major projects that have bettered life for millions of the poor. Today iDE is a global effort that spans 14 countries, encompassing four social enterprises in agriculture, water, sanitation, hygiene, and finance.

Katalysis North/South Development Partnership

1331 North Commerce St. (209) 943-6165
Stockton, CA 95202
www.katalysis.org jrgontard@katalysis

Katalysis was founded in 1984 and helped pioneer the microcredit model of economic development: the 'Bootstrap Banking' model that the organization still practices today. Instead of offering handouts that increase dependency and yield short-term results, Katalysis nurtures sustainable self-help enterprises, providing microloans and training to small businesspeople who already have tiny businesses, but lack the resources to make them profitable and sustainable—thereby building self-sufficiency and self-confidence.

LDS Church Welfare Department
(The Church of Jesus Christ of Latter-day Saints)

>50 East North Temple St., 7th Floor   801) 240-3001
>Salt Lake City, UT 84150

This department of the church provides temporal relief to Latter-day Saints and others around the globe, including food, clothing, and medical supplies in response to natural disasters, civil wars, and other emergencies. The department also operates farms, canneries, distribution centers, and employment services, primarily in the United States.

LDS Humanitarian Services/Latter-day Saint Charities

>50 East North Temple St., 8th Floor   (801) 240-1201
>Salt Lake City, UT 84150

As an outreach effort of the LDS Church, the LDS Humanitarian Services and LDS Charities are heavily involved in providing aid and technical assistance to both non-LDS and LDS needy, especially internationally. Often working in conjunction with other NGOs, this organization has helped channel relief to crisis areas such as Ethiopia, Somalia, Rwanda, and Kosovo, as well as supporting grassroots development projects in Central American and elsewhere.

Mentores Empresariales

6 Ave. 13-43 Zona 9
Guatemala City
Guatemala 01009

011-502-332-2678
011-502-332-1902 (fax)

This affiliated foundation of Enterprise Mentors in Guatemala provides training, consulting, and microloans to the poor.

Mentors International

65 Wadsworth Park Dr., Suite 207
Draper, UT 84020

(801) 676-7776
www.mentorsinternational.org

Founded in 1990 by a mostly LDS group of individuals, Mentors International is a human development foundation designed "to build self-reliance and entrepreneurial spirit within those who struggle for sufficiency in developing countries." Working first in the Philippines and now expanding to Latin America, Enterprise Mentors works with indigenous staff, building increased self-reliance. Efforts are made to charge for consulting services based on ability to pay, transforming the donor-receiver dependency relationship into a character-building, consultant-client relationship. A nonprofit, tax-exempt organization, Mentors depends on individual, foundation, and corporate donations to achieve its goals. Primary interventions include training, consulting, walk-in services, professional referrals, and access to microcredit loans.

MicroBusiness Mentors

UVU Small Business Development Center
815 West 1250 South
Orem, UT 84058

(801) 863-8230
sbdc@uvu.edu
https://microbusinessmentors.org/

MicroBusiness Mentors was founded in the Marriott School at BYU to address economic challenges, mostly of refugees and immigrants from Latin America. Operated by graduate and undergraduate students from several campuses, MBM, as it is known, offers business training, mentoring, and microloans starting at $500 to individuals seeking to become economically self-reliant. Offering tools and skills to assist Latino families in enjoying a better quality of life, MBM has succeeded for nearly two decades in enhancing people's well-being.

Mindanao Enterprise Development Foundation

Room 7, 2nd Floor
Vega Quitain Bldg., Anda Street
Davao City, Philippines 8000

011-63-82-221-0910
medf@interasia.com.ph

Affiliated foundation of Enterprise Mentors in the southern islands of the Philippines, it provides training, consulting, and microloans to the poor.

Ouelessebougou Alliance

525 East 4500 South
Salt Lake City, UT 84107
https://www.lifteachother.org/

(801) 983-6254

info@lifteachother.org

The Alliance was begun in 1985 to develop a long-term relationship with a group of villages in Mali, the West African country. The Alliance undertakes projects requested by the villagers, who define their own needs, contribute labor to projects, and provide their own leadership. Projects include constructing wells, fencing gardens, providing basic healthcare training, teaching literacy, and establishing a village bank, various microenterprises, and producer cooperatives.

Philippines Enterprise Development Foundation

791-CF Manalo St.
Barangay Bambang
Pasig City
Metro Manila, Philippines 1600

011-63-2-642-3895
011-63-2-641-2207 (fax)
pedf@compass.com.ph

The first overseas partner of Enterprise Mentors, PEDF is engaged in small-business formation, job creation, microcredit services, and technical assistance to cooperatives.

Russian Enterprise Development, Inc. (REDI)

2602 East 6200 South
Salt Lake City, UT 84121

(801) 227-1130
jdrather@msn.com

REDI is a nonprofit charitable organization established in the 1990s to assist in the development of small employee-owned enterprises in the Russian Republic and Baltic region, beginning in the city of St. Petersburg. The two primary purposes of REDI are to provide affordable business management consultation and training, and to offer access to credit to entrepreneurial groups seeking to start or improve small enterprises.

Sustain Haiti

Marriott School, BYU
Provo, UT 84602

(801) 422-1211
www.sustain-haiti.org

This student-managed NGO arose after a massive 10.1 earthquake wreaked havoc on the island nation of Haiti in the Caribbean Ocean in 2010. From a course taught by Dr. Warner Woodworth, several hundred MBA, accounting, social science, economics, and other majors for students were organized and trained to travel as volunteers beginning in spring 2010 to help rebuild communities with construction skills, microfinance, business plans, family agriculture, environmental strategies, water purification technologies, orphanage support, and more. Teaching health and hygiene, as well as providing education in schools, while also rebuilding damaged orphanages were all vital programs. U.S. teams raised funding in the states and sent summer volunteers, while the indigenous Haitian staff managed multiple programs, mostly in the town of Leogane, the earthquake's epicenter. The organization has collaborated for a decade with other NGO partners like FINCA International to assist the people of Haiti in regaining their lives and livelihoods.

Unitus
Unitus Labs, Unitus Ventures, Unitus Equity Fund, Unitus Capital, Patamar Capital, and Unitus Ventures

Seattle office	Bangalore office
815 1st Ave., #302	16/1, Haudin Rd.,
Seattle, WA 98104	Yellappa Chetty Layout,
+1 206 486 5701	Sivanchetti Gardens
	Bengaluru, Karnataka 560042
Mauritius office	www.unitus.com
9th Floor, Medine Mews	
La Chaussée Street	
Port Louis, Mauritius	
Tel: +230 203 4300	

UNITUS, a 501(c)(3) nonprofit organization, is working to find permanent solutions to poverty with an emphasis on accelerating microfinance. Having evolved over 20 years, it continues to uplift the global poor. Its staff and volunteers call the organization UNITUS (pronounced 'Unite-Us') because they believe that unity is a key to eliminating poverty. They believe that greater global unity will motivate and enable more people to get involved in helping their brothers and sisters in lasting ways. Unitus fulfills its mission in a variety of ways, including a comprehensive website, semiannual development conferences, local action groups, and sponsorship of innovative new organizations.

Visayas Enterprise Foundation

Cinco Centrum, Room 307 011-63-32-254-1979
Fuente Osmena
Cebu City, Philippines 6000 vef@cnms.net

VEF is an Enterprise Mentors affiliated foundation, which serves the central islands of the Philippines, providing job creation through training, consulting, and microcredit.

Wave of Hope

2013 North 500 East (801) 377-7576
Provo, Utah 84604

Current Offices: Original website:
455 N University Ave. https://empoweringnations.org
Provo, Utah 84601 Current website
  www.help-international.org

Wave of Hope, an organization within the NGO calling itself Empowering Nations, was launched to assist survivors of the late-2004 Indian Ocean underwater earthquake and resulting tsunami that impacted 11 countries. Organized out of Professor Warner Woodworth's class on "Becoming a Social Entrepreneur," it mobilized and trained several hundred students at BYU and other universities to volunteer in Khao Lak, Thailand, beginning in spring 2005, and continuing there and also to additional nations for a few years. Eventually, considering how it overlapped with another BYU student NGO, called HELP International, the two NGOs finally merged into a single organization.

Yehu Microfinance

P.O. Box 82120 - 80100
Mombasa Kenya

0708-343434
info@yehu.org

Yehu was established by the Provo resident Louis Pope and his Pope Family Foundation. Later it became folded into a new, much larger nonprofit called the Asante Foundation, working in Africa. Over several decades Louis Pope and his children have dedicated millions of dollars to economic and humanitarian programs while living in East Africa and hiring a large indigenous staff to help them serve rural families in the region. They have funded many thousands of microenterprises for poor women in particular, as well as established other ventures. These include a large agroforestry business to create jobs for rural farmers; a lumber mill; a charcoal-producing facility; Coast Cocoanut Farms, a factory producing women's creams and lotions sold throughout Europe and America; and in recent years Asante purchased farmland to produce plants for making essential oils, becoming a major supplier for doTerra, Inc. products sold worldwide.

Non-Economic Development with a Latter-day Saint Connection

The organizations listed within this category are working in worthy areas of humanitarian services *other than* economic development—including education, literacy, healthcare, short-term relief, and more. These organizations also have a Latter-day Saint connection on either the giving or receiving end of their work.

Academy of LDS Dentists

PO Box 483 (801) 889-7012
Pleasant Grove, UT 84062 academyofldsdentists@gmail.com
https://academyofldsdentists.com/

Founded in 1977, this organization exists to instruct and support LDS dentists. Its members have also given volunteer services in Africa, China, Israel, Mexico, South America, the Republic of Georgia, Thailand, the West Indies, and the United States.

Alliance for Youth Service

178 Springfield St. (702) 568-0088
Henderson, NV 89014
www.ays.org ebingham@ays.org

AYS (Alliance for Youth Service) is a nonprofit volunteer organization of parents, leaders, and volunteers that offers LDS teens unique service opportunities in the U.S. and abroad. They work with existing high-quality nonprofit organizations that they call Alliance Partners, such as Habitat for Humanity and Amizade, to form exclusively LDS programs. AYS provides life-changing experiences through service to others while strengthening testimonies; learning about other peoples, places, and cultures; and making new friends while helping others.

American Indian Services

3115 Lion Ln, Suite 320 (801) 375-1777
Salt Lake City, UT 84121
https://americanindianservices.org/

AIS began in 1958 to provide scholarships and other needed services to Native Americans through Brigham Young University's Indian Education Department. In 1989, AIS was established as a private charitable 501(c)(3) foundation so that it could expand its reach to Native Americans throughout the country. Its mission is to assist Native Americans in developing their human and natural resources in order to help them make a contribution to society without detracting from the culture and background from which they have emerged. AIS does this by providing scholarships, leadership and motivational seminars, agricultural projects, humanitarian projects, educational projects, and even Christmas projects for Native Americans.

Beehive Foundation

1011 West Mermod
Carlsbad, NM 88220
www.beehivefoundation.com

(800) 524-2799
(505) 885-2179
beehive_nm@hotmail.com

The Beehive Foundation organizes volunteers who supply millions of pounds of clothes to Mexico and Central America each year. It has also planted gardens and supported orphanages and children's hospitals. The Foundation seeks volunteers who want to give time, money, effort, or all three to help wipe out poverty and sickness around the world.

Bennion Center-University of Utah

200 South Central Campus Dr., Room 101
University of Utah
Salt Lake City, UT 84112

(801) 581-4811
(801) 585-9241
https://bennioncenter.org

Since its founding, the Bennion Center has been providing service opportunities to the students, faculty, staff, and alumni of the University of Utah. More than 5,000 people donate more than 100,000 hours annually to a variety of projects. Some give an hour of their time, and others give weeks or even months. In each case, volunteers learn from projects dealing with poverty, the environment, at-risk youth, the elderly, the disabled, and the like.

Benson Institute

Brigham Young University   (801) 422-2607
Provo, UT 84602
http://benson.byu.edu   benson_institute@byu.edu

The institute is now primarily connected with LDS Philanthropies
1450 N. University Ave.   Provo, UT 84604

Formally known as the Ezra Taft Benson Agriculture & Food Institute, the Benson Institute is now a LDS Church-owned organization, still a somewhat BYU-affiliated outreach program, which conducts research and provides technical assistance to small farmers, primarily in Mexico and Central America.

Charity Anywhere Foundation

PO Box 2747   (208) 734-8041
Twin Falls, ID 83303   www.charityanywhere.org
    gordon@charityanywhere.org

The Charity Anywhere Foundation has the goal of arranging service projects to anyone, anywhere, who has a real need for charitable relief. CAF offers a variety of projects including service trips to Mexico and Nicaragua as well as domestic service opportunities. CAF is looking for people who have ideas for service projects but don't know how to get started, or for volunteers for its current projects.

Collegium Aesculapium Foundation, Inc.

200 North 11 East   (801) 802-0449
Orem, UT 84057   www.collegiumaesculapium.org

The foundation is an international organization of LDS health professionals. Besides its journal and regular meetings, the foundation participates in humanitarian service by providing medical and financial support and other programs such as Adopt-A-Saint.

Deseret International Foundation

1282 East Cambridge Court   (801) 374-0167
Provo, UT 84604

Started in the Philippines in 1990, and now operating in 13 countries throughout Central and South America, Africa, Asia, and the Pacific, the foundation is "a private, nondenominational charity whose goal is to provide surgical and dental assistance primarily for children in emerging nations." Its participants are primarily medical professionals who help local medical practitioners establish adequate health facilities, perform surgeries, and reduce overhead costs by soliciting donations of medical and dental supplies.

Dolls of Hope

Orem, Utah   (801) 369-0915
https://www.dollsofhope.org

Started by Sarah Carmichael Parson, a former graduate student in neurology who joined our class to design and launch a new NGO after the 2004 Asian tsunami, this organization grew out of her managing the new organization we established, Wave of Hope, in both Thailand and the United States, for several years. She worked with others to mobilize volunteers, raise money, and help coastal villagers who survived the earthquake and waves of destruction to recover. She then was inspired to begin making soft, cuddly, homemade dolls for children who suffered, first in Asia, then in Africa, and finally worldwide. She's generated many thousands of teddy bears and/or soft, indigenous-looking dolls for children, not only those in international villages and communities, but also in refugee camps for kids in Syria, Iraq, Afghanistan, Bangladesh, Jordan, and more nations. So far, the women volunteers have produced dolls for more than 52,000 children in 41 countries. Under Sarah's leadership, LDS women across the USA and Europe have volunteered to help, producing sweet dolls for sad children. They also offer many types of patterns, describe the best materials, and collect thousands to ship abroad each month.

Families Helping Families, Inc.

    4040 East Greenway   (480) 807-0750
    Mesa, AZ 85205   gwalker@azmesalaw.com

Families Helping Families grew out of a 10-day work-expedition of families, including young people, to repair and rebuild homes on the eastern coast of Honduras in the aftermath of Hurricane Mitch. The families and youth organized this work expedition to build homes but have since expanded its efforts to promote education, literacy, family, healthcare, and community gardens. It asks all recipients who are able-bodied individuals to work on its projects to earn shoes, clothes, tools, and garden supplies. Families Helping Families hopes to include other areas of Honduras and eventually spread throughout Central America.

First Hope

    4936 Viewmont St.   (801) 272-7045
    Salt Lake City, UT 84117   fsthope@aros.net

Founded in 1986 by Cecile Pelous when she was Relief Society president of the Paris, France, LDS Stake, this group supports an orphanage and school in Nepal that was built by and is operated by a native Nepalese woman who is LDS.

Food for Everyone

    848 Woodruff Way   (801) 583-4449
    Salt Lake City, UT 84108
    www.growfood.com   gforder@growfood.com

Today there are many people around the globe who do not know how to grow their own food and be self-reliant. Millions are undernourished, impoverished, or even starving, due to their inability to provide for their food needs. The solution can be found in complete, field-tested growing procedures prepared for the family-size gardener, taught professionally in the native language, with daily lab work in the garden. Dr. Jacob Mittleider has conducted 75 major garden teaching projects in 27 countries for the past 36 years. His documented experience is in 10 books, on CD ROM discs, in student manuals, and in video lectures for a complete gardening course usable anywhere in the world. Food for Everyone welcomes the involvement of all who want to learn home-based family agriculture. It also trains people everywhere.

H2O for Humanity

340 N 19th Street
Hamilton, IL 62341

http://www.h2oforhumanity.com/
info@h2oforhumanity.com

In 2010, two brothers, Kevin and Eric Cluff, decided to launch a new social business using their father's research to support water purification technology. Funded with personal savings, a home refinance, and a seed grant from the Deshpande Foundation, H2O was launched in Karnataka, India—and a sustainable social business was born. It soon grew to operate in some 150 villages serving over 140,000 customers daily. The social business ultimately began setting up AquaSafi water stores. Soon it shifted from being an NGO to become a Low-Profit Limited Liability Company (LC3), an innovative new form of American business that is a hybrid between a nonprofit and a for-profit organization. H2O provides necessary equipment, technical support, and expertise for a small monthly charge and no up-front capital costs. The clean water being produced can total 1,300 liters per hour, and the new technology is tested three times per day to ensure villagers' safety. Today purified water is available to many more villages and over a million rural Indians.

Hands with Hope

11777 Autumn Ridge Cove (801) 501-7676
Sandy, UT 84092 handswithhope@aol.com

Hands with Hope is an organization whose mission is to help foster the well-being of the children of Africa. It believes that by helping to provide the fundamental needs requisite to the success of any child—food, shelter, education, and medical care—it gives that child the opportunity to step beyond the borders of poverty and ignorance to live a life of hope and promise for generations to come.

Hope Humanitarian

Sarah Franklin, MD (801) 449-0359
University of Utah info@hopehumanitarian.info
  www.Hopehumanitarian.org

Hope Humanitarian was founded by a young Utah medical researcher, Sarah Franklin, who mobilized her peers to carry out refugee expeditions, initially in the Middle East, after the September 11, 2001, attacks on the U.S. Since then, her volunteers—mostly well-educated professionals in their 30s—have worked annually in several Afghan and Iraqi refugee camps in Greece, as well as helped other groups such as the Rohingya people who fled from Myanmar's attacks, burned villages, and killings by the military junta to refugee camps in Bangladesh, as well as serving Syrian refugees in Turkey, and also helping children in orphanages in Haiti, Dominican Republic, and Belize.

Humanitarian Aid Relief Team (HART)

3650 N. University Ave., Suite 200   (801) 377-7835
Provo, UT 84604

A BYU student-founded, student-run nonprofit group, HART is committed to providing medical relief to the less fortunate. Currently, HART is working on a health project to eradicate the Buruli ulcer medical disaster in West Africa.

Humanitarian Resource Center of North America

1600 South Empire Rd., Suite 700   (801) 977-0444
Salt Lake City, UT 84104
www.hrcna.org   HRCNA@worldnet.att.net

The Humanitarian Resource Center of North America (HRCNA) is a 501(c)(3) publicly supported organization. Its mission is to relieve human suffering by providing humanitarian supplies to qualified relief organizations. It is a matchmaker, gathering appropriate humanitarian resources and providing them to effective relief efforts here at home and around the world. HRCNA focuses on five specific areas of relief: (1) Literacy and Education, (2) Health, (3) Microenterprise, (4) Water and Environment, and (5) Local Leadership.

International Aid Serving Kids

432 E. 1200 N.   (801) 226-2695
Orem, UT 84097   kaaia@yahoo.com

International Aid Serving Kids is an organization designed to get members of the community involved in service. Made up almost entirely of teenagers, the organization works to improve the lives of children in the Third World, mostly those in orphanages. Working through adoption agencies, adoptive parents, and orphanage directors, it organizes projects to gather donations for the children, as well as assisting in locating good, safe homes for the children.

International Development Network

786 TNRB (801) 422-6834
Brigham Young University
Provo, UT 84602

This informal group meets semiannually at BYU to discuss LDS-related issues, Third World development, and humanitarian programs being carried out by LDS family foundations, charities, NGOs, and other entities. It facilitates interaction, networking, student internships, and other opportunities by Latter-day Saints and others seeking to make a difference in the world.

Jacobsen Center for Service and Learning

2010 WSC (801) 422-8686
Brigham Young University
Provo, UT 84602
www.byu.edu/jacobsencenter jim_backman@byu.edu

The Jacobsen Center for Service and Learning was organized in October 1999. It supports and promotes service and learning through volunteer community service, service-learning courses, academic internships, semester-away programs, and international study programs. It attracts donor contributions and grants to be distributed primarily to students to reduce their costs in participating in service and learning experiences.

It provides funding connected to community service in its local community and also in worldwide LDS Church communities. It is a resource for advising new faculty and student initiatives in reaching out to extend the blessings of education by providing service connected to a student's academic studies.

Kids Who Care

4 Calle Serra (949) 459-9233
Rancho Santa Margarita, CA 92688
www.kids-who-care.org karen.baker@kids-who-care.org

KidServe, Inc., is a nonprofit organization that provides monthly service activities for families through a program called Kids Who Care. The aim of Kids Who Care is to teach children that they can make a difference in the world by serving in the community—and have fun doing it! A different type of service activity specifically geared to children is featured each month so that the children are exposed to a wide variety of service opportunities. Children discover which service activities they like most while interacting in a positive and fun way with family and friends. In addition, neighborhoods draw closer as they work together in a good cause.

Laubach Literacy

Box 131 (888) 528-2224
1320 Jamesville Ave. www.laubach.org
Syracuse, NY 13210 info@laubach.org

Founded in 1955, this nonprofit, educational corporation works to enable adults and older youths to acquire literacy, communication, and both mathematics and technology skills through partner programs throughout the U.S. and in 36 developing countries. Its programs include coordinating with volunteer tutors and publishing special, easy-to-read books.

Lifting Hands International

2543 So. 1700 East hayley@liftinghandsinternational.org
Salt Lake City, UT 84106 https://www.liftinghandsinternational.org/

Lifting Hands International is dedicated to helping refugees at home and abroad by seeking to create a world where compassion transcends divides and where global refugees are assisted in gaining a better future. Established in 2016 by a Utah college student studying Arabic, Hayley Smith, it has grown to assist hundreds of thousands of refugees. From its original focus on Middle Eastern refugees fleeing civil war and genocide in Afghanistan, Iraq, and Syria due to ISIS and other terrorists, it has served victims in the huge camps in Jordan, Turkey, and Greece. It has also also assisted victims of destroyed communities such as Rohingya villagers fleeing Myanmar to camps in Bangladesh, groups suffering in African countries, and Central Americans seeking asylum at the U.S. southern border.

Mothers Without Borders

125 E. Main St., Suite 402 (801) 607-564
American Fork, UT 84003 office@motherswithoutborders.org
https://motherswithoutborders.org/

This Utah County-based NGO offers hope to orphaned and vulnerable children by nurturing and caring for them in Zambia. It was founded by Kathy Headlee, a Utah mother, who felt a need to care for African kids. She traveled to Africa and began to partner with and support several organizations there, empowering women and caring for vulnerable children. MWB provides food, housing, and education for kids while also offering adult caregivers literacy and business skills training. By funding local schools and salaries for Zambian teachers and staff, lives are improved and the future is more hopeful.

Musana International; Ethikco

http://www.musanaintl.com https://ethikco.com/
https://www.facebook.com/melissa.sevy.94

The first of these two organizations, Musana International, was founded in 2009 by Melissa Sevy, a BYU student who at first helped build the NGO called HELP International. After living and working to lead HELP in Uganda with me in 2004 and 2005, she decided to establish Musana, a women's cooperative supporting numerous rural Ugandan women whose crafts she began acquiring and selling in Utah and beyond. The main products were jewelry and clothing: fashionable African products. For a decade, it was a successful co-op enterprise with its brands working to break the cycle of poverty in Uganda. Handmade products supported the employment and education of Ugandan women and their children. Through stable employment and classes in English, business, and health, Musana artisans were empowered to break the cycle of poverty for themselves and their families.

After a few years, this young entrepreneur turned to launching a new organization to seek, buy, and market high-quality crafts from various Third World nations. Ethical sourcing has been a growing phenomenon, and Melissa Sevy has been at the forefront of the movement. Core values include cocreation that builds on the natural talent, capabilities, and traditional skills artisans already have, using quality control and design aesthetics to create high-quality handmade products and textiles that can compete in Western markets. Results are that consumers in developed nations enjoy high-quality products while indigenous women who create them are paid more fairly, work in improved conditions, gain better education and new skills, earn higher incomes, and enjoy a more-sustainable future.

Norma Love Foundation

5107 Atlantis Terrace   (817) 540-1954
Arlington, TX 76016

This project is focused on aiding impoverished Misquito Indians in Honduras. Volunteers gather and send various goods, such as clothing, medicine, and children's toys, to the rural poor. The eventual goals include improving the Indians' education, teaching better farming techniques, and establishing medical clinics.

One Hundred Humanitarians

> Located somewhere in rural East Africa
> https://100humanitarians.com/
> https://www.facebook.com/heiditotten

A BYU graduate named Heidi Totten established this NGO in 2015 to help rural Kenyans, especially the Maasai tribal villages in East Africa. Gradually she gathered a community of entrepreneurs, small businesses, and individuals to help preserve indigenous culture and build education through sustainable projects that support communities and preserve the culture of indigenous tribes. One of its objectives is to help prevent human trafficking within families by eradicating the practice of female genital mutilation and early marriage of young girls. Building a school initially, the NGO has labored to empower women, create strong families, and educate the next generation.

Radiant Futures

> 7001 Fairfield Greens Ct., NE (505) 822-0704
> Albuquerque, NM 87111 radiantfutures@juno.com

Radiant Futures is a nonprofit organization whose purpose is to provide a "radiant future" for orphaned and abandoned children in the Americas by furnishing them with a home, family, love, education, and opportunities for success.

Reach the Children

578 East 9650 South
Salem, UT 84653
www.reachthechildren.org

(801) 423-1147

Africakid1@aol.com

Reach the Children, Inc., was started in 1998. It is incorporated in the state of New York and is registered with the IRS as a 501(c)(3) nonprofit charitable organization. It is an organization dedicated to strengthening families by providing education and healthcare for children, offering vocational training for adults, and teaching self-reliance and principle-based values. These tools and skills will enable people to overcome the shackles of extreme poverty and promote community leadership as they reach for a brighter tomorrow.

Rebuild for Peace

https://www.facebook.com/rebuildforpeace
https://www.rebuildforpeace.org/

Rebuild for Peace is an NGO working in Jordanian communities that was founded by Chris Udall, of Arizona. Collaborating with poor communities and the government of Jordan, it aims to help youth and others in disadvantaged circumstances, particularly those fleeing conflict-torn regions. Rebuild for Peace provides an opportunity to forge positive identities and strengthen families through peacebuilding training and community service. Its overarching goals are to rebuild lives and communities, largely through vocational training projects. Among other programs, it has established some small enterprises such as bicycle collectives, aided impoverished schools, and founded two vocational training centers on the border between Jordan and Syria. All these are strategies intended to help build regional peace.

Saving A Generation

1260 East 50 North   (801) 491-2207
Springville, UT 84663   www.savingageneration.org

Saving A Generation is a nonprofit humanitarian organization that believes people in need deserve help without regard to race, religious belief, gender, or political affiliation. With an emphasis on orphans, Saving A Generation is dedicated to improving the lives of the people of Africa. By providing school fees, uniform costs, other school expenses, and higher education opportunities in other parts of the world, Saving A Generation strives to do just that—to save a generation from hopelessness and despair and to provide a foundation for them to be productive citizens.

Starlight UK of Utah, Inc.

1870 High Pointe Drive   (801) 292-0607
Bountiful, UT 84010

In response to the civil war in Bosnia, an English-LDS Relief Society President named Carol Gray organized a relief mission in England to generate donated goods for the victims of the civil conflict, especially widows and orphans. Obtaining 40 tons of goods, she sold the family car in order to buy a truck to transport food, clothing, and medical supplies. Since then, with others' help, Gray has led over 20 humanitarian missions on the 5,000-mile road trip to aid the destitute people of Bosnia, and the group is expanding its efforts to Honduras and Kosovo. Most recently, she has carried her mission into Liberia to address the fierce civil war that is going on there. She currently has plans for an orphanage, a school, and a hospital in Liberia.

Students for International Development (SID)

237 HRCB, Brigham Young University (801) 422-3377
Provo, UT 84602

A BYU-student run program, SID conducts charitable drives on the Provo campus. It also organizes international development conferences, seminars, and outreach efforts.

Thrasher Research Fund

15 East South Temple St. (801) 240-4753
Salt Lake City, UT 84150-6910

In 1973, E. W. "Al" Thrasher, a non-LDS Utahn, provided a substantial endowment to be administered through the LDS Church for humanitarian, child-related research projects. The Thrasher Fund supports research in two separate categories: (1) academic research on nutrition and pediatric infectious diseases and (2) field applications appropriate to local cultures that, through careful documentation, can be transferred to other cultures.

World Wide Canneries

PO Box 2311 (208) 233-1937
Pocatello, ID 83206 worldwidecanneries@paraglobal.com

The purpose of World Wide Canneries, a nonprofit organization, is to build small canneries to help people who live in poor economic conditions help themselves. Providing used equipment and technically trained volunteers, it uses donated funds to cover the expenses. In many places around the world there is a lack of food processing. In some areas, there is a minimal amount being done with old, worn-out equipment. The objective of World Wide Canneries is to help people in struggling countries (LDS as well as non-LDS) to establish small food processing plants. It reports: "We have found that old, unused equipment in the U.S. can be of great value in these places. Our goal is to bring this cast off equipment in the U.S. to people in developing countries. We want to assist the Latter-day Saints in underdeveloped countries. We would like to build a cannery in such a country and then turn it over to people."

Economic Development without a Latter-day Saint Connection

Organizations in the following category focus on economic development but do not necessarily have a Latter-day Saint connection. Most of these are national and international organizations that may have worked with members of the church on an individual basis before, but nothing specifically related to Latter-day Saints.

Acción International

120 Beacon Street
Somerville, MA 02143

(617) 492-4930
www.accion.org
info@accion.org

Founded in 1961, Acción is a nonprofit, private organization, which provides small, short-term loans to self-employed poor through its network of affiliated organizations in 13 Latin American countries and 6 U.S. cities. Recently, Acción has created fully commercial financial institutions in Bolivia and Colombia whose sole clientele are members of the microenterprise sector.

ACDI/VOCA

1008 "S" Street, Suite B
Sacramento, CA 95814

(800) 556-1620
www.acdivoca.org

ACDI/VOCA identifies and opens economic opportunities for farmers and other entrepreneurs worldwide by promoting democratic principles and market liberalization, building international cooperative partnerships, and encouraging the sound management of natural resources.

Cashpor, Inc. (Network for Credit and Savings for the Hardcore Poor in Asia-Pacific)

6 Larong 4/1, Taman Permata (Lobok)
70200 Seremban N.S., Malaysia

011-60-6-764-5116
011-60-6-764-2307 (fax)

Cashpor aims to further reduce hardcore poverty in the region by providing technical assistance to scale up existing credit and savings programs for the poor and by promoting new Grameen Bank replications where they are needed.

CDRO (Cooperative Association for Western rural Development, Cooperacion para el Desarrollo Rural de Occidente)

Paraje Tierra Blanca
Totonicapán, Guatemala

011-502-766-2175
011-502-766-2183 (fax)

CDRO is a consortium of horizontal organization integrated into 45 rural communities. Its fundamental purpose is to support development in those communities through both a methodology of community participation, which is the basis of the Maya Kiché culture, and the use of available science and technology.

FINCA (Foundation for International Community Assistance)

    1101 14th St. N.W. 11th Floor   (202) 682-1510
    Washington, D.C. 20005   www.villagebanking.org
        finca@villagebanking.org

Founded in 1984, FINCA now serves 121,120 borrowers through approximately 6,092 village banking groups. FINCA's mission is to support the economic and human development of families trapped in severe poverty. To do this, it creates what it calls "village banks": peer groups of 10 to 50 members, predominantly women, who receive three critical services: working capital loans to finance self-employment activities, an effective mechanism for promoting family savings, and a community-based system that provides mutual support and encourages self-worth.

Freedom From Hunger

    1644 DaVinci Court   (800) 708-2555
    Davis, CA 95617   www.freefromhunger.org
        info@freefromhunger.org

Originally founded in 1944 to develop and distribute a nutrition supplement, Freedom From Hunger now concentrates on providing microenterprise training and credit programs for women in several Third World countries.

Grameen America

    150 West 30th Street   (718) 704-0426
    New York City, NY 10001   https://www.grameenamerica.org/
        info@grameenamerica.org

Grameen America was founded in New York City as an off-shoot of the Grameen Bank in Bangladesh. Seeking to empower poor women, especially refugees and migrants, it began offering training and microloans in 2008 and has gradually expanded to another 14 large U.S. cities, having invested over $1.8 billion to some 134,000 women to start and grow their tiny microenterprises.

Grameen Trust Bank

Grameen Foundation USA (202) 628-3560
1709 New York Ave., NW, Suite 101 (202) 628-3880 (fax)
Washington, D.C. 20006 (888) 764-3872
www.grameenfoundation.org info@grameenfoundation.org

Grameen Bank Bhaban 011-880-2-9005257-68
Mirpur-2 www.grameen.org
Dhaka 1216, Bangladesh grameen.bank@grameen.net

This trust bank is one of the world's leading microenterprise financial institutions, founded by Dr. Muhammad Yunus in the 1980s. The work of the bank is supported in the U.S. by the Grameen Foundation USA at the address above.

Inter-American Foundation

901 North Stuart St., 10th Floor (703) 306-4301
Arlington, VA 22203 www.iaf.gov

An independent agency of the U.S. Government, formed in 1969, IAF offers an alternative to traditional U.S. foreign aid programs. It provides extensive support for grassroots economic development projects throughout Latin America and the Caribbean, including grants, training, and other services to cooperatives and other local groups.

International Executive Service Corps

333 Ludlow St. (203) 967-6000
Stamford, CT 06902 www.iesc.org
  iesc@iesc.org

IESC is the largest nonprofit business development organization in the world, utilizing its 13,000-strong database of senior-level professionals, who donate their time and experience to improve private and public enterprises in more than 50 developing countries and emerging markets. IESC has provided effective, results-oriented assistance to businesses, nonprofits, and governmental agencies in more than 120 countries over the last 34 years.

Mondragon Corporacion Cooperativa

Paseo Jose Maria Arizmendiarrieta, No. 5
20500 Mondragon
Gipuzkoa, Spain

011-34-43-77-93-00
011-34-43-79-66-32 (fax)
info@mondragon.mcc.es
www.mondragon.mcc.es

This cooperative is the center for information on the Mondragon cooperative complex in the Basque country of northern Spain, a large network of some 200 worker-owned companies. The center provides literature and arranges visits to Mondragon or visits by Mondragon representatives elsewhere.

Opportunity International/Women's Opportunity Fund

2122 York Road, Suite 340
Oak Brook, IL 60523
www.opportunity.org

(800) 793-9455
(630) 645-4100
getinfo@opportunity.org

Opportunity International was founded over 35 years ago by an international business executive, Alfred Whitaker, who felt inspired by his Christian faith to leave his luxurious executive lifestyle to find constructive ways to help lift the poor. It provides microloans to both individuals and affinity groups throughout the Third World and Eastern Europe.

Philippines Rural Reconstruction Movement

Kayumanggi Press Building
940 Quezon Avenue
Quezon City, Philippines 1103

The Philippines Rural Reconstruction Movement is a nongovernmental organization that focuses on grassroots training and community organizing to empower peasants as well as rural farmers.

Programa de Economia del Trabajo

Santo Domingo 526
Santiago, Chile 632-6128

The Programa de Economia del Trabajo is an NGO involved in workers' self-management and microenterprise projects in Chile.

Results International

440 First Street, NW Suite 450
Washington, D.C. 20001

(202) 783-7100
www.action.org
results@action.org

Educational Fund
440 First Street, NW Suite 460
Washington, D.C. 20001

(202) 637-9600

info@microcreditsummit.org   www.microcreditsummit.org

Results International is a citizens advocacy group that lobbies governments to create political strategies for ending global hunger and poverty. It trains volunteers to influence public officials, media, and local communities, promoting the immunization of children, the advancement of education, and effective microlending programs. Its Educational Fund has organized two widely publicized global microcredit summits.

San Dionisio Credit Cooperative

0554 Quirino Avenue
San Dionisio, Paranaque, Philippines

One of the oldest and most successful Filipino credit-union type organizations, the San Dionisio Credit Cooperative serves many of its poverty-stricken members in the community of Paranaque.

Scott Bader Commonwealth, Ltd.

Wollaston, Wellingborough
Northhamptonshire, NN29-7RL
U.K.

011-44-1933-663100
011-44-1933-664592 (fax)
info@scottbader.com
www.scottbader.com

Scott Bader Commonwealth is a British chemical company that paved the way to sharing wealth through employee ownership and worker representation on the board of directors, allowing employee input regarding the firm's corporate strategy and allocation of profits.

SEWA Bank (Self-Employed Women's Association)

SEWA Reception Center
Opp. Victoria Garden
Bhadra, Ahmedabad 380-001 India
sewa.mahila@gnahd.globalnet.ems.vsnl.net.in

011-91-79-5506444
011-91-79-5506446 (fax)

SEWA is a trade union registered in 1972. It is an organization of poor, self-employed women workers. These are women who earn a living through their own labor or small business. SEWA's main goals are to organize women workers for full employment and self-reliance.

Trickle-Up Program

    121 West 27th Street, Suite 504   (212) 362-7958
    New York, NY 10001   info@trickleup.org
        www.trickleup.org

Created in 1979, Trickle-Up provides training and credit assistance to micro-entrepreneurs through local development agencies in over 50 countries.

Women's World Banking

    8 West 40th Street, 9th Floor   (212) 768-8513
    New York, NY 10018   (888) 768-8513
        wwb@igc.apc.org

Established in 1979 and supported by many major private and governmental donors, WWB promotes microcredit for poor women in almost 40 countries (including the U.S. and Europe as well as the Third World) through education, policy initiatives, and assistance to microfinance institutions.

Non-Economic Development without a Latter-day Saint Connection

The following is only a small list of the thousands of humanitarian organizations that have been created worldwide. These have been included because while they do not necessarily concentrate on economic development or Latter-day Saints, they *do* provide a great deal of service to those in need. This is by no means a comprehensive list for this category, though they are worthy and well-known organizations that the author felt necessary to include.

Business for Social Responsibility

609 Mission St., 2nd Floor (415) 537-0888
San Francisco, CA 94105 www.bsr.org

BSR is a national trade association for large and small companies that wish to become more socially responsible on such issues as diversity, ecology, ethics, and employee relations.

CARE

151 Ellis St. NE (404) 681-2552
Atlanta, GA 30303-2426 www.care.org
 info@care.org

Founded after the Second World War to send relief supplies to Europe and Asia, CARE has since helped more than *one billion people* in 121 countries to improve their lives through emergency disaster relief as well as agriculture, environment, health, nutrition, population, and small-business development programs. One of its largest supporters is the LDS Church, through the donation of surplus production from the church's welfare farms.

Catholic Relief Services Headquarters

209 West Fayette St. (800) 235-2772
Baltimore, MD 21201-3443 (410) 625-2220
www.catholicrelief.org (410) 234-2983 (fax)

CRS is a large, effective charity of the Roman Catholic Church that coordinates and funds relief efforts of numerous Catholic charities throughout the world, often partnering with the LDS Church on global projects.

City of Joy Aid

A-58 Nizamuddin East
New Delhi 100 013 - India

www.cityofjoy.org

City of Joy Aid is a nonprofit humanitarian organization dedicated to helping some of the world's most underprivileged. Based in Calcutta, India, this network of clinics, schools, rehabilitation centers, and hospital boats has brought relief to the poorest of the poor since 1981.

Co-Op America

1612 K Street, N.W., Suite 600
Washington, D.C. 20006

(800) 58-GREEN
www.coopamerica.org
info@coopamerica.org

This nonprofit organization links consumer members with socially and environmentally responsible businesses through directories, newsletters, and other information programs.

Habitat for Humanity International

121 Habitat St.
Americus, GA 31709

(912) 924-6935
public_info@habitat.org
www.habitat.org

Habitat for Humanity International is a nonprofit, ecumenical Christian housing ministry. HFHI seeks to eliminate poverty housing and homelessness from the world, and to make decent shelter a matter of conscience and action. Habitat invites people of all backgrounds, races, and religions to build houses together in partnership with families in need. Contact Habitat for Humanity for local chapter information.

Intermediate Technology Development Group

9 King Street
London WC2E 8HN
United Kingdom

011-44-171-4369761
011-44-171-4362013 (fax)

Associated with the pioneering work of the British economist E. F. Schumacher (author of the pioneering best-selling book *Small Is Beautiful*), ITDG strives to assist people in living more simply, using appropriate technologies and indigenous methods.

International Rescue Committee

122 East 42nd St.
New York, NY 10168-1289

(212) 551-3000
www.intrescom.org
irc@theIRC.org

Founded in 1933, the International Rescue Committee (IRC) is a leading nonsectarian, voluntary organization providing relief, protection, and resettlement services for refugees and victims of oppression or violent conflict.

Mi Refugio

4908 Jasmine Drive
Rockville, MD 20853-1632

(301) 929-1267

Mi Refugio describes itself as a nondenominational Christian ministry that provides education, food, clothing, and medical assistance to children and their families who live in the Guatemala City garbage dump. The ministry provides preschool through high school academic education, as well as trade school education in carpentry, baking, and sewing, which will assist the children to leave a lifetime barely surviving on the garbage dump.

Missionaries of Charity

54 A.J.C. Bose Road
Calcutta 700016, India

335 East 145th Street
Bronx, NY 10451
(718) 292-0019

This world-renowned, humanitarian, service-oriented Catholic religious order was founded in 1950 by the late Nobel Peace Prize winner Mother Teresa of Calcutta.

National Center for Employee Ownership

1736 Franklin St., 8th Floor
Oakland, CA 94612-1217

(510) 208-1300
www.nceo.org
nceo@nceo.org

The NCEO is a nonprofit clearinghouse that advises executives, unions, and companies on employee stock-ownership programs and other employee ownership methods. It organizes conferences and workshops and provides many publications, including a professional journal on the financial and legal aspects of employee ownership.

Operation Smile

6435 Tidewater Dr.
Norfolk, VA 23509

(757) 321-7645
www.operationsmile.org

Operation Smile describes itself as a private, nonprofit volunteer medical services organization providing reconstructive surgery and related healthcare to indigent children and young adults in developing countries and the U.S. It offers education and training around the world to physicians and other healthcare professionals to achieve long-term self-sufficiency.

Water for People

6666 West Quincy Ave.
Denver, CO 80235

(303) 734-3494
www.water4people.org
info@waterforpeople.org

Water for People is a nonprofit, charitable organization in the U.S. and Canada that helps people in developing countries obtain safe drinking water. It works with local partner organizations to provide financial and technical assistance to communities, depending on their needs. Water for People's commitment is to "help people help themselves."

World Neighbors

4127 NW 122nd St.
Oklahoma City, OK 73120
www.wn.org

(405) 752-9700
(800) 242-6387
info@wn.org

A private volunteer agency, World Neighbors works to improve farming and other conditions in rural villages in Asia, Africa, and Latin America.

Appendix II

Global Change Agents, Inc.

Ever dream about combating Third World suffering? GCA is a nonprofit consulting firm that provides technical assistance to Third World NGOs. We draw on two decades of experience in the creation, growth, and sustainability of poor peoples' institutions to alleviate human suffering. The list below conveys the range of services we have successfully provided around the world—Latin America, Africa, Asia, and the former USSR. The most powerful force for global change is a new idea in the hands of a social entrepreneur!

- Inspiring young global change agents to transform the world through H.E.L.P. International
- Building participatory systems for self-determination
- Integrating theory with action: praxis
- Encouraging new forms of compassionate capitalism, such as Ben & Jerry's Ice Cream, that are based on the highest human values
- Combating oppressive trends in globalization
- Fostering humane, grassroots indigenous development
- Drafting advocacy papers for conferences and symposia such as the OD Network, OD Institute, and SHRM

- Strengthening poor, marginalized families around the globe by building a new social sector or "third way" for solving global problems
- Expanding service learning opportunities for college-age students through H.E.L.P. International as we grow to 500 change agents in Latin America volunteering each summer
- Integrating the spiritual with the temporal in international development so that practices are holistic
- Moving people from dependency to dignity through Enterprise Mentors International
- Promoting socially responsible business practices such as Guru's Restaurants and Tom's of Maine
- Becoming peacemakers through grassroots organizing that reduces social conflicts and violence
- Providing tools for building capacity among the poor, such as the Microcredit Summit
- Conducting action research on NGO best practices that ensure self-sufficiency, such as the Grameen Bank in Bangladesh and the Acción Comunitaria del Peru in Peru
- Advocating and radicalizing on behalf of the world's "have-nots," as the World Social Forum is doing in Brazil and India
- Networking between progressive individuals, donors, and NGOs as carried out by CEO entrepreneurs like Anita Roddick of The Body Shop
- Ensuring NGO transparency and integrity that guide ethical social change
- Carrying out relevant, hands-on practitioner research that leads beyond mere publication to a better world
- Becoming a catalyst for microcredit acceleration through Unitus

- Calling to action humanitarian volunteers who have real passion and fire in the belly to make a difference in the world, such as with the Ouelessebougou Alliance in Mali, West Africa
- Facilitating the rise of new social-purpose ventures with values of stewardship and service to humanity
- Developing NGO paradigms that ensure long-term sustainability, like Engage Now in Ethiopia
- Fostering new economic and business models, like Semco in Brazil, that engender cooperation rather than competition, and encouraging servant leadership rather than authoritarian management
- Empowering impoverished people in their struggle for equality and socioeconomic justice
- Accelerating the rise of the emerging NGO movement around the world
- Fostering microcredit strategies and conducting studies on the impacts of village banking in the informal economy with nonprofit enterprises like FINCA and Katalysis
- Mobilizing potential social entrepreneurs in living out their dreams to improve life on this planet by becoming Ashoka Fellows
- Creating partnerships like Cause for Hope between First World middle-class "haves" and the Third World/Fourth World impoverished "have-nots" who suffer
- Building innovative systems and frameworks for fighting poverty and moving toward human fulfillment, like the Academy for Creating Enterprise in the Philippines

Would you like to have a more meaningful experience in your professional career? Consider the following words of Peter Drucker, Stephen Covey, Warner Woodworth, and Social Entrepreneurs of India:

Peter F. Drucker
Harvard Business Review, March/April 1999, pp. 65–74

Peter Drucker in 1999 wrote a classic *Harvard Business Review* article, "Managing Oneself," about consultants "knowing how and when to change the work we do." He talks of the many professionals who "after 20 years of doing very much the same kind of work ... are not learning or contributing or deriving challenge and satisfaction from the job. And yet they are still likely to face another 20 if not 25 years of work. [This] increasingly leads one to begin a second career ... as a social entrepreneur. ... Such people have substantial skills and they know how to work. They need a community. ... These social entrepreneurs are society's true change agents. But above all they need challenge." Drucker points out that "If one does not begin to volunteer before one is 40 or so, one will not volunteer once past 60. ... All the social entrepreneurs I know began to work in their chosen second enterprise long before they reached their peak in their original business." Finally Drucker concludes with the insight that "This need to manage oneself is therefore creating a revolution in human affairs."

Stephen Covey
BYU Microfinance speech, March 20, 2003, and subsequent 2004 book

Stephen Covey, Warner Woodworth's dear colleague since the time that both were Organizational Behavior professors at BYU, authored the classic best-seller *The Seven Habits of Highly Effective People*. Woodworth brought Dr. Muhammad Yunus, founder of the Grameen Bank in Bangladesh, to BYU many times, an institution that is owned by the "poorest of the poor," having loaned out over $4 billion in microcredit to 2.4 million microentrepreneurs. On one occasion Woodworth introduced Yunus to Covey, who was astounded at Yunus's vision, leadership, and great mission to eliminate global poverty. Covey then began to see the new social entrepreneurship work carried out by global change agents as a wonderful way to use their craft on behalf of the world's "have-nots." When Covey wrote his last book, *The 8th Habit: From*

Effectiveness to Greatness, he featured Professor Yunus in the introductory chapter as one who went beyond the "seven habits" to a higher level of human achievement in changing the world. The latter book's theme was Yunus-inspired with Covey's words to "Find your voice and inspire others to find theirs." In the process, declared Covey, the poor become empowered, and the ripple-effects of change expand.

Warner Woodworth
Professor of Organizational Behavior, Marriott School of Management, BYU

Warner Woodworth often argued that "To radically change the world by identifying social problems and inventing new solutions requires determination and a committed vision of transformation. In the past two decades there has been an explosion of social entrepreneurship and the rise of a new Third Way, neither private enterprise nor government agencies. For example, today there are over a million social sector organizations in the U.S., 70 percent of which did not exist in the 1960s.

Social Entrepreneurs of India
April 2000

Global Change Agents, Inc., a Woodworth NGO consulting firm, finds problems that are not being solved and develops new strategies by changing the overall system, disseminating new solutions, and convincing entire societies to take new leaps. These change agents are not satisfied to just "give a person a fish," or to teach how to fish. They move to a whole new level by revolutionizing the fishing industry itself.

From Calcutta: "While a business entrepreneur may thrive on competition and profit, a social entrepreneur has a different motivation: a commitment to leading through inclusiveness of all actions in society and a dedication to changing the systems and patterns of society."

Appendix III

Sample NGO Work Expectations

(Contract for each student wanting to serve in Thailand in 2005)

[Please carefully read the following paragraphs. When done, sign, tear out, and give the original to Wave of Hope managers, retaining the second copy signed, but left in your handbook.]

To be successful in Thailand, we need to have the full cooperation and commitment of all volunteer social entrepreneurs so that the experience is positive for tsunami victims and our partner NGOs, as well as members of our own group. We have sought your expression of your own expectations and will strive to help you meet your goals! We believe in the Power of One. We also believe in the leveraged power of a united group. Your support is needed so that we all enjoy a safe, productive, and high-impact experience. An ultimate objective of our Wave of Hope effort is to have a life-changing experience that continues to nourish us throughout a lifetime of service to those who suffer, both locally and globally. This requires some simple ground rules that everyone adheres to. It also requires structure to ensure effective teamwork, as well as genuine cooperation.

The items below describe our expectations agreed to by the Coordinating Team, to be carried out by our in-country managers. Remember: You are not to just do your "own thing" this summer. Rather, each of you is working under the auspices of Empowering Nations and HELP International. Beyond that, you also represent your country, university, and church. As a result, you will be perceived as an unofficial ambassador of each of these organizations, so we hope you will be kind, be considerate, and offer the best we have to give to the world.

Clearly, there are pluses in providing our humanitarian services as a collective group, because the greater leverage we can achieve, the greater impact we can have. New change agent synergies may even emerge by your collaborating with one another and uniting your skills, intellectual capacity, and ethical values in a larger cause than your individual self.

Work Plan

- We ask that all volunteers commit to working for a period of 4 weeks minimum.
- Volunteers should commit to working 5 days a week (barring sickness), with Saturdays and Sundays off.
- To offer some flexibility and to allow volunteers to enjoy a little travel within the country, volunteers will be allotted 3 free days for travel within Thailand during the month. Of course, afterward, more in-country touring is available for those who have the extra time and money.
- Free days (time off) need to be requested at least 2 days in advance, thus facilitating the planning and organizing of projects and volunteers by the in-country managers.
- Traveling outside of Thailand is to only occur after the volunteer's 4-week commitment.
- Volunteers will work and travel at least in pairs, at all times. No solo work or travel is permitted.

Work Week
- The daily schedule is subject to local work habits, project requirements, and so forth, but will be from approximately 7 or 8 a.m. to 6 p.m., including travel time and meals. (Why? Because the summer sun comes up early; projects start working early due to climate and work habits of natives and projects; we don't want people traveling after dark; also, hitchhiking and mosquitoes start to come out during the evenings.)
- Absolutely no one should be out after dark alone; our buddy system is a *must* to ensure everyone's safety.
- Morning and evening prayers are held; group prayers are said 7 a.m. and 10 p.m. (nightly prayer will include a spiritual thought and a sharing of some experiences of the day).
- Family Home Evening occurs on Monday nights, time to be determined.
- House-cleaning assignments will be determined on arrival in Khao Lak.

Safety
- Volunteers should limit being outside at night due to mosquitoes, as well as security concerns.
- No one is to travel, hitchhike, or work alone.
- All drinking water must be bottled and sealed.

Projects
- Individual volunteers will be assigned to work on projects according to their skills and abilities.
- Projects to be determined by in-country managers, according to Khao Lak needs and problems, as well as each volunteer's skill and ability.
- Volunteers can be proactive and involved with projects they are interested in by actively seeking out the needs of Thai locals. Therefore, we have created

a proposal system for projects that can be submitted to the in-country managers for review and approval.
- In-country managers determine allocation of funds and volunteer labor.
- Volunteers will be assigned to projects in groups; there must be a minimum of 2 persons working on each project at all times.
- Again, we would ask that all individuals work in pairs, so that no individual is ever working alone, or off by themselves. This is primarily for safety, but also for accountability reasons.

In-Country Managers

- Based on individual talents, commitments of time and energy, and their participation in planning the Wave of Hope project, in-country managers were chosen prior to departure for Thailand.
- Their roles?
  - Responsible for safety and well-being of volunteers
  - Responsible for securing housing, travel, and food arrangements for volunteers
  - Responsible for determining projects in which volunteers will be involved
  - Responsible for allocation of funds and volunteer labor
- In-country managers will report to the U.S.-based Support Team on a weekly and monthly basis.

Project Leaders

- Depending on individual volunteer energy, skill, and ability, one volunteer will be chosen as the project leader for each Thai project.
- Project leaders will report to the in-country managers daily regarding:
  - assessment of the day's pluses and minuses

- volunteer hours worked
- next day's on-site plans
- volunteer concerns and individual well-being (accountability of volunteers)
- Project leaders will usually be changed or rotated weekly.

Communication Chain
- On-site volunteer talks to project leader
- Project leader talks to in-country manager
- In-country managers talk to U.S. support team manager

Buddy System
- We insist that all volunteers adhere to the buddy system at all times, working on projects, out during the day, and especially at night.

Living Arrangements and Food
- Housing will be taken care of by the in-country managers. (Exact accommodations will be secured by the lead team, which is going ahead to set things up by May 1.)
- Volunteers will be given a food and incidentals cash allotment per week.

Miscellaneous
- We expect that we won't have to throw water on you in the morning to get you out of bed...
- We expect that you have come to Thailand because you want to help others, and not merely because you wanted to get a better tan.
- We expect that you want to work hard and also have fun.
- And last but not least.... We expect that you'll be responsible, caring, and committed to the cause, working as representatives of Wave of Hope and your

family/church/country. We assume that all of us seek to give the world the very best we have to offer as social entrepreneurs. We expect not only that we can successfully serve and uplift the impoverished victims of the tsunami, but also that our lives will be more meaningful, as well. Thus, this will be a shared process in which both parties benefit each other. We expect to learn from the wonderful people of Thailand, as much as they will hopefully learn from us, too. If this occurs, the summer of 2005 may launch tiny ripples of joy that will spread and grow into waves of strength and beauty throughout our lives!

Printed Name: _____

Signature of Agreement: _____

Date: _____

Appendix IV

Sample NGO Legal Liabilities

Help International / Empowering Nations Liability Document

Volunteer Agreement Consent
Liability & Waiver Release Form

Duties and Responsibilities
- Volunteer agrees to volunteer services for the full and complete 4-week duration of the Empowering Nations/ Wave of Hope Tsunami Relief Project and to participate in all activities following the team schedule.
- The primary concern of each and every Volunteer is their own health and safety, as well as that of others.
- The Volunteer is expected to be with tsunami victims and accessible to their needs.
- The Volunteer is expected to behave in an exemplary and competent manner at all times.
- The Volunteer shall honor the laws, rules, and regulations of Thailand.

- The Volunteer is prohibited from using foul or abusive language.
- The use of tobacco products and alcohol is prohibited.
- The use and consumption of illegal drugs is absolutely prohibited. This policy will be strictly enforced, and any violation of this policy will subject the Volunteer to immediate expulsion.
- A Volunteer's failure to behave in accordance with these and any such policies as Empowering Nations/ HELP International may adopt will result in immediate termination of services.

Travel Responsibilities
- Volunteer acknowledges that it is her or his sole responsibility to raise funds to provide and pay for her or his own travel expenses to Thailand, including travel fares, meals, lodging, and incidental expenses to travel.
- Each volunteer is solely responsible for her or his travel that may occur after leaving Khao Lak to travel in other countries or areas in the region as she or he returns to the U.S.

Cancellation and Refund
- Wave of Hope reserves the right to cancel any of its programs at any time. In such event, rather than refund monies to volunteers, surplus funds may be passed on to Thailand partner NGOs or other worthy humanitarian programs.

Governing Law
- This Agreement shall be governed, enforced, and the legality and validity of each term and condition shall be determined in accordance with the internal, substantive laws of the State of Utah applicable to agreements fully executed and performed entirely in Utah.

- In the event that a suit is instituted against any party to this Agreement or any other Agreements with Empowering Nations/HELP International, the sole jurisdiction and venue for such action shall be the superior or Municipal Courts of Utah County, State of Utah.
- I have carefully read this Agreement and fully understand its content and agree to abide by its terms and conditions.
- I, _____, acknowledge that I am in good health, with no present medical or psychiatric conditions that would prevent my full participation as an Empowering Nations volunteer.
- I have my own health insurance and travel insurance, and I will either purchase my round-trip airline ticket to and from Thailand, or will raise equivalent donations before the trip begins.
- I will hold Empowering Nations and HELP International and their boards, officers, and employees harmless from any and all injuries, accidents, or losses that may befall me, whether from natural or human-made causes, foreseeable or unforeseeable, expected or unexpected.
- I assume full responsibility for my own safety, health, and well-being during my flights and/or other travel to and from any residence, during my time in Thailand and other countries, and also on my way to and from the region.
- In the event of an accident or costs, expenses, or any damages whatsoever, I shall not seek compensation in any way, or seek any legal redress claim or action, causes of action, or costs from Empowering Nations and HELP International, their boards, officers, or employees or individually, nor be entitled to any attorney's fees that may accrue from any claim arising out of any accident during May–August 2005, or on any

other dates relating to my travel from home until I return home.
- The undersigned further declares and represents that no promise, inducement, or agreement not herein expressed has been made to the undersigned, and that this Release & Waiver contains the entire agreement between the parties hereto, and that the terms of this Release & Waiver are contractual and not merely recital.
- In consideration of my rights as a volunteer in Wave of Hope's Thailand Project, and for other good and valuable consideration, the receipt and sufficiency of which is hereby acknowledged, I hereby acknowledge and agree to the provisions of this Consent and Release form as follows:

Voluntary Participation
- I acknowledge that I am volunteering to be a Wave of Hope volunteer for at least four weeks during summer 2005.

Assumption of Risk
- I am aware that the role of being a humanitarian volunteer in Thailand may be a hazardous activity. I am voluntarily participating in this activity with knowledge of the danger involved and hereby agree to accept any and all risks of injury associated therewith including, but not limited to, personal injury, bodily injury, or death.

Release
- As consideration for being permitted to be a Volunteer by Empowering Nations and HELP International, their respective officers, directors, agents, and employees (individually and collectively referred to herein as "Releasees"), I hereby agree that I, my assignees,

heirs, distributees, guardians, and legal representatives will not make a claim against, sue, attach the property of, or make any other demand on Releasees or any of their affiliated organizations for injury or damage resulting from negligence or other acts, howsoever caused, by any employee, agent, or contractor of Releasees or any of their affiliated organizations as a result of my participation as a Volunteer. I hereby release Releasees and any of their affiliated organizations, including Brigham Young University and the Church of Jesus Christ of Latter-day Saints, from all actions, claims, or demands that I, my assignees, heirs, distributees, guardians, and legal representatives now have or may hereafter have for injury or damage resulting from my participation as a Wave of Hope Volunteer.

Knowing and Voluntary Execution

- I HAVE CAREFULLY READ THIS CONSENT AND RELEASE AND FULLY UNDERSTAND ITS CONTENTS. I AM AWARE THAT THIS IS A RELEASE OF LIABILITY AND A CONTRACT BETWEEN MYSELF AND RELEASEES AND/OR AFFILIATED ORGANIZATIONS, AND I SIGN THIS OF MY OWN FREE WILL.

_____   _____   _____

Volunteer Signature   Volunteer Printed Name   Date

Appendix IV

Sample NGO Handout

(Woodworth handout used at Cambridge, Harvard, Oxford, Yale, Stanford, and other universities)

Changing the World
One Person, One Family,
One Community at a Time

Never doubt that a small group of thoughtful,
committed citizens can change the world.
Indeed, it's the only thing that ever has.
—Margaret Mead

Dr. Warner Woodworth
Marriott School of Business, Brigham Young University
Darden School of Business, University of Virginia, 2020

Ever dreamed of changing the world? This handout summarizes some of the microcredit work we have been doing over the past 30 years as change agents, entrepreneurs, professionals, college students, and friends to design courses, apply concepts, develop action models, and offer pro bono consulting to fight poverty and to address social problems. I hope they will suggest applications that more individuals like you may want to consider. These efforts grow out of the projects we have designed and implemented with our partners through the Marriott School at BYU—teaching courses, offering mentoring and service learning opportunities while doing research and publication. Some of these social ventures have resulted in public recognition—including those from President Bill Clinton's Global Initiative Award, Grameen Foundation's Practitioner Excellence Award, Fast Company Magazine/ Monitor Consulting Group's Social Capital Award, the Drucker Centennial Professorship at Claremont University, and the Faculty Pioneer Award for social impacts from the Aspen Institute in New York City, and the Church of Jesus Christ of Latter-day Saints' First Presidency. In some cases, we've had involvement of students from other universities, as well as our own alumni to help as project advisors, to provide service on NGO boards of directors, to donate their personal money and time.

The resources and links below show areas that may be of interest to you and your associates regarding our activities in Asia, Africa, and Latin America. They foster microcredit strategies, scale up social entrepreneurship, strengthen family well-being, build social capital and generate Third World improvements. They show examples of how individuals, NGOs, and businesses may partner as resource systems for combating poverty, thus enabling people and groups to become incubators in which to design, create, assess, and then spin-off social enterprises. Hopefully, this will open a dialogue as to what others may accomplish as we collaborate in future actions that transform people's capacity for achieving economic self-reliance, and solving global problems.

Why

With so much suffering and extreme poverty, the world has a great need for social innovations, conscious capitalism, and skilled people with a passion for improving society to become engaged in empowering the poor and building better communities.

Strategies
Microfinance, Self-Reliance, Economic Development, Social Entrepreneurship, Capacity-Building, Organizational Design, Action Learning, Social and Economic Impacts, Women's Empowerment, Leadership, NGO Management

Where
Starting at Brigham Young University (http://www.byu.edu) and going far beyond, around the globe

Programs
Over the past three decades, I have sought to recruit, train, and send out more than 3,200 BYU students, along with dozens from other universities such as Stanford, VATech, USU, Harvard, Utah, Yale, USC, Colorado State, MIT, and others to labor as global change agents—partnering with businesses, creating new NGOs, working with existing social enterprises, and striving to foster sustainable strategies to empower the poor. We have designed and implemented some 60 projects to build civil society and reduce poverty. As of now, 41 have become NGOs that operate in many countries. A few others are social businesses that utilize leading-edge management tools to serve the poor, not to make a profit. In 2018 alone, through all of these efforts, we collectively raised some $27 million in donations and investment capital, trained 340,000 poor women, and grew the NGOs' microentrepreneur bases to help over 8.5 million clients. I'm a founder of Unitus, Enterprise Mentors, Help International, and other NGOs. You may wish to involve your friends and colleagues in these programs. At BYU, in addition to new courses, training modules, dozens of student theses, and faculty mentoring, we have produced several tools for change. Much of this has occurred because of individuals becoming committed to making a difference.

What
- Established the $3 million Ballard Center for Economic Self-Reliance: https://marriottschool.byu.edu/ballard/
- Held 12 annual conferences, bringing together top practitioners, donors, NGOs, students, faculty, and others: http://marriottschool.byu.edu/selfreliance
- Published books such as *Small Really Is Beautiful: Micro Approaches to Third World Development* (Third World Think Tank)
- Founding editor of the *Journal of Microfinance*, the first of its kind: http://marriottschool.byu.edu/microfinance
- Published author of 11 books and more than 123 articles, and presented some 240 conference papers around the globe

Who
Dr. Warner Woodworth (Social Entrepreneur and Professor), Marriott School, Brigham Young University
590 Tanner Bldg., BYU, Provo, UT 84602, USA

Email
- warnerwoodworth@gmail.com
- warner_woodworth@byu.edu

Websites
- Personal: http://warnerwoodworth.com
- BYU: http://marriottschool.byu.edu/emp/wpw

Facebook
- http://www.facebook.com/profile.php?id=762100466
- https://www.facebook.com/NGOs-Worldwide-1908668009406210/
- https://www.facebook.com/Social-Entrepreneurship-Global-Consulting-LLC-653592988008896/

LinkedIn
- https://www.linkedin.com/in/warner-woodworth-b775a4/

> Earth provides enough to satisfy every man's
> need but not enough for every man's greed.
> —Mahatma Gandhi

MFIs & Social Entrepreneurship NGOs
Groups I have cofounded and/or been deeply involved with include:

- CHOICE Humanitarian (7 countries): http://www.choicehumanitarian.org/
- Sustain Haiti (Post-Earthquake Haiti): http://www.sustain-haiti.org/
- Care for Life (Mozambique): http://careforlife.org
- Reach the Children (9 African nations): www.reachthechildren.org
- Hope Humanitarian (Mobilizing volunteers to serve in refugee camps Middle East, Europe, Bangladesh Turkey, and beyond): https://hopehumanitarian.info
- H.E.L.P. International (Throughout Asia, Africa, Latin America, Jordan, and others): http://help-international.org
- Ascend Alliance (Ethiopia, Bolivia, Perú, and Ecuador): http://ascendalliance.org
- Cause For Hope (Honduras and Nicaragua): http://causeforhope.org
- Singular Humanitarian (Ecuador): https://www.singularhumanitarian.org/
- Eagle Condor Humanitarian (Peru): http://eagle-condor.org

- Academy for Creating Enterprise (Philippines and Mexico): http://creatingenterprise.com
- Empowering Nations (Wave of Hope Thailand, plus Ghana and Panama): http://empoweringnations.org
- PIN (Purpose Investor Network: Social Venture Impacts—Utah): http://pin-svp.org
- MicroBusiness Mentors (Mentores para la Microempresa/Utah Latino Community): http://microbusinessmentors.org
- Their Story Is Our Story (Tales of refugees from Iraq, Syria, and other countries, to bridge the gap): https://tsosrefugees.org
- Rising Star Outreach (Leprosy communities in India): http://risingstaroutreach.org
- DoTerra (Utah firm with social impacts) https://www.doterra.com/
- Mentors International (Central America, Africa, and the Philippines): http://mentorsinternational.org
- Ouelessebougou Alliance (Mali, West Africa): http://sistercommunity.org
- Yehu Microfinance (Kenya) Also, small-scale farming projects and reforestation: http://yehu.org   http://www.asante-foundation.org
- Lifting Hands International (Refuges globally): https://www.liftinghandsinternational.org
- Grameen America (New York): http://grameenamerica.com
- Micro-Business USA (Florida immigrants): http://microbusinessusa.org
- AMAR Foundation (Middle East refugees): https://www.amarfoundation.org/en-us/
- Microcredit Summit Campaign (Global): http://microcreditsummit.org
- Cotopaxi (SLC company doing good): http://cotopaxi.org

- Musana International (Uganda): http://musanaintl.com
- Unitus (India, Mexico, Argentina, Indonesia, Philippines, Tanzania, Kenya, and 12 other nations): http://unitus.com
- Mali Rising Foundation (Schools in West Africa): http://www.malirisingfdn.org/

Note: My latest personal social business enterprises for consulting and training include

- NGOs Worldwide: https://www.facebook.com/NGOs-Worldwide-1908668009406210/
- Social Entrepreneurship Global Consulting LLC: https://www.facebook.com/Social-Entrepreneurship-Global-Consulting-LLC-653592988008896

Other smaller Projects and NGOs include SOAR (China), Acción Contra La Pobreza (Honduras), SOL (Sustainability NGO rural Parana, Brazil), Liahona Economic Development Foundation (Nigeria), Achatina Snail Farms (Ghana), Nova Geração (southern Brazil), Paramita Group (Asia), and Grupo Roble (Argentina).

Each microloan is a voyage of self-discovery.
All human beings have unlimited potential.
These little monies give women an opportunity
to discover their self-worth.
—Muhammad Yunus,
founder of Grameen Bank,
Nobel Peace Prize Laureate

Major Microfinance Organizations

Major MFIs with which I have ongoing relationships:

- FINCA International (Global): http://villagebanking.org
- Grameen Bank (Bangladesh): http://grameen-info.org
- Grameen America (New York): http://grameenamerica.com
- Acción (Latin America): https://www.accion.org
- Making Cents (Training): http://makingcents.org
- Kiva (Crowdfunding microloans globally): https://www.kiva.org
- Grameen Foundation USA: https://grameenfoundation.org
- Micro-Business USA (Florida immigrants): http://microbusinessusa.org
- Microcredit Summit Campaign (Global): http://microcreditsummit.org
- Opportunity International (Global): http://opportunity.org

Collaborating Organizations and Academic Programs

Below are a number of other institutions with which I've been involved in research, funding, or promoting change agentry or social entrepreneurship:

- Aspen Institute (social innovation): http://aspeninstitute.org
- Program on Social Enterprise (Yale): http://mba.yale.edu
- Idealist Org: http://idealist.org
- Harvard Initiative on Social Enterprise: http://hbs.edu./socialenterprise
- Institute for Social Entrepreneurs: http://socialent.org
- Peter Drucker School of Management (Claremont University): https://www.cgu.edu/school/drucker-school-of-management
- Social Edge (online magazine): http://socialedge.org

- Wharton Social Impact Initiative (University of Pennsylvania): https://socialimpact.wharton.upenn.edu
- Ashoka (Innovations for the Public): http://ashoka.org
- Net Impact (MBAs doing good): http://netimpact.org
- Duke University (Innovation and Entrepreneurship Initiative): https://entrepreneurship.duke.edu

Utah-focused Nonprofits

Here are my favorite NGOs doing community work among the locally disenfranchised:

- Bennion Community Service Center: http://bennioncenter.org
- The Other Side Academy (TOSA): http://www.theothersideacademy.com
- Utah Climate Action Network: https://www.utahclimateactionnetwork.com/
- Coalition Of Religious Communities (CORC): https://www.crossroadsurbancenter.org/corc.html
- Refugee Justice League of Utah: https://www.refugeejustice.org
- Mormon Women for Ethical Government (MWEG) (Nonpartisan, nondenominational advocates for better politics): https://www.mormonwomenforethicalgovernment.org/
- Utah Diné Bikéyah (Protecting and preserving native lands): http://utahdinebikeyah.org
- The Road Home (serving the homeless): https://www.theroadhome.org
- Southern Utah Wilderness Alliance (SUWA): https://suwa.org/
- Utah Women's Coalition (UWC) (Public policy, advocacy, and education): http://utahwomenscoalition.org
- Food and Care Coalition (Provo): https://foodandcare.org

- Adopt-A-Native-Elder Program (fostering an indigenous weavers' market): http://www.anelder.org
- Utah Valley Earth Forum: http://uvef.org
- Women of the World: https://www.womenofworld.org

Film

A one-hour PBS documentary we produced, titled "Small Fortunes," is accessible on the internet that features some of our NGOs and partner MFIs around the world. It also highlights concrete ways to establish action groups and to fight poverty. See http://kbyutv.org/smallfortunes or http://pbs.org/kbyu/smallfortunes

JOIN US IN BUILDING A MOVEMENT OF GLOBAL CHANGE AGENTS TO TRANSFORM THE WORLD!

You must do the things you think you cannot do.
—Eleanor Roosevelt

Dr. Warner Woodworth is a global social entrepreneur who has helped raise some $1.3 billion over four decades to combat poverty and reduce human suffering. He has mobilized more than 3,400 volunteers among college students, business associates, schoolteachers, homemakers, executives, and others, as volunteers throughout the world. Whether laboring in the trenches after cyclones, earthquakes, floods, or civil wars, he has sought to link many associates as investors in achieving beneficial social and economic impacts. He is author of 11 books and 300 articles while engaged in empowering the poor. He holds M.A. and Ph.D. degrees in Organizational Behavior from the University of Michigan, Ann Arbor. Dr. Woodworth has consulted in launching the worker ownership movement in the U.S. through ESOPs (Employee Stock Ownership Plans), and lobbied the U.S. Congress to create the National Cooperative Bank, both of which empower members of lower-income blue-collar sectors of America.

He next turned to the global poor to design and teach the first U.S. courses in Microcredit and Social Entrepreneurship, by using sustainable business strategies, topics now taught at over 600 American college campuses. With collaborators he founded or served on the boards of some 41 NGOs, including Mentors International (7 countries), Ouelessebougou Alliance (Mali), Unitus (23 countries), and HELP International

(11 countries). In 2019 alone the NGOs and MFIs that he and associates established during recent decades have grown to serve more than 7.6 million clients in living sustainably. They collectively raised $28 million and trained some 348,000 microentrepreneurs.

Professor Woodworth achieved tenure and was a full professor at the Marriott School at Brigham Young University for four decades. In addition to universities worldwide, he is currently a visiting faculty member at the University of Utah. Dr. Woodworth has been honored with the Faculty Pioneer Award for global impacts by the Aspen Institute in New York and the Social Entrepreneurship Teaching Award at the Skoll World Forum at Oxford University. He was named the first Peter Drucker Visiting Scholar in Social Entrepreneurship at the Drucker School, Claremont University, in Los Angeles, and has received many more honors as well. The work of various NGOs he cofounded has been recognized by the LDS First Presidency, *Fast Company Magazine*, the Clinton Foundation, the Red Cross, various city and state governments, numerous university teaching and research associations around the globe, and others. Along with his association with various NGOs and professional groups, he was appointed by the Nobel Peace Prize Laureate Muhammad Yunus to the Advisory Board of Grameen America in New York City.

www.ingramcontent.com/pod-product-compliance
Lightning Source LLC
Chambersburg PA
CBHW050310120526
44592CB00014B/1849